EUGENIO BARBA

....

THEATRE
Solitude
Craft
Revolt

....

THEATRE : *Solitude, Craft, Revolt*
Edited by Lluís Masgrau
Translated from the Italian by Judy Barba

Photos: Fiora Bemporad: nos. 1, 5, 16, 37, 42, 44; Peter
Bysted: no. 26; Tony D'Urso: nos. 3, 7, 17-20, 23, 28-34, 36,
38-41, 45, 50-53, 55, 59, 60, 63; Christoph Falke: no.
13(a+b);Francesco Galli: nos. 65, 66; Adenor Gondim: nos.
21, 46; Torben Huss: nos. 12, 25; Emidio Luisi: no. 24;
Riccardo Musacchio: no. 61; Odin Teatret: nos. 2, 4, 6, 9-
11, 15, 27, 35, 47, 49, 57; Roald Pay: nos. 8, 14a, 48; Bernd
Uhlig: no. 14b; Jan Rüsz: nos. 54, 56, 58, 64, 67; Morten
Schandorff: no. 43; Saul Shapiro: no. 22; Carlo Sperati: no.
62.

All texts have been translated by Judy Barba except for
*Written Silence, Dialogue with Brecht, Theatre-Culture, The
Shadow of Antigone, The Part of Us which Lives in Exile* and
Eurasian Theatre which were originally translated by
Richard Fowler and revised for this book by the author
and Judy Barba.

First published in 1999 by Black Mountain Press
Centre for Performance Research · 8 Science Park ·
Aberystwyth · SY23 3AH · Wales · UK

Typeset in Berkeley Old Style
Printed and Bound in Great Britain by
The Lavenham Press, Suffolk
Designed at The Design Stage · Cardiff Bay · Wales

British Library Cataloguing in Publication Data
A catalogue record for this book is available from the
British Library

Library of Congress Cataloguing in Publication Data
A catalogue record for this book has been requested

ISBN 1 902867 02 5 (hbk)
ISBN 1 902867 03 3 (pbk)

European Contemporary Classics
Series Editor : Richard Gough
BLACK MOUNTAIN PRESS
Black Mountain Press is a division of
the Centre for Performance Research Ltd

EUROPEAN contemporary CLASSICS THEATRE

THEATRE
Solitude, Craft, Revolt

CONTENTS

CONTENTS

*Whatever I say should not
be taken as an assertion
but as a question.*
Niels Bohr

1. *Eugenio Barba during a work demonstration at the University of Eurasian Theatre, Fara Sabina, Italy, 1993.*

This book is a collection of twenty-eight texts by Eugenio Barba dating from 1964 to 1995, the years which shaped his life's work as director of Odin Teatret. They were written at different times and focus on various topics and concerns; but despite their apparent diversity, they all emerge from an essential core: the meaning of theatre practice. From this point of view *Theatre. Solitude, Craft and Revolt* can be seen as complementary to Barba's other book, *The Paper Canoe.*

To me these two books present the two faces of the same professional life: *The Paper Canoe* expounds Eugenio Barba's theories on the work of the actor; *Theatre. Solitude, Craft and Revolt* makes visible the 'why', the meaning. *The Paper Canoe* is a guide to theatre anthropology; *Theatre. Solitude, Craft and Revolt* is a meandering professional autobiography.

This book is both the result and the transformation of Barba's previous book, *Beyond the Floating Islands* (1985). It is divided into five chapters. The first part of the title of each chapter defines the theme; the second part, the manner in which this theme is revealed through the author's way of thinking.

The chapters follow a chronological system in which each new article refers back to a precise period, representing a theme with the perspective of the sixties, seventies, eighties, and nineties. Each chapter usually begins with a brief text (an interview, the commentary to a didactic film, a speech) constituting a first attempt to formulate, in personal terms, a particular theme, and closes with a long reflective article, opening up onto a horizon where reflection on an experience seeks to become a legacy.

In this way, each individual chapter shows the development of the theme proposed at the beginning which is sometimes studied in depth, sometimes becomes something different, and sometimes is even rejected. It is a characteristic of the book that the questions dealt with are constantly undergoing a process of transformation, taking on diverse forms of expression, perspectives, images and topics which do not exclude contradiction.

I believe the key to the whole of Eugenio Barba's professional biography - and also to Odin Teatret's longevity - is a singular capacity for mutation. It is a 'strange' capacity, because in Barba's universe mutation never seems to be associated with the idea of change, but rather with the will to remain oneself. The constant swerves in his discourse are not changes but a way of having a dialogue with his time, refusing its spirit in order to protect his own identity. It is a strategy for interrogating History while avoiding being stripped of what he regards as essential.

What is most revealing about this book is not merely the contents of the individual texts, but the vision we are able to glimpse in between the leaps from one text to another.

Lluís Masgrau

SHIPS OF STONE
AND FLOATING ISLANDS

Barba's introductory text opens with a list of circumstances which have conditioned his and Odin Teatret's work. But what lies beyond these circumstances? Barba answers: the complementarity of opposites which becomes creative wisdom in artistic fiction, and sanguinary reality in the world of men and women. How, then, should we react to the ferocious lacerations of history? Can the artistic fiction of theatre curb the frenzied race of history? Memories from his youth seem to illuminate the vision of the sixty year-old director who dreams of a theatre able to transcend itself.

This text was first published in the special issue of Máscara *dedicated to Odin Teatret's thirtieth anniversary (No 19-20, Mexico City, 1995). It contains a few fragments from* Beyond the Floating Islands, *originally an article written in 1985 which, in this book, appears with slight modifications, under the title* Written Silence.

After the last page comes the first: this premise, which could be the end of the book, is its beginning.

The book contains texts concerning my professional biography and the activity of my theatre group, both distinguished by particular necessities and conditions. Here are some of them:

- the fact of not being accepted for a long time by the theatre milieu;
- the fact of accepting that others might not consider our work necessary;
- the need to change ourselves without presuming to change others;
- the necessity to invent our own theatrical knowledge, since we started as autodidacts;
- the demand for a discipline which might make us free;
- the desire to remain foreigners;
- the impulse to travel far from the territories in which theatre normally lives;
- the meeting with other 'emigrants';
- the deep conviction that the theatre can only be a revolt;
- the search for a way to pass on the meaning of revolt without being suppressed;
- the realisation that there exists a bond between us and others who live in conditions similar to those in which we live or have lived;
- the discovery of a common foundation which we share with masters far removed in time and space;
- the awareness that our craft belongs to the transcultural country of the profession and is shaped by an attitude towards existence.

13

For a long time, I thought of this country as an archipelago, and of its islands as floating islands. I used a historical analogy from a minor episode in the history of the New World in which men and women abandoned the security of terra firma to lead a precarious life on floating islands. In order to remain faithful to their need to live in a different way, they built villages and cities or wretched dwellings with a handful of dirt for a garden, there where it seemed impossible to construct or cultivate anything: on the water and in the currents. They were people who, either because of personal necessity or external circumstances, seemed destined to be asocial, yet they succeeded in creating alternative models of sociability. The floating islands are that uncertain terrain which can disappear under your feet, but where personal limits can be overcome, and where encounters are possible.

But what exists beyond the floating islands? Who or what do you meet there?

Contraria sunt Complementa

My theatre has two emblems: one is a reproduction of an ancient bas-relief representing the Nordic god Odin on his horse Sleipner, accompanied by two ravens, Hugin and Munin, who symbolise thought and memory. The other is the coat of arms that Niels Bohr designed for himself when he was knighted by the Danish King for his scientific achievements. He chose the Chinese sign of Yin and Yang and surrounded it by a Latin text: Contraria sunt complementa.

Nature teaches us that opposites are complementary. Art also teaches this. In our own century, subatomic particles taught it to Niels Bohr. The alchemy of herbs taught it to Friar Laurence who, with his potions and wise counsels, spread death and despair amongst the younger members of the Montague and Capulet families, crazy with love.

How do they appear in History, these opposites that become complementary?

The last time I was in the Mausoleum, in Moscow, was in November 1985. Outside the temperature was eleven degrees below zero. Inside I contemplated the face of History. The embalmed cadaver of Lenin, one of the most long-lived myths of our century, had the skin of a celluloid doll with eczema. Behind him, tombs and tombstones pell-mell: Stalin beside Kamenev, his rehabilitated victim, and Gorki beside Zhdanov, who had him poisoned in 1936.

At the time, my actors were in some country in Europe which was still governed by the fear of the cold war and by the oppression of an insurmountable wall. They were performing *The Gospel according to Oxyhrincus* where a Hassidic Jew went, dancing, in search of the Messiah and met people who had already found their own Messiah.

In that performance, all values blended and went mad before the eyes of the humble tailor Zusha Malâk. Great luminous ideals generated nights of assassinations; ecstasy and faith were the new earth from which ferocity grew; the immolated victim on the cross became a flag of war. All opposites reverted – amid blood – to their complementary aspects. Because, unlike what happens in the invisible world of atoms and in art, in the world of men and women opposites embrace in a sanguinary way.

The performance transformed into dance, song and action that which, in the Mausoleum, was represented in the solemn hibernation of history. And as I looked about me, I was amazed that some spectators judged our performance to be incomprehensible. We continued to perform it until 1987, stopping just in time, before its content became too obvious. History from 1989 on has made us familiar with the crumbling of the faiths. And peace has broken out amid blood-baths.

What can theatre do in the face of all this?

Ships of Stone

In the Imperial Palace in Beijing; in a few squares in Rome; in the gardens of the Vatican; in the desert where once Lake Aral was situated; on the mountain where the poet Gabriele D'Annunzio built his princely abode; on the roof of a supermarket; in a novel by Garcia Marquez; underneath an oak tree, in a dream, I have seen ships of stone.

At times they sail the grass and pebbles of gardens, at others they are stranded at the centre of fountains, lapped by a few centimetres of water.

They are solid stone fixed to their pedestals, striving to represent movement.

A few of them have ample sails of marble swollen by ghosts of winds, benign and impetuous yet imperceptible to us inconstant beings. It is easy to indulge our fantasy and imagine that those winds blow in another world, parallel to our own, where the ships of stone sail. They are the symbol of how to travel in the world of Art.

Theatres are ships of stone which have the power to make us travel and dream.

In the normal way of thinking, of organising society and of making laws, an awareness now prevails that Art, in its diverse manifestations, is a social asset to be protected. With time, this mentality has also begun to be applied in favour of the theatre.

Thus the ships of stone have welcomed generations of artists with open arms.

And those who, for one reason or another, remain outside, risk being ignored and forgotten.

The Two Faces of Tradition

All theatres are archaic in our times. But in this archaic and noble art there is an even more archaic attitude: the urge to transcend theatre.

If the ships of stone with their ancient and amazing features represent an anachronistic luxury, the urge to transcend theatre is represented by those floating gardens, those homes constructed on fragile islands of reed which up to now have inspired my writings: *The Floating Islands* and *Beyond the Floating Islands*.

The floating islands are not a sumptuous representation of navigation – they really navigate. But their consistency and their geography do not appear worthy of admiration. At times, I imagine the ships of stone perched on the summit of an iceberg. They are safe, while it is the massive body of ice beneath the water that moves.

There is a part of the theatre that is submerged and that we do not see or do not want to see. Whoever writes chronicles and history tends only to see the translucent pinnacles of the mountains of ice as they pass by, carrying with them the motionless ships. They ignore the infinite and obscure ways in which a multitude of theatres is present in society, often anonymous, without the names of famous artists, or with artists who only become known after their death. Here theatre is a means to weave relationships, to lead a life independent of the impositions of circumstance, to preserve the thirst for a future which seems impossible, to create an oasis of 'normal' life amid the relentless course of history, to bring the fragrance of liberty into prisons and to nourish, non-destructively, one's own revolt.

Nobody is naïve enough to believe that the wind of Art blows from one side only, that it cannot set in motion the ships of stone, or that it does not reach, with its secret tremor, the floating islands and their precarious inhabitants.

When I have spoken of Third Theatre, some people thought that I was denying the value of those theatres which Julian Beck called 'respected'; that I had rejected the great tradition of European theatre and its sophisticated avant-garde. When I began to reflect on Theatre Anthropology, often using such examples as the classical Asian theatres or a brilliant master and outsider like Etienne Decroux, some people thought that the aesthetic results of the other theatres did not seem to me to be worthy of my attention.

But for me it was not a question of aesthetics, but one of essence.

Quite apart from aesthetic results, success and well-deserved fame, there is the essential question of the presence of the theatre in its historical context, of its meaning. And theatre is not merely performances; it is not just an artistic form, but a form of being and of reacting. It is both tradition and the invention of tradition.

The concept of 'tradition' is ambiguous; it would seem to refer to the past, but in reality it is always a retrospective creation. It is constituted by the men or the women and the history which we look back upon, in which we recognise ourselves and from which we move away while accepting and transforming their legacy.

Jacques Copeau said that there were two ways to refer to tradition: one looks to the results, and the other - which he defined as *la tradition de la naissance*, 'birth tradition' - is inspired by the processes. He was not interested in reconstructing the great works of the past, but in finding the necessity which engendered them. He wanted to uncover the need for action by writers and actors who were capable of altering circumstances and opposing the currents of their times. *La tradition de la naissance*, for example, does not imply the preservation of the original values of Molière's works, but the continuation of the endeavours of a rebel who knew how to hide a wound, as well as his desire to inflict wounds under a soft cocoon of irony.

For me that is synonymous with the 'tradition of revolt'.

Stones which Dream

Revolt means continuing to dream actively and rationally, taking care that the dream does not turn into a monument or a regret.

Only once have I visited the theatre of Epidaurus, and I have never wanted to return.

In the spring of 1958, nearly 22 years old, I had not the least suspicion that in the near future I would begin to be interested in theatre. I was working in Norway as a welder, and went on a trip hitch-hiking my way around Turkey and Greece. One morning a young English couple gave me a lift in a big car in which they used to sleep at night. They too were visiting ancient monuments. When night fell, they stopped in a solitary spot. I walked off in the dark so as not to disturb them. I made my way through the undergrowth and emerged in an area that was open yet sheltered, hardly able to see a couple of paces in front of me. I climbed into my sleeping bag and fell into a deep sleep.

I was awakened by the chirping of birds and looking around me in the drowsiness of awakening, I saw stones dreaming. It was a solitude inhabited by benign forces, a space of harmony and beauty, a world of stone, immense yet intimate. My eyes took in the surroundings while noting the tiniest details as though I could reach out and touch them. Everything was made for human beings as if they lived in a more just universe.

In those days the theatre of Epidaurus was not protected by fences and unknowingly I had walked in there to sleep. I have never wanted to go back either as a tourist or man of theatre, to that place which had awakened me with an enlightenment.

Enlightenment is not only made up of light. It is set in a dark frame of death. Beauty is not always beautiful, said Baudelaire, with his sarcastic and blasé smile.

One of his most famous poems is about a carcass:

Remember the sight we saw,
My soul, that fine mild, summer morning:
Round a turning in the path
A disgusting carcass on a bed
scattered with stones ...

This fundamental text within the revolution of modern poetry is also one of the most original lessons on the nature of Beauty, and on the way we think and reflect upon culture and its values.

Baudelaire alternates two ways of seeing: one which regards the corpse with dismay and emotion considering it 'disgusting', and another, clear-sighted, uncontaminated by feelings and good taste. He discovers the realm of death in that rotting carcass while at the same time thousands of teeming maggots transform it into a dwelling, nourishment and birth-place for other forms of life.

As a spectacle, in the eyes of those two refined observers - the poet and his loved one - the carcass is revolting. Seen with the eyes of science, it is a living organism which transcends itself.

It is of no importance that theatre is an archaic leftover of another era. What matters is what it becomes. It can be a ship of stone to be admired among other monuments. It can become the privileged abode which nourishes and protects our thirst for liberty.

Epidaurus, which is the greatest stone ship of all, is not petrified - it is action even within immobility. In my memory, those stones continue to dream and confirm my dream that Epidaurus is in the future.

Thirty Years

There were five of us in *Ornitofilene*, our first production: four actors and the director. Of those five, three are still with Odin Teatret.

We are very different thirty years on, and do very different things in order to remain the same.

The possibility of remaining close to one's own origins, to the dreams and the will which possessed us in the early days, coincides with the capacity to change without losing oneself. Louis Jouvet's expression 'the legacy from us to ourselves', fascinates me on the one hand because it is filled with shadows, and on the other I recognise it because I have experienced its consistency in practice.

Change is the only way to discover what remains constant, what is the unrenounceable legacy which we of yesterday transmit to us of today. But 'today' is an abstraction. In fact, either we speak of our past or of our future, of that which we were, or of that which we would like to become.

Thirty years is a long time for a group. It is not an interest in the present that can keep it alive for so long. It is nostalgia for the future.

But if one attempts to explain which nostalgia and which future, words begin to deceive. It is not a good idea to try to throw light on one's own secret. It is vulnerable. For this reason it is hard to safeguard. It is painful to remember it even when, with the years, we acquire strength and experience, and have learned to forge our own perfect coat of armour.

But why, as Copeau said, is duration or longevity an essential component in the value of a theatre? Is it because changes allow us in time to draw near to this mysterious legacy from us to ourselves?

I also ask myself: do I exaggerate? Am I too proud of these thirty years? Do I attribute some merit to the longevity of my Odin Teatret which instead is due to chance or luck? Or is there a technique or a science of duration?

I don't believe that it is just a question of luck. And I don't think there is reason to be particularly proud. It is a problem of unadaptability. A group remains alive so long as it does not adapt to its own times - an attitude considered by many to be a childhood ailment.

And yet I believe that the only possibility we have to cultivate our floating island and bequeath something to our unknown heirs is linked to the child in us who even now bewitches us and compels us to be out of place and out of time.

In our first production, a daughter committed suicide because her father was too sympathetic towards the inevitable progress of history, and decided to cooperate for the prosperity of the community. His village stood to gain. His daughter remained empty-handed because he had stripped her of the values for which he had once fought.

An understanding of history can corrupt. One must be familiar with it in order to know how to reject the history of which we are a part. Reject it and stay alive, without being destroyed and, if possible, without destroying.

The Wall

That first production of ours, *Ornitofilene* by Jens Björneboe, dealt with the theme that today I find condensed in the phrase 'the legacy from us to ourselves'. But when I think of those beginnings, I don't think of the place where, thirty years ago, we worked on Jens Björneboe's text, trying to disentangle the inescapable contradiction between a daughter who commits suicide and a father who, in an excess of common sense, frees himself of the legacy that he had transmitted to himself.

I don't think of that damp and windowless room where we took our first hesitant steps in our profession (it was an atomic air-raid shelter, a monument to the anxieties of those years, which for us youngsters with no place to work, became a hospitable refuge). Nor do I think of the theatre. Instead I feel the freezing air on the steeply sloping roofs of Oslo, heavy with snow, in the winter of 1955.

There, a man is moving cautiously, repairing the gutters. He leans on the edge, secured to a rope held by a young man. The young man is not up on the roof, he runs no risk of falling, he is in safety as he leans out of a skylight. He has to slacken the rope so that the other man can move freely, but at the same time he must keep it fairly taut in order to be able to save him if he should fall.

The older man, who is more expert, working on the gutters, entrusts himself to the hands and the attention of the younger one who is a foreigner.

The man intent on repairing the guttering had spent his youth during the war years, when the land of Peer Gynt was occupied by the Nazis. He had been active in the Resistance and had been interned in the concentration camp at Sachsenhausen. He died in 1985. I arrived just in time to give him a last embrace. He was light, fragile. But not when he had walked and worked on the roofs; then he was heavy and it was not easy to hold on to him. His name was Eigil Winje. He was my first master. The young man leaning out through the skylight was me.

I imagine a journalist asking me point-blank: 'But how is it that after thirty years you are still doing theatre?'

'Because of the rope', I would reply.

It would be an incomprehensible answer, and therefore rude.

But I imagine that the journalist is a close friend who would not hesitate to protest. Then the right answer would be: transcendence.

My friend would reply: 'Isn't that rather pompous?' No, it's humble, simple, almost infantile.

The urge for transcendence is the child within us, who stands on tiptoe in order to look over the wall that is higher than us.

I believe that if I continue to do theatre after thirty years, it is because my feet and those of my actors are not tired. They push us towards the place we cannot reach. The wall is still there, massive, protective, with all the ambiguity of a house and a prison, of something that defines us and yet prevents us from reaching ourselves.

On Tiptoe

Theatre is unbearable if it is reduced merely to performance. The craft, precision and pleasure of invention are not enough. Nor are the solidarity, the sense of duty, one's companions. Nor is the awareness of the pleasure, or of the knowledge that we induce in the spectators. All of this is theatre, our privileged abode, the wall which protects us and encloses us.

When we stretch up on tiptoe in front of our wall, what are we trying to reach? Something higher up or something beyond?

There is no difference between horizontal transcendence and vertical transcendence. Theatre can be a place where it is worthwhile living for a long time, because it allows us to remain on tiptoe. It represents the tension to lean over the limits: the limit between the 'present' of the performance and the 'past' of the story being represented, between the intention and the action, the actor and the spectator, between us and our 'shadow'.

The word transcendence, which conjures up thoughts of heaven and hell, makes me think above all of Ayacucho, the town in the Peruvian Andes which for many years has lived in the grip of a ruthless civil war. The warring parties - the army and the guerrillas of the Shining Path - both equally brutal, wanted to destroy the normality of daily life. Their terror aimed at paralysing towns and villages. Instead of the normal rhythm of work and rest, they wanted curfews, fear, subdued acceptance.

There in Ayacucho I came to know a theatre group I shall never be able to forget. It was called Yawar Sonko and consisted of only three actors. In the beginning there were about twenty, a couple of years before I met them. Then some of them had left with the guerrillas, others had been killed, yet others imprisoned. Others were 'desaparecidos'.

21

The three who were left persisted doggedly in doing theatre. Their performance was raw, simplistic in its way of indicating the good on one side (the exploited peoples of the Andes) and the evil on the other (the Yankee imperialists). But their generous and almost suicidal courage in order to safeguard, through theatre, the relationships which belong to the normality of everyday life, has always been for me the most extreme example of theatre which transcends itself.

When I asked them why they risked so much to bring together a handful of people, they looked at me in astonishment: 'Because a normal theatre ought to be able to exist here too'.

With the distance of several years, the words of that humble group are re-echoed in the writer Susan Sontag's account of the months she spent in the bombed out and besieged Sarajevo, working on a production of Beckett's *Waiting for Godot*: 'To put on a performance here - she said - far from being frivolous, is a serious expression of normality'.

Eigil

Faced with those three actors from Ayacucho, who would deny that theatre can possess a sacred dimension?

Transcendence is more perceptible in those situations in which theatre is visibly a matter of life and death. But ought it not also to be our ambition, deep in the tranquillity and satiety of our more fortunate lives?

I believe that I continue to do theatre because it gives me the chance to meet men and women who do not feel at ease in their condition, and who keep standing on tiptoe as though, one day, they were going to fly.

And indeed we can fly: like flying fish who, from time to time, get a glimpse of the world which lies beyond their own element and which keeps them alive.

In order to remain alive, a group has to be an organisation for flying. That which transcends theatre - the sense which each of us gives to the craft - is different for every individual, and is almost always incommunicable. It has nothing to do with methods and organisation. All one can organise is a respect for incommunicability which becomes performance, and solidarity amongst egoisms which becomes social action.

I mentioned that Eigil was my first master. For a long time I didn't know it. Eigil had nothing to do with theatre. He was a metal worker who opened the doors of his workshop to me when, as a teenager, I was looking for work in Oslo and could barely utter a word in Norwegian. He taught me the rudiments of the welder's craft, patiently making me watch and try, watch and try again. He applied justice to the elementary matters of every day, from the punctuality with which he paid us to the respect he showed all of us, even an unskilled foreigner like myself. He was the owner and we were a group of five or six workers. But everybody did everything. There was no difference in our duties. No one was assigned to the more humble and unpleasant tasks while others, because of their 'superior' abilities, were exempted. There were no words for grand values, only words for work.

A few years later I recognised a familiar air, the same atmosphere of an artisan's workshop, that search for quality in the craft and in relationships when I arrived in Opole, Poland, in that tiny group of young actors led by Ludwik Flaszen, a well-known critic, and Jerzy Grotowski, a young director who many people considered too sure of himself.

Today I look at our latest production, simple and obscure like the meanderings of our stories and explicit in its title. It is called *Kaosmos*: knowing, and knowing that you don't know.

We are ten: nine actors and myself amongst the spectators, the director's place once his work is finished.

Now it is for the actors alone to reach out towards that unknown world waiting on the surrounding benches. At times I see them, the one and the other, actor and spectator, on tiptoe, one being the wall for the other. I feel that my actors are carrying me too in the midst of that tension where two solitudes, two foreign bodies - actor and spectator - can just for a moment discover a secret and involuntary bond.

This is theatre. But I am unaware of it. In reality I feel between my fingers something rough, resistant and precarious like a rope.

I

ORIGINS
VOCATION

*You must make people pay you well to do
the theatre they want, but you must pay out of your
own pocket to do the theatre you want.*

Vsevolod Meyerhold:
Conversations with Gladkov

2. *Torgeir Wethal in* The Book of Dances, *Carpignano, Italy, 1974.*

A RIFT THEATRE

This is an unpublished text, written in 1964, when Eugenio Barba was twenty-eight years old and Odin Teatret was a group of young amateurs which had existed for only a few months in Oslo. It is a historical document because it represents Barba's first attempt to formulate the spirit of his group and his idea of a vocational theatre with strongly motivated actors. Some of the fundamental ideas which are to characterise Barba's way of thinking and make up Odin Teatret's identity are already present here, although in the somewhat aggressive and fanatical style of a young outsider. These ideas are: the ethical dimension of the craft, the vision of the theatre as an unending school, and the will to separate oneself from the mainstream in order to build one's own independence.

In order to appraise this text, it is essential to keep in mind the context in which it was written: in 1964, Barba, who is Italian, returns to Oslo after four years in Poland with Grotowski, who, at that time, is unknown; theatre groups do not exist in Europe; Odin Teatret is an anonymous group of amateurs; 'Che' Guevara is still a minister in Cuba and not yet a myth; the revolution of '68 and the guerrilla movements are still to come.

Written originally in English under the title The Creation of a Rift Theatre, *this text was sent by the young Barba to the Flemish playwright, Tone Brulin, who had requested it for a Dutch magazine. It was not published and Barba forgot about it. In 1994, while I was working on Odin Teatret's archives, Ferdinando Taviani gave me a copy of the original text which was in his possession. Two years later, while preparing this book with Eugenio Barba, it seemed to me appropriate to recover his first manifesto from oblivion.*

I worked with Grotowski for three years, immersed in a very special atmosphere, isolated from every trend and artistic fashion. It was in that tiny room which constituted the famous Teatr-Laboratorium of Opole - a small town of 60,000 inhabitants situated 250 miles from Warsaw and 150 miles from Cracow.

The working conditions were clearly laid out. Grotowski directed a theatre which was supported by the State, thus leaving him comparatively free from economic worries. His actors had studied at the national drama schools and were willing to accept an austere discipline. Also collaborating with Grotowski were a couple of the most interesting artistic personalities, namely Ludwik Flaszen, a well-known theatre and literary critic, and Jerzy Gurawski, a young architect whose original ideas provided a continual source of inspiration. Personalities from every branch of the arts followed Grotowski's activities, from Warsaw to Cracow, from Poznan to Lódź, often visiting the Laboratory and thus presenting a stimulating front of 'internal' criticism and dialogue.

The term 'laboratory', therefore, had a genuine significance. A group of qualified artists were dedicating themselves to specific research on the basis of a clearly defined aesthetic and technical method, backed up by people from cultural circles all over Poland.

Once back in Norway, my new 'base', the situation was entirely different. During my three years spent in the anonymity of a small provincial town buried in Silesia, I had nevertheless been at the focal point of one of the most original experiences in contemporary theatre. In Oslo, however, the administrative and artistic capital of Norway, I really found myself 'in the provinces', not because of geography or customs, but the 'artistic' provinces which vegetate, having no ambitions, satisfied with their fortuitous achievements, simply because they are no worse than those of their colleagues. The only creativity of these 'provinces' was to adorn its own sterility behind ponderous verbosity, frustrating debates or, at best, behind impudent loans from the most recent hits on the Parisian 'boulevards' or from London's West End. The only initiatives of these 'provinces' were to trim themselves with feathers borrowed from others' successes, or to rejoice in the mistakes of others without having the courage to bear the consequences of their own.

But let's dot our i's and cross our t's! Norwegian 'provinciality' is in no way different from that of any other European country. Independent artistic research which creates and does not consume, patiently elaborating new visions and paths in dramatic art, has disappeared from the majority of European stages. The spectators' need to be confronted with an artistic work and a critical reflection of their own condition still exists. But 'this need of the public is continually being smothered by directors avid for money, and by a certain kind of 'actor-soloist' who likes to tickle the entrails of his public in an attempt to imitate life, but who is far from being a disciplined member of an artistically creative group. Then there are the 'realistic' directors, utterly unconscious of the aims of their own production, searching blindly for unusual innovations and new shivers yet without any aesthetic coherence, and without being in a position to distinguish between formal and realistic effects. Their work is wasted, disorientating both public and actors, not to mention the confused critic who mumbles empty phrases in a frantic effort to understand the casual finds of the directors, themselves ignorant of the true sense of their own work.'

This analysis made by Witkacy in 1938 does not appear outmoded. It may be applied to the entire 'theatrical Norway' or, similarly, to the whole of that artistic 'province' which is Theatrical Europe, content with its own power of inertia and the suggestive mirages of some prophet (Artaud and Co.), and which survives thanks to the clumsy financing of some Arts Council.

My return to Norway not only represented a proselytic expansion of the method of Grotowski. It also involved an interesting cultural and socio-logical experiment. What would be the reaction of the Norwegians to the attempt at a break with the brief traditions of their national theatre, rooted in naturalism and in psychologism, though masked by the fragmentary results of other artistic techniques - film, painting, dramatic literature, architecture? What would happen in a country which has not seen the birth and evolution of a purely local avant-garde movement, where Joyce and the Surrealists, Artaud and the complete works of Brecht have never even been translated; a country where avant-garde theatres do not exist and where the entire theatrical life revolves around six permanent stages and three travelling companies?

Apparently the circumstances and the cultural climate are not propi-tious to the formation and development of a 'rift-theatre'. Such a theatre, through the actors' means of expression, proposes a new sociological function and a psychological content which does not describe the charac-ters' states of mind, but conveys an emotional shock to the spectators.

Two postulates, however, decided my choice to remain in Norway and create my own theatre. The first was borrowed from the *Guerrilla Manual* by Ernesto 'Che' Guevara. It states: 'One should not always wait for favourable conditions to start a revolution. The actual breaking out of the insurrection can create them'.

But let me make myself clear: far be it from me to say that the theatre should serve a 'revolution'. This remark by Guevara combines a form of heroism and an abnegation which should distinguish honesty in art. It is not necessary to hope in order to undertake. A 'rift-theatre' is a refusal of any short-sighted pragmatism and brings coherently to life the models of one's own professional conscience. Like the 'guerrillas', its actors live in isolation, always on the offensive, pursued by public opinion and by those artists who, too self-assured and proud of their talent, react against such an unruly band that dares to question the value of their art.

The second postulate derives from the parallel we have just made with a guerrilla movement. A 'rift-theatre' cannot base its strategy and tactics on the traditional conception of the academic theatre. The difference between them lies in the organisation, the artistic and social function, the working methods, and the finality of their activities. It is not a question of the 'rift-theatre' forcibly imposing its own artistic norms or seizing power. Its aim is to convey to its spectators an awareness of what sense and purpose theatre should have for them, and of what spiritual and intellectual needs this art should satisfy in our time.

A 'rift-theatre' exposes itself to the wrath of the spectators who are unwilling to be disturbed in their intellectual lethargy; it attracts the anger of the critics who suddenly find all the pretty ready-made phrases with which they are accustomed to label every new trend slipping through their fingers. It is a thorn in the foot of the academic theatre with its tendency to idleness and self-complacency.

The tactics of such a 'rift-theatre' consist in working in complete isolation, far from any official artistic circles, never content with its achievements, and obstinately fighting to overcome every professional obstacle. Through long months of hard work it prepares for the performance with which it will launch its attack on the academic theatre, not by means of an aesthetic theory but with technical quality and artistic sincerity. Then, after this confrontation, the theatre retires once again to its arduous labours for the next production which must destroy all the labels that categorised its previous results, and deny every form of dogmatic evolution in its own working methods. The 'rift-theatre' is not a slavish medium for preconceived ideas but is subjected to the evolution embodied in the artistic affinity of a group of actors.

Hence it is a theatre which is based on the sacrifice of each of its members who are totally dedicated and ready to give themselves to the group, working to the limits of their strength. It is an artistic community in which the actors do not feel themselves alienated as in the vast administrative and commercial machine of academic theatre with its intrigues, cliques and aberrant publicity. It does not develop solely from an aesthetic closeness between its members; it is at the same time a true school of ethics for the actor as an individual.

The actors in this theatre must be amateurs, young people who have not undergone the demoralising experience of theatre schools and who have never learned laziness on academic stages. The 'rift-theatre' trains its own actors, and its activities present two distinctive aspects: the internal one being a professional training and the external being the performance which reflects the results of this training. In reality the theatre will remain a school throughout its existence, never ceasing to confront its actors with new tasks relating to their psycho-physical possibilities.

After some years, this school elaborates adequate means of research resulting in a higher level of work, whose achievements are regularly presented to the public in the form of performances. We can imagine the 'rift-theatre' evolving into an institute for research, or a laboratory, once its members have acquired their own methodological approach and developed the technical capacities needed to carry forward this research. This will be possible after ten or so years of work in common.

Talent is not necessary in order to belong to such a theatre. Talent in the theatre does not exist. There only exists a will to work and to give one's all for one's work. To render this assertion valid it is enough to quote the example of the Asian classical theatre in which six-, eight- or ten-year-old children are admitted to the acting profession. After ten years of grinding apprenticeship and austere discipline they emerge as artists whose suggestive expressivity will remain the greatest dream of every great European actor. The 'rift-theatre' selects its members not on the basis of their talent but according to their will to work.

But this is not all. These young people must be fully aware of the hard task they have chosen, and must consider it as the highest possible honour to participate in this theatrical adventure. The actors themselves entirely finance the theatre during the early stages of work or during the absence of the spectators. The artistic credo of the actors is contained in two principles:
- Please, God, give me the strength always to choose the most difficult path;
- If I miss one day's training, only my conscience will know; if I miss three day's training, only my colleagues will know; if I miss a week's training, all the spectators will know.

I can well imagine the reader's cynical smile on reading these 'commandments' of professional ethics with their ascetic tang, which will probably be considered as an idealistic dream. I think the moment has come to deal with some concrete facts.

On a quiet street in Oslo there exists a theatre unknown to all: Odin Teatret. Here a very small group of actors is preparing itself to put into practice the 'idealistic' views expressed above. The members have been selected from amongst the applicants who were refused admission to Oslo's Drama School. They work from 9 a.m. until 4 p.m. and from 5 p.m. until 8 p.m.. Their training consists only of practical subjects: acrobatics, gymnastics, sports, ballet, rythmics, plastique, improvisation, naturalistic studies, vocal hygiene and exercises in concentration (psycho-technics). Each student is responsible for a given sector of the training under the guidance of the theatre's artistic director. Here there are no external

31

pedagogues to teach the student-actors, but each pupil becomes his own pedagogue under the guidance of the director. By pedagogy is meant a conscious study of one's own body, of the muscular mechanisms, of the psycho-physical laws which determine these mechanisms and of the ways of controlling them and transforming them into means of artistic expression.

The economy of the theatre is assured by weekly contributions which every member of the group pays into a common kitty. None of the actors can take up temporary work in another theatre, nor in films nor on television without the consent of the other members. They may agree to this on three conditions:
- The work must be useful from a technical point of view;
- The actor works extra time thus making up for the hours of training lost;
- Half the earnings go to the actor's own theatre.

Another method of incrementing the economy of the theatre is to periodically enforce a week's work outside the theatre, turning the salary over to the common kitty. An attempt is made to avoid such a method, however, in order not to interrupt the rhythm of the training.

Odin Teatret has now been in existence for six months. In spite of the hard discipline and its economical difficulties, it shows no sign of all the symptoms which afflict the academic theatres. The actors consider with calm good humour the long years of training that await them. They have fully accepted the singular working atmosphere in which anonymity and sacrifice are the common rule, and they are beginning to develop that special form of professional integrity which consists in considering one's own conscience as the only critical authority.

Contact with the outside is limited, yet the theatre gains only valuable stimulation from this. But the fact that Jens Bjørneboe, a noted and much discussed Norwegian author, has given one of his unpublished plays - *Ornitofilene* - to us gratis to be our first production, or rather our 'launching of hostilities', constitutes a proof of confidence and a source of encouragement. The premiere will take place only when the group is sure that at the present stage of its technical capacities it has nothing more to give.

To what degree does a theatre such as this stand a chance of survival in a welfare state where material standards have replaced spiritual ones? I believe that amongst the youth there will always be a tiny group in search of a refuge, or rather a path leading to an openly articulated protest and revolt against a society in which they feel foreign. It is therefore a matter of knowing how to direct this revolt into channels which are useful to society and which represent for the actor a school of moral self-discipline.

It is no longer a question of a correct professional preparation, but of new professional ethics. For us it is a natural conclusion that technique and aesthetics are the results of a specific ethical attitude. Why do I want to become an actor? What does this represent for me and what should it represent for my spectators? What is the meaning of the theatre, and what function must it defend at a time when new forms of entertainment have assumed the ancient sociological role of this art?

Such are the questions that must be answered by this group of young people whose disinterested labours are diagnosed as madness by a sane society.

Yes, it is madness, yet there is method in it.

LETTER TO ACTOR D.

Eugenio Barba wrote this letter to one of his actors in 1967. It illustrates his vision of theatre, particularly with regard to the attitude of an actor who is nourished by deep personal needs: 'the eternally unanswered questions'. Here, Barba sees the vocational theatre as a catacomb, the secret place where the birth of another theatre and another tradition is prepared.

This text, first published in Synspunkter om Kunst, Brøndums Forlag, Copenhagen 1968, was immediately translated into many languages. With time, its wide diffusion and its dense and emblematic character have transformed it into a manifesto.

I have often been struck by a lack of seriousness in your work. This is not the same as a lack of concentration or good will. It is the expression of two attitudes.

First of all, it seems as if your actions are not driven by any inner conviction or irresistible need which leaves its mark on your exercises, improvisations and performance. You may be concentrated in your work, without sparing your energies, your gestures may be technically correct and precise, but your actions remain empty. I don't believe in what you are doing. Your body clearly says: 'I have been told to do this'. Your nerves, your brain, your spine are not totally engaged, and with this skin-deep commitment you want to make me believe that what you are doing is vital to you. You yourself do not sense the importance of what you want to share with the spectators.

How then can you expect the spectator to be gripped by your actions? How can you, with this attitude, uphold the understanding of theatre as a place where social inhibitions and conventions are annihilated to make way for an open-hearted and absolute communication? You represent the community within this space, with the humiliations you have undergone, your cynicism as self-defence and your optimism as the essence of irresponsibility, your guilt, your need for love, the longing for a lost paradise hidden in the past, close to the person who could make you forget fear.

Everybody present with you in this space will be affected if you succeed in rediscovering these sources, this common ground of human experience, the hidden motherland. This is the bond that unites you to the others, a treasure that lies buried deep within all of us, never unearthed, because it is our only comfort, and because it hurts when we touch it.

The second attitude I see in you, is your embarrassment in considering the seriousness of your work. You feel the need to laugh, to sneer, and come with humorous comments about what you and your colleagues are doing. It is as if you want to flee from the responsibility that you feel is inherent in your craft, which consists in establishing communication with human beings, and in assuming responsibility for what you are uncovering. You are afraid of seriousness, of the awareness that you are on the fringes of the permissible. You are afraid that everything you do is synonymous with tediousness, fanaticism, or over-specialisation. But in a world where people around us either no longer believe in anything, or only pretend to believe in order to be left in peace, those who dig deep within themselves to reach a clarity about their own situation, their absence of ideals, their need for spiritual life, will always be called fanatic or naive. In a world where cheating is a norm, those who seek their own truth are taken for hypocrites.

You must accept that everything you create, everything liberated and given form by your work is also a part of life and deserves care and respect. Your actions before the community of the spectators should possess the power of the flame hidden in the red-hot iron, or of the voice in the burning bush. Only then will your actions live on in the senses and the memory of the spectator, fermenting into unforeseeable consequences.

While Dullin lay on his deathbed, his face contorted and assumed all the important roles he had played: Smerdiakov, Volpone, Richard III. It was not just the man Dullin who was dying but also the actor, the many phases of his life.

If I ask you why you became an actor, you will reply: 'To fulfil myself, to express myself'. But what does this mean? Who has fulfilled himself? Was it Mr. Smith who lived a quiet life, respectable and without problems, never tormented by unanswerable questions? Or the romantic Gauguin, who broke with all the social norms and ended his life in poverty in a Polynesian village, convinced that he had found the lost freedom, Noa-Noa? In an age where belief in God is diagnosed as a neurosis, we lack the scales to weigh our life and tell us whether we have been fulfilled or not. No matter which personal and hidden motives have led you to the theatre, once you have entered the profession, you must find a meaning which, stretching beyond your own person, confronts you socially with others.

It is only within the catacombs that we can prepare a new life. This is the place for those who in our time seek spiritual commitment measuring themselves with the eternally unanswered questions. It presupposes courage: the majority of people do not need us. Your work is a sort of social meditation upon yourself, your human condition and the events that touch you to the quick through the experiences of our age. In such a precarious theatre which disturbs the normal psychic well-being, every performance can be your last. You should consider it as such, the final possibility of reaching out to others, crying out your last word, your testament, the reckoning of your actions.

If being an actor can mean all this to you, then a new theatre will be born. A new approach to tradition will spring forth, a new technique and a new relationship between you and the spectators who come in the evening to see you because they need you.

WAITING FOR THE REVOLUTION

Developing the discourse from A Rift Theatre *and* Letter to the Actor D.*, this text sums up the perspective of the sixties on vocation, the springboard on which theatre should stand. Any theatre revolution sinks its roots into a vocational theatre because personal motivations and needs are the secret motor which can transform us through theatre. Theatre practice cannot change society in general; it can change only that part of society which we call 'theatre'. Not theatre within revolution, but revolution within theatre.*

First published in Odin Teatret's magazine Teatrets Teori og Teknikk, 8, *Holstebro 1968.*

To claim that theatre must once again become a popular art is proof that one is ill-acquainted with its history. We find only two eras in the past when theatre represented a social event embracing the entire community: Greek drama and the passion plays of the Middle Ages. But in those days, theatre was not so much an aesthetic fact as a manifestation of moral and religious edification.

Only a community bound together by strong and profound ties and by a common vision of life can react unanimously to a performance which, inasmuch as it touches on the sources of its faith and of its spiritual life, can become a model for action. Today, there no longer exists a homogeneous audience, but audiences reflecting our dispersed society. Once the common ground has disappeared - that is to say the religious faith and a deeply felt moral code - no form of theatre can claim to be popular or, in other words, capable of engaging the community totally.

Theatre is no longer the only form of performance. There exist others which are more exciting and more suitable to the rhythm of our life: sport, television, cinema and even foreign travel, where an hour's flight - the time required to reach a theatre in the centre of town from the suburbs - takes us to a new country. It is a fantastic world which is not made of papier mâché, but of real exotic scenery, animated by human beings who do not play at being, but are authentically spontaneous, a world which frees us from the constraints and the taboos that restrict us in our everyday surroundings.

What I have in mind when speaking of theatre is neither a place of pure entertainment nor a didactic or revolutionary centre. To fulfil these two functions there exist, on the one hand, discotheques, night-clubs and cabarets, and, on the other, evening classes, political party schools and the streets.

Theatre is fiction, vision. Its intensity of suggestion is the one thing which acts on the spectator. When it applies itself to becoming what it endeavours to suggest, it loses its effect. In the twenties, there were dozens of agit-prop communist theatres in Germany. They were unable to check Hitler's advance and are now all forgotten. But Piscator and Brecht, who were voicing the same appeal in an artistic manner, are part of our political and cultural heritage.

Today, the value of the theatre no longer lies in its sociological function, which is diffuse and undefinable, but in the precise and distinct psychological meaning it takes on for each actor and for each spectator.

We have all seen performances where the actors play in an uncontrolled physical whirl - they call it spontaneity - with piercing cries and convulsive movements. At the very moment when they seek to express their total being, they go to pieces in a shapeless nonentity. And although the fundamental aspirations of such a theatre are worthy of respect, this form of communication brings out nothing new in the way of articulate consciousness of ourselves. Everything gets bogged down in a biological chaos, in impotence.

Theatre, like all artistic activities, is discipline. All visionary explosion must be mastered: the actor must ride on the tiger, he must not let himself be devoured by it. The physical exteriorization of the emotions must be canalised, controlled, and thus become a wave of explicit signs. It must not be allowed to get the upper hand and plunge the actor into confused actions which ape suffering. This false agony, this epidermic sentimentalism akin to hysteria, this aping of the afflictions of contemporary man and, above all, this alibi for a good conscience felt by the actor, show up the squalidness and the hypocrisy of our whole age, of our whole society. The theatre then becomes the true reflection of a condition which must be destroyed, beginning with itself. The spectators smile at such a performance and feel reassured: this place is not dangerous, the deception continues. The impossible is not made manifest, the cries, the political slogans, the naked bodies on the stage are rags in which the actors clothe their inner void. Lucidity and knowledge are required in order to be a revolutionary: amateurs have never changed the course of history.

Theatre is not an exact science, a field in which one can attain, transmit and develop certain objective results. The results achieved and the solutions found by the actors die and disappear with them. The spectator perceives as objective signs the articulate actions of the actor which are, however, the result of a subjective process. How can the actors be the matrix of these actions and at the same time be able to shape them into objective signs whose origin is in their own subjectivity? This is the essence of the actor's art and methodology. It is impossible to discover the formula, the tools, the instruments which might provide a definitive answer to this question.

During the process of training - which cannot be limited to three or four years - there is only one possibility: that of discovering, and then surmounting, the obstacles which hinder communication. The rest is incertitude.

The misapprehension begins with apprenticeship, that intimate situation in which one generation offers its experience - of art and of life - to another generation. It is entirely illusory to teach a series of elements which, in reality, are only clichés and stereotypes: a little diction, a little theatre history, a little psychology and, possibly, some notions of modern dancing and acrobatics. A fresh approach to our craft can only be determined by a continual renewal of our consciousness and of our personal attitude towards life. It is the process which transforms us, the day-by-day manner with which we share our work.

Meanwhile, let the young people who have chosen theatre furnish daily proof of the necessity of their choice, even by means of this inconsequential programme. Let them clash with a profession which imposes such inhuman demands that only a few persevere: those who are animated by an indomitable need, those who are not satisfied with superficial solutions, the demons for work who overcome the inertia which contents itself with futile results. Let them attain, with their own personalities, their bodies and souls, the ultimate judgement on themselves as representatives of this society which still proclaims: thou shalt love thy neighbour. And let this be achieved without chaos and emotional overflow, but with lucidity and in cold blood.

It is no longer a question of being a missionary or an original artist, but of being realistic. Our profession gives us the possibility of changing ourselves, and thereby changing society. One must not ask: what does theatre mean for the people? This is a demagogic and unfruitful question. But rather, what does theatre mean for me? The answer, converted into ruthless and uncompromising action, will be revolution in the theatre.

THE DISCIPLE WHO WALKED ON THE WATER

In this text, Eugenio Barba reflects upon theatre and revolution in the intensely politicised context of the seventies. The activities of Odin Teatret's first ten years are a response to overt political theatre, underlining yet again the importance of motivation. Theatre is not political because it attempts to change society through eloquent discourse, but rather because it provides the means to embody personal needs. In the sixties vocation was a springboard; now it has become a political 'compass'. Vocational theatre is no longer a secret place, but a separate one; nowadays it is a reservation where one's own needs have the right to exist.

The following text is a montage of fragments from The Park and the Reservation *(in Ferdinando Taviani's* Il libro dell'Odin, Feltrinelli, Milan 1975); Not a Political Theatre but, through Theatre, a Policy *('Mezzogiorno', 4, Bari 1975) and* Without Illusions *('Rinascita - Il contemporaneo', 9, Rome 1978).*

Like mice hanging on the bell-ropes, we often delude ourselves that we are ringing the bells, that it is up to us whether they chime or are silent.

One can speak of theatre in general, of its function, of the crisis and the vast problems of our art in present-day society.

I do not wish to judge, merely to observe. And this simply on the basis of a decade's experience with my companions from Odin Teatret, a group which is trying to put into practice its own 'politics', which wants to live out its own 'no' and follow its own vision.

Showing your Back

A precept of the theatre in the past obliged the actors never to turn their backs on the audience. For the spectator, the actor was not supposed to have a back.

An analogous tendency to hide one's own back seems today to characterise the life of certain groups from so-called 'political theatre'. These define themselves according to acceptable ideas on society, on how to accomplish through theatre what they believe it is right to give the audience. They affirm their utility to others, but hide the motivations which brought them together, the demands and the needs which impelled each individual to unite in a group and do theatre.

Often the fact of clinging to 'political theatre' means escaping from the problem of pursuing a policy through theatre.

The forging of a policy involves socialising one's own needs and, through these, reaching out to and making a mark on others. Each individual transforms into moments of exchange and encounter the choices which made him or her become an actor, without hiding them behind the supposed answers to the supposed needs of the spectators, or behind a prefabricated image imposed by a faceless audience. The actor should not hide behind static representations of how a theatre that is useful to society should be. Those who justify their work by speaking of what society wants from them, are not able to mutate their personal needs into a public act capable at times, like a ghost, of haunting the spectator.

We have to start from ourselves and for ourselves. Only by so doing can we confront others and be recognised.

The Reservation

Does theatre still constitute a genuine cultural need?

Anyone who knows what is going on among the new generations knows that our craft has acquired a whole new sense. This sense arises not only from the need to *see another theatre*, but also from the need to *create another theatre*, establish new relationships between the actors and the spectators.

This formula sums up the mutation that theatre is undergoing. One could investigate the motives which have driven ideologists, critics, professionals and scholars to refute this simple truth: that theatre has lost its character of functional use to a specific community or particular social strata. This situation has been concealed under elaborate aesthetic or ideological encrustations which presumed a social and revolutionary utility, in spite of it being evident that theatre had no tangible influence on the surrounding reality.

The encrustations are often pearls. But the pearl grows around a wound which we are trying to hide: the indifference as to whether the theatre lives or dies, either as a place of tradition or of cultural experiment.

The theatre has an audience which is often numerous. But the audience, as such, is not the problem. Who, amongst those spectators, would genuinely feel intellectually or spiritually diminished if it became impossible to go to a performance? Nowadays the so-called 'need for theatre' is an artificial one. It is useless to continue to hide behind a false rhetoric instead of identifying that which is new, springing from the withering of our art.

On other occasions I have used the term Third Theatre to describe those groups which exhibit needs and contradictions that may only belong to a limited number of individuals, but are nevertheless profound.

New relationships, and not new aesthetics or contents, invade the identifiable habitat of the theatre, occupying the peripheries and penetrating places and environments that would previously have been unthinkable. This is not the birth of 'another theatre'. Other situations are now being called theatre.

Theatre becomes a reservation which gives the right of existence to personal needs and permits their manifestation. It is a reservation whose inhabitants live out their own utopia which has the right of citizenship only in this apparent isolation. This reservation can only be protected through a craft and a coherence associated with technical and artistic criteria. Personal necessity becomes action, crosses frontiers and enters into history.

The Guru and the Disciple

There was once a guru who attracted a multitude of disciples whose hope was one day to become his equal. Many of them seemed unfit for the task, as though predestined never to approach the Great Deed. The guru, always patient, welcomed even the unsuitable.

As the years went by, strange rumours began circulating concerning one of these. It was said he worked miracles. People told how he persisted in going down to the river bank at night where he walked on the water. The guru was curious and wanted to verify these stories. In the dark of the night, he watched as his most humble disciple entered the river, walking on the water.

On his return to the bank, the guru asked him how on earth he was able to do such a thing. Confused, the disciple mumbled: 'It is not me who does it - it is you. As I walk on the water I cling tirelessly to your name. It is your name that sustains me.'

Theatre is the name of the guru.

Me and my Odin companions attempt to walk on the river, on the swirling waters of history and of our vulnerable convictions.

WRITTEN SILENCE

Written Silence *takes up again the theme of vocation from the perspective of the eighties. After two decades of work, vocation appears as the origin which guides us through the craft and to which one has to remain loyal. Personal needs are no longer a springboard or a compass, but the very roots. 'It is our first day of work which determines the meaning of our path', writes Barba. Referring to the vocational theatre, Barba uses the image of the floating islands from the New World: minute pieces of land which detach themselves from terra firma, but which remain arable. Vocational theatre is now defined as precarious yet fertile space.*

First published in Alfabeta, 69, Milan 1985, under the title: Odin Teatret: storia e oggi, *and later as* A Premise on Written Silence *in* Beyond the Floating Islands, *PAJ, New York 1986. In this book, the first part of the text has been changed.*

The Travellers of Speed

There are people who live in a nation or in a culture. And there are people who live in their own bodies. They are the travellers who cross the Country of Speed, a space and time which have nothing to do with the landscape and the season of the place they happen to be travelling through. One can stay in the same place for months and years and still be 'a traveller of speed' journeying through regions and cultures thousands of years and thousands of kilometres distant, in unison with the thoughts and reactions of men and women far removed from oneself because of skin colour or history. Speed is a personal dimension which cannot be measured by scientific criteria, although science and progress themselves have roots in this immeasurable dimension.

In this personal dimension, in the centre of this country, which is confined to our living bodies, there is a capital, and in it the Palace of the Emperor, and in this palace is a secret room, and in this room is the heart. The heart of this country, which is our body-in-life, is a constellation of fixed ideas, of very particular problems, of individual obsessions and hidden illnesses.

The travellers of speed can also be met in theatre. The significance of their lives and the meaning of their revolt, have been forgotten. Sometimes they themselves have been forgotten. At other times they have merely become famous.

One of them, for example, had a very personal obsession: how to repeat his role every night with the flowing quality of life, without any mechanical predetermination.

One of them looked for the New Man in the actor.

One of them wanted theatre to reveal transcendent realities, realities truer than those we call true, and which lie behind the veil of our world and psychology.

One of them exhausted his life building a theatre like a Great Wall of China, a defence against the irrational and emotional waves which throw the days and years into confusion and obscure the inscrutable dialectics of history.

And finally, one of them, the one closest and dearest to me, began by wanting to change Poland, then changed the theatre and his profession. And then he sought to change the lives of individual people.

The inhabitants of the great traditions and the travellers of speed live together on the map of theatres and their histories, and it is difficult to tell them apart. The former live inside a heredity which they pass on to successive generations, sometimes in an impoverished form, sometimes altered or enriched. The latter, having arrived at a certain point on their path, look at their hands, and discover that with them they have built something very different from what they had in mind.

For a long time, as a traveller of speed, I walked in a group. Then I discovered that I had been walking alone among other solitary people. I keep on going.

But what do I see beyond the faces I know?

Secrecy and Barter

Odin Teatret is twenty years old. Twenty years for a group are like sixty years for an individual. Looking around me, I can safely say: we did not die young. In the history of the theatre, this is exceptional.

I ask myself what concrete and unprogrammed facts have resulted in the fragile equilibrium which has allowed us not only to get through our youth, but to continue to grow and change, even in maturity. I ask myself what logic can be detected behind the succession of episodes dictated by circumstance. I ask myself if fragments of information useful to others can be discerned behind the smokescreen of a group's biography.

There are apparently two distinct periods in the life of our group. The first period began in 1964, when Odin Teatret was formed, and lasted for ten years. It was characterised by work which we remember as being very hard, so hard that today we suspect we would no longer be able to endure it: training several hours a day, preparations for each new production lasting one or two years. It was through its performances that the group opened itself to the outside world. These were presented to sixty spectators, the maximum number that could be fitted into our work room. They were above all our performances and we refused to change them when we were on tour and it would have been possible to accommodate a larger audience. They always stayed within the borders of the small area in which they had been born: with only sixty spectators.

All the actors' work, their training and personal research took place isolated from any extraneous observation. Our two work rooms in Holstebro were separate ('secret,' etymologically speaking) environments in which the actor's research could develop, protected from external disturbances in reciprocal trust, without being subjected to the tyranny of premature judgements and the haste to produce. In addition to the performances, the activities which made us visible to the outside world were not, at that time, normally associated with a theatre: organisation of courses, seminars, tours of foreign productions, publication of a magazine and books, sociological surveys, production of didactic films.

The second period of our group life began in 1974 with a long stay in a village in southern Italy. It seemed natural to behave there as we did at home: 'secret' training and 'secret' preparations for a new production, activities not intended for the outside. But in that situation, in that village in southern Italy, secrecy generated curiosity. And the curiosity pressured us into asking ourselves if secrecy was actually still necessary. We discovered that it no longer was.

Our daily work, our training, which we believed concerned only the individual actors in the group, turned into something else as soon as we opened it up to the outside. It revealed the web of our internal relationships, that which defined us not as performers, but as a small group of people who had a history in common and shared attitudes (perhaps not explicit, but certainly concrete and evident) with respect to the reality which surrounded us.

The secrecy, which we had sought only in order to guarantee ourselves the best possible conditions for our professional development, had produced an unexpected result: the crystallisation of a group culture.

'Group culture' - when I write this term now, it bothers me somewhat. It has been quite a few years since I have talked or written about it, and now there is a danger of it becoming hollow, a slogan. Group culture is nothing more than a prouder and more eloquent way of saying that a group has knowledge and experience in common, has developed its own training, has found its own artistic vision and chosen its objectives. This is as it should be, if one is dealing with a theatre group.

Both the 'secret' activity and the use of theatre in places without theatre, showed us that it was possible to turn our craft into an instrument for change - for ourselves as well as for others - provided that we stayed either on the outskirts of the theatre ('secret' activity) or beyond theatre's reach ('barter'). What in the past were two complementary periods are today the two poles of a single line of action.

Beyond theatre was 'barter': the exchange of our theatrical presence - training, performances, pedagogical experience - for the 'culture' of other theatre groups or communities. It was also a different way of using theatre in a variety of contexts. But it was above all the means to revitalise an otherwise worn-out relationship: the means to pass from a meeting with a ghost-audience which came and disappeared in one evening, to a meeting with spectators who showed and presented themselves as well as watching the actors.

On the outskirts of theatre was the 'secret' theatre, secret in the sense of separated: a place where a small group of people - some actors and a few spectators - gathered together. They had chosen each other in order to dissect the forces governing human and social realities, to confront themselves with their own questions, their unresolved enigmas, and to look at the fragments of the past and the imminent future, deformed and magnified in the performance's mirror.

Both the 'secret' activity and the 'barter' are based on reciprocal interest and expectations, not on a vague and general artistic curiosity. The barter contains the secret of simultaneously using and wasting theatre. And the 'secret' contains the high point of an exchange.

* * *

These two periods in the life of our group often appear to observers as two very distinct and contrasting phases. From the point of view of the results, this is right. From the point of view of the process, however, it has been a consistent and unbroken development.

First the group laid the solid foundations of its internal and external life. Then it constructed activities on these foundations which broke through the confines of the theatre. Only on the surface do there seem to be contradictions and divisions between these two periods, one, when the theatre was concentrated on itself, and the other when it seemed to project itself into the outside world. It is only because we concentrated on the conditions of our work for ten years, and succeeded in changing ourselves before considering changing theatre or society, that today we are more or less able to free ourselves from the ties of a specialised type of theatrical organisation.

In the life of a group, as in the life of an individual, there comes a time when the conditions for a certain security are consolidated. One then finds oneself faced with an alternative: to stay in a secure routine or to accumulate even more stability. In order to avoid being caught in the grip of this vice-like situation, it is important to know in which direction one's energies should be projected. It is the critical moment when the thread may break at any time. Each person looks for his own path, the pressure becomes so centrifugal that the group fragments into individual projects or into escapes towards the outside in search of fresh oxygen, new challenges, other relationships.

It is often thought that a theatre group has unity because its members resemble each other. On the contrary, it is necessary to look for reciprocal differentiation in order to achieve totality. It is through this process of differentiation, founded on the trust of each individual in all the others and on the lack of illusions, that a common ground is built in spite of all differences. Superficial agreement on the other hand, even when it is a unity of ideas and intentions, is swept away by the first wind.

This can be translated into professional terms as follows: if when looking at a group of actors, one sees that the work of one actor resembles the work of the others and vice versa, it nearly always means that they merely have certain theories in common. When these theories fade, artistic development is in danger of wasting away. It is a good sign when the work of the individual actors in a group begins to develop in such different directions that, from the technical and aesthetic point of view, they no longer seem to have any relationship to each other. This difference, this lack of similarity in the results, is perhaps one of the most reliable proofs of a deep methodological unity.

This methodological unity consists in nothing more than feeding the impulse which pushes the individual actors to follow their own path until they meet themselves and their own vision, not the teacher's vision. What then is left of the relationship between the teacher and the pupil?

Does the search for one's own path lead irrevocably to solitude?

Telling Kite Stories

I was once told about a discussion which took place among members of certain theatre groups. Someone maintained that the Odin had opened up a route along which other groups could also travel. The Odin, he said, was an avant-garde, in the political, not in the artistic sense. Someone else

47

then said: 'We can't relate to a group like the Odin that way'.

'And why not?' said another.

'Because the Odin is like a kite' answered the first. The I Ching had told him so, he went on. I imagine that some of the people present started to smile. But the one who had spoken up, ever more sure of himself, began to explain. It was not his personal opinion, he pointed out; whether they wanted to believe it or not was up to them, but it was what the I Ching had said. So they should at least listen. It was a mistake to believe that the Odin was a strong group. The Odin did not have strong ties anchoring it to the world. It was much more fragile than people thought, much less powerful than it appeared: it was held to the earth by nothing more than a slender thread. But the Odin was important because it explored the winds. Then the I Ching had added: 'Let the winds guide you, but follow the water-ways'.

It is in fact impossible to bequeath the harmony of the winds, their continuous and ever-changing interplay.

The history of the theatre contains many journeys whose routes are not passed on.

In spite of the great distance which separated the Berliner Ensemble's productions in the fifties and Grotowski's in the sixties, the spectator was left with the same impression of rightness, the same sense of a 'harmony' by means of which a personal search had become something objective. But this search followed such individual routes - like the winds which guide the flight of a solitary kite - that it seemed to exclude all possibility of anyone repeating the process that gave birth to the results.

Stanislavski's spectators too, at the beginning of the century, must have received the same sense of a new, highly personal harmony.

Harmony is not static beauty, but active proportion, movement in still-ness.

The need for harmony is not the need to solve a problem. It is an impulse to change things around in a way which is often difficult to explain even to oneself.

Harmony is accord between tensions. If I feel the lack of something essential to me, then there is no harmony within me. It is as if there is a fragment of emptiness within me and I am compelled to fill it, and for this reason I set myself in motion. This being on the move in order to find out how to placate the emptiness, reveals the meaning of what pushes and nourishes me.

Let us imagine a man with a weak constitution, with one partially disabled hand, with eyes that can barely see, living in a time when the stars and planets were studied with the naked eye and dogged endurance was required in order to stay up night after night scrutinising the skies. Johannes Kepler was such a man, seemingly unfit for astronomy.

He was obsessed with the need to solve the mystery of Creation and the secrets of its harmony. Why, he asked himself, are there six planets (as many as were known at that time) and not twenty or thirty-three? Why are they separated by precisely those distances? Why are they moving at that given speed?

These were useless questions, and even stranger were the ways in which he looked for answers. He thought that the different distances between the six planets corresponded to the succession of the regular polyhedrons and to the intervals of the notes in the musical scale.

What method for future scientific discoveries would Johannes Kepler ever have been able to pass on to his pupils? And yet, because of the extremely personal, mystical and Pythagorean obsessions which drove him, he discovered that the orbits of the planets are elliptical, that Copernicus' hypothesis, which made the sun the centre of the universe, was demonstrable, and many other facts that showed for the first time that the same physical laws apply to the earth as to the heavens. These were the bases for the theory of universal gravity which Newton would define less than a century later.

Today many scholars are demonstrating that there exists a private, secret context within scientific discovery which does not fall within the belief that ideas evolve rationally. Paradoxes, arguments which seem irrational, prejudices, personal passions, and the tenacity to search, sometimes combine to create a new harmony between solitary challenge and its openly convincing results.

A personal struggle, which could never be translated into a universally valid method, leads the greatest mathematicians to seek a kind of beauty, an aesthetic symmetry. This struggle is similar to what drove the musician in Thomas Mann's novel to look for a figurative concordance among the notes arranged in his score.

Poincaré said that for mathematicians the search for an aesthetic harmony, 'unknown to the uninitiated', is fundamental to the birth of new ideas.

As in the history of science, so in the history of art and theatre, the essential is hidden underneath the development of methods, underneath the pedagogical intentions and the handing on of knowledge. The word 'harmony', symbolises the meaning of this personal fight in the search for new tensions which can re-create life, giving a renewed meaning to that which has lost or is losing meaning. Not new facts, but new relationships between the facts.

When kites fly in art and in science, when these tensions and searches lead to new results which also have value for the surrounding environment, it seems that a hoard of knowledge is accumulated to be bequeathed to those who will come after us, or who want to follow us.

So, apparently, there is much to teach. Yet we know that results always risk becoming ballast, dead weight. What is essential is the meeting between our personal sense of emptiness, our obstinacy in placating it, and the winds.

None of this can be passed on. It is the zone of silence.

Yet it is one's duty to speak. Precisely because the essential is mute.

How the Essential is kept Silent

Results are determined by motivations, not just by the routes of the search. And yet, the only thing that can be passed on is the route that one has followed.

But not always. Throughout a long, person-to-person relationship, it is possible to pass on to someone else all that one has accumulated in years of experience without ever speaking about the essential. This is the case in the *guru-shishya* relationships in the Asian theatre tradition. And yet, in the end, this silence transmits something, unknown to either person, in an unexpected way, according to a logic which is superior to the logic of all pedagogical knowledge.

Such a relationship is built up over years and years, with a precise attitude on the part of the pupil towards the values which the master represents. Thus, more than the master it is time, the currents of the winds, which leave an imprint. And more than the pupil's awareness, it is his subliminal consciousness which absorbs hints of what is essential.

Such a relationship can involve only a very few people. What passes between them is fundamentally a seed of active silence, hidden inside the fruit of an almost scientifically explainable knowledge. When the pedagogical relationship opens up to include a wider circle of people, only the pulp of the fruit is left. And when one then passes from a direct relationship to the written word, and he who is writing cannot know for whom he is writing, the words become marble and lose their active silence.

For this reason, Stanislavski or Brecht, Copeau or Grotowski, and many others who once were masters and travellers in the Country of Speed, today seem to be statues.

Is there a way to pass on one's own experience, to hint at the essential in it, yet avoid the degradation which menaces every enlargement of the radius of our words?

It would be necessary for the words, no longer communicated person-to-person, to give up the pretence of translating a will to speak. They would have to retreat, to lie in ambush. Written words can convey this sense of lying in ambush, waiting to grasp something about which nothing is said. They will dress themselves up in artistic knowledge and experience, pointing out rules and discoveries. But their truest value, if one succeeds in achieving it, will lie in their being a form of not-saying by saying.

The more one tries to use the written word to get close to the meaning of oral transmission, the further away one gets. And the further away one gets, the closer one comes.

So I told myself: do not try to teach anything about artistic expression. Lie in ambush in the territories of pre-expressive work. Do not try to transmit heat with warm words. Seek to capture heat in the cold grip of a way of speaking devoid of emotion. Do not try to describe what has been the most fertile part of your experience. Speak of the arid work which precedes experience.

But why? For whom?

Why, if I myself came to the theatre like a man who was hungry for the wind, to placate the emptiness, to live like a floating island far from terra firma?

To pass it on to whom?

On different occasions during the years of my professional life, various people have asked me the same question: for whom do you do theatre?

I have answered in different ways. I have bypassed the question, or I have analysed it. I have let it be understood that I did theatre only for myself, or for two or three people I knew well, or for an absent spectator whom I always imagine standing beside me during the work and whose judgement is my measure of objectivity.

Today I think often of doing theatre for those who will be twenty years old in 1994, those who were born when Odin Teatret was performing *My Father's House*.

For the moment this is the answer to that question so often asked of me. But it is also the answer which reveals the emptiness because it means working for a theatre which will disappear, for spectators who have not yet appeared.

In the Heart

'Each time the ground begins to shake under your feet, each time you are no longer sure of the stability of your past experiences' - Grotowski advised me - 'go back to your origins, to where you started.' We were sitting in a Polish railway station restaurant, a quarter of a century ago. And he added: 'This is also what Stanislavski advised, to go back to the first days in the theatre'.

It is our first day of work which determines the meaning of our path.

Whenever I think of this advice, the image of a five-year-old child comes to mind, a backward child who could hardly speak, and who thought he was seeing a miracle when his father gave him a pocket compass. Sixty-two years later, Einstein writes in his autobiography: 'That experience made a profound and lasting impression on me. Everything must have something hidden deep within it.'

What then are my origins? Which was my first day in the theatre?

Perhaps it was the day of separation, the day I lost my mother tongue and made myself into a foreigner, in a country which was not the country of my birth.

It was undoubtedly the day when, without realising it, I became a 'floating island', a traveller of speed, citizen of a single country: my body-in-life. At home in different cultures, yet always a foreigner. Wanting to meet other similar islands, other archipelagos. On that day I began my search to overcome individual limitations, to meet the reality which was all around, to try to bring about a new way of life: a theatre group like a little island which can detach itself from the solid ground of terra firma yet remain cultivable, becoming strong by exploiting its weaknesses, rediscovering its own identity, its own being, through difference from others.

Looking back for a moment I think: What a long preparation!

I ask myself: for what? And I answer recalling a sarcastic saying: 'It takes sixty years to make a man, and when he's finished, he isn't good for anything but dying.'

***

Looking ahead, I see the Great Theatre: useless and unreasonable.

Jacek Woszczerowicz was small, old, had never been handsome. His face was devastated by wrinkles and he was nearly bald. He was Polish and an actor. After a heart attack, the doctors told him to stop performing. He kept on and had a second attack. The doctors said he would surely die if he continued on the stage. He persisted. Twice a week, wearing heavy armour, dragging himself along as if weighed down by a well-hidden secret, he was Richard III. He prepared for each performance two days in advance, eating only soup and drinking only water. In his room, he walked back and forth, up and down, never stopping, as if to reassure his body: 'We'll make it!'

The day of the performance he fasted like a monk preparing for mass. But he was only thinking of lightening his stomach before the effort of the performance. At three in the afternoon, he left his house and set off for the theatre on foot. He lived in the suburbs and walked into town with a determined step, muttering his lines. People who saw him passing by thought he was drunk, or disturbed.

He put his armour on again. The time had come when he was no longer looking at his co-actors, no longer looking at the audience, but was peering all around him, looking for death.

'I do not perform for the public. But for God.'

In Warsaw, in the theatre school where I spent my first day of apprenticeship, it occurred to me that perhaps only people with heart disease should be actors.

THE THEATRE OF THE POLIS AND
THE SANCTUARY OF THE METROPOLIS

Ancient Athens is seen here as a contrast to our technocratic society where theatre appears to be a mere archaeological relic, a piece of seaweed stranded on the beach of progress. In the nineties the artisan-like and archaic dimension of theatre no longer constitutes a secret, separate or precarious yet fertile space. Theatre becomes a privileged place where one can live in accordance with other values. Barba now sees vocation as 'blind demons', 'mute worms' which drive him to remain a communist in a society which has no place for such ideals. The Theatre of the Polis and the Sanctuary of the Metropolis *is, in the nineties, what* Waiting for the Revolution *was in the sixties.*

Throughout Eugenio Barba's professional life, the image of vocational theatre reverberates as 'catacomb', 'reservation', 'floating island' and, in this text from 1990, as 'sanctuary'. Paradoxically, this sanctuary is built to protect the same reality which, in the beginning, was hidden in the catacomb.

This text is a re-elaboration of Holstebro come Atene, *first published in* Teatro Città, *Mestre 1991.*

> No one searched for what he found.
> Halfdan Rasmussen, *Sabine Synger*

I would be lying if I said what I was searching for. I would even be lying if I affirmed that I was searching for something. Am I really searching for something? For what?

In order to try to answer these questions I must go back in history and look with shrewd eyes at certain situations, names, concepts: 'laboratory' for example. Odin Teatret is designated as a 'theatre laboratory'.

The Laboratory

It was Stanislavski who first used this word in connection with the theatre. His first laboratory came into being with the specific aim of broadening and probing deeper into acting techniques in a previously established context - the Art Theatre - which, at that time, was a recognised artistic institution, where people queued for hours to obtain tickets.

Successive laboratories, those of Meyerhold or Stanislavski's collaborators, were guided by a vision of the world that inspired technical research, but did not last for long. They didn't apply the consequences of their results within the actual context of the theatre, in front of spectators, evening after evening.

The same can be said of another laboratory, Copeau's Vieux Colombier. For as long as he thought in terms of technique, Copeau maintained the theatre, the school and the laboratory. As soon as he distanced himself from the craft and began to concentrate on inner needs, he left the school and retired to the provinces. Copeau, however, always operated within the theatre that was recognised as an artistic institution.

The Berliner Ensemble too was a large laboratory. Brecht's way of working was the opposite of the normal practice of the German theatre. He was a renowned playwright, an original poet, an intuitive director working with well known actors and collaborating with Erich Engel, a 'historic' director. Yet again it was theatre with the stamp of artistic legitimacy.

The case of Grotowski was similar when he started out. He completed the school for actors in Cracow, then the one for directors. He directed some productions in traditional theatres in Cracow and Poznan, keeping within the normal rehearsal time of two or three months. Then he moved to Opole in the provinces to direct the Theatre of the 13 Rows. During the first year he directed six plays, two of which were for radio. Then something happened. Over the next two or three years Grotowski extended the rehearsal period to at least six months per performance, defining his theatre as a 'laboratory'. He justified this change of name by relating it to Stanislavski, partly because the Russian reformer was a point of reference for him, but also in order to avoid problems with the Polish authorities who were unhappy with his meagre productivity. Grotowski confronted them on their own ground. Stanislavski was above all criticism in socialist Poland, and he too had laboratories delving into the art of the actor. Grotowski's laboratory was born through subterfuge, yet within theatre, a recognisable and accredited artistic field.

The problems begin with the arrival of the barbarians, those with little learning, who had not attended a school but had, on the contrary, been rejected by one. When these nameless people get together and have the impertinence to call their theatre a 'laboratory', how can such behaviour be defined? Impudence, childishness, ingenuousness, revolt? When inexperienced beginners call themselves a 'theatre laboratory', it is evident that the term loses the legitimacy and the value that historic models and examples have bestowed upon it.

When we speak of laboratories, we must remember that a gap exists between the historical laboratories created by trained people in a theatrical milieu and operating with the recognition of these milieus, and the laboratories created by inexperienced young people who get together and declare: we are a theatre laboratory. Such was the case with Odin Teatret.

The Arrival of the Barbarians

In 1964 when Odin Teatret began its activity in Oslo it was a group of amateurs, young Norwegians presenting a contemporary Norwegian author to Norwegian spectators. The traumatic moment came when our theatre decided to move from Norway to Denmark; it lost its language and could no longer be understood by its spectators. So it shamelessly adopted the term 'theatre laboratory'. We could do everything except for one thing: 'research' into the art of the actor because, as actors, we had little experience.

With the Odin Teatret, another tradition of the theatre laboratory was born: a milieu which did not merely concentrate on an autodidactic apprenticeship, technique and scenic behaviour, but which transformed the ensemble, the group, into a centre of theatre culture with a multiplicity of activities. It did not limit itself to the preparation and presentation of performances, but set in motion what today is taken for granted: workshops, conferences, sociological research, theoretical and practical seminars, activities in schools, production of didactic films (before the video became a cheap and easy piece of equipment). It was a whole new way of conceiving the activity, economy and politics of a theatre.

Here lies the difference: Stanislavski, Copeau and the Berliner Ensemble were accepted. The Odin was a reject, like those groups which, following in its footsteps, called themselves 'theatre laboratories'. This term was a camouflage, an original yet groundless term to justify the fact that doing theatre sprang from a desire to refuse traditional theatre; or to embellish a failure: the forbidden access to traditional theatre.

It is fundamental to keep in mind these historical facts, and also that the historic laboratories - except for that of Grotowski - were all short-lived. I believe that the life-span of a theatre laboratory is a decisive factor for the significance it acquires.

At the moment of writing - 1990 - Odin Teatret has been active for twenty-four years in a small town of twenty thousand inhabitants in north-west Denmark. The town didn't have a theatre when, in 1966, this group of Norwegian 'barbarians' arrived, calling themselves a theatre laboratory. The story of the relationship with the town is a saga in itself. The Odin has aroused sudden passions and violent reactions, but with time things have changed. In Holstebro today, even those who have never set foot in our theatre, are proud of it.

Athens and Holstebro

The Odin taking root in Holstebro reminds me of Athens, the place our civilisation considers to be the cradle of the theatre. The city of Athens, with its surrounding territory, Attica, had about three hundred thousand inhabitants. Of these, one hundred and fifty thousand were slaves, thirty to forty thousand were *metekois* - foreigners who didn't have the same rights as the Athenians - and of the hundred and ten to hundred and twenty thousand people remaining, at least a half were women who could not participate in political life. The so-called Athenian democracy was in the hands of forty to fifty thousand men whose standard of education could hardly be compared to that of the citizens of Holstebro. Only a very few had the knowledge possessed by today's students on completing middle school.

In Athens, theatre was performed outside, not during the summer but in January or March when it was cold. The summer was the season the Athenians devoted to travel and commerce. Performances took place during the day. Historians affirm that between ten and fifteen thousand people attended each performance, including women and slaves.

What is it that strikes one when comparing my theatre (where the people know it and are proud of it because it gives the town prestige, although they don't flock to see it) with that of the Athenians who went to watch theatre without taking a conscious pride in it? It should not be forgotten, since we are looking at the theatre through shrewd eyes, that in Greece it was forbidden to deal with topical themes. *The Fall of Miletus*, which recalled the massacre of the people of that town, was punished with an exorbitant fine by the Athenian jury. Of all the Greek tragedies, the only one that mentioned contemporary events is *The Persians*, and that did not take place in Greece but in Persia, a land of barbarians. There was no repertoire. The plays were not performed more than once. The actors could alter their own lines. Respect for the text did not exist. The only version was the one elaborated by the actors. It was only in the fourth century BC that it was decided to fix texts as points of reference.

The Athenian theatre is based on an oral tradition and culture. It is typical of a context with common beliefs and norms and one which accepts waste as a value of social life: waste of time, money, energy, writing. A play is written to be presented only once and no more.

I reflect upon what the theatre in Athens was once, and what the theatre in Holstebro is today. Here I continually find myself confronted with politicians, experts and citizens who ask: what use is your theatre? What does the Odin give to the population of Holstebro? These questions echo around me all the time. After all, we are living in a society where value is measured by output. The need which urged people to change the world - the Sermon on the Mount, anarchism, communism - presupposed the wasting of energy. The Italian *Festa dell'Unità*, the pilgrimages, the volunteers who left their families and jobs to fight in Spain during the Civil War, the building of the cathedrals are all reminiscences of an archaeological park. The theatre is an archaeological ruin from a society whose way of thinking and building relationships presupposed a reality that transcended the material one. The theatre remains as an archaic residue amongst men and women who entrust their life to tangible and commensurable results.

This archaic residue no longer has any justification, and goes in search of its identity, like Oedipus. Stanislavski, Meyerhold, Copeau, Brecht, Artaud and Grotowski, are all unabashed Sisyphuses who have undertaken the immense effort of rooting theatre in the functional and technological civilisation of the twentieth century.

The Reformers
The reformers of the twentieth century were looking for techniques and arguments to justify their political, spiritual, artistic, religious or nihilistic motivations.

Each of them found an image-symbol, an emblematic seal, a poetic knot which they left as a legacy and which contained one of the absolute truths of artistic creation: the oxymoron, the embrace of contrasts, the simultaneous presence of opposites. In painting, in poetry or in theatre there is a use of colour, of language, of the body which is not the usual daily one. An extra-daily language becomes poetry. A painting by Van Gogh is an extra-daily reproduction of reality. Similarly, the physical presence of the actor or the dancer on stage is an extra-daily presence because it does not follow the normal and strictly functional modes of behaviour.

Another technical process singled out by the Russian formalists and which is to be found in different artistic fields is the alienation effect: the ability to remove a word, a concept or a situation from its usual context and present it anew by means of a process based on contrasts. What Meyerhold called 'grotesque'.

We see in all the reformers of the twentieth century the urge to find and perfect effective technical procedures. But it has to be understood that this research is indissolubly linked with their need to give a value to theatre. For Stanislavski, Meyerhold, Brecht or Grotowski it is impossible to separate the how from the why. The complementarity of the one with the other is an organic force with the great reformers, something which brings to life their writings and their performances for those who have seen them. The how is the way of capturing and making visible their why.

Theatre is something that does not have a rational justification of its own according to the categories which apply in an industrial society. It is revealing that subsidies for the theatre are rare in the United States or Japan, two of the most technologically advanced countries. Research consists not only in finding the material means to exercise our art, but also in giving ourselves and those who come after us a value which transcends every alibi, all the rhetoric and all the petty arguments that we use when we talk to politicians or with private patrons. Our own personal justification, even if it is nebulous, becomes a value if it leaves traces, if it succeeds in building examples which others can use for orientation and as a shield in their own struggle, just as Stanislavski's laboratory did for Grotowski.

The real research is into why we do theatre. At the root of everything there are no genres, no traditional theatre or theatre of research - only personal needs.

Resistance

So what am I searching for?

I am trying to prolong an archaic presence no longer suited to the time in which we live. The theatre is the squaring of the circle which permits me to remain a communist, like the early monks who retreated to the desert, like certain eighteenth century philosophers dreamed of being, like the Catalan anarchists or Luis Carlos Prestes. I am waging a war against a large part of society, a war under the camouflage of art. It is a permanent struggle because the majority of the values which exist outside my theatre are the opposite of those which guide me in the profession I have chosen. It would be understandable if the politicians were no longer to give me money.

The last elections in Holstebro were won by the Conservatives and the Progress Party whose policy is to stop subsidising culture and to get rid of all the foreigners in Denmark. This conservative victory, which wipes out 24 years of cultural politics by the social democrats, is for me a warning that the search continues. The search for how to resist while being considered a parasite by the newly elected politicians; the search into how to succeed in being *present* here and now with my own way of thinking and doing; the search for a society which allows me to keep my sense of dignity and guides me in my human, professional, political and economic relationships; the search for a communism which will never be victorious, but which it is up to me to ensure never suffers defeat. My search is for how to become a legend.

I am not pursuing an ideology, but a legacy. I speak of ancestors, of Stanislavski and Meyerhold, of Brecht and Artaud.

Endurance in time is essential. For a theatre laboratory, duration signifies *resistance*.

Sanctuary

Once in Japan some friends told me about the radical changes that had taken place in their society. Young people no longer wanted one permanent job, but took two or three at the same time. They earned a lot. In Tokyo I sometimes had the impression of being at a huge fashion show. I had never seen so many well dressed people. It was a generation that had grown up with the video; they had a thousand, two thousand, some even up to five thousand tapes. They spoke little amongst themselves. Youths of seventeen or eighteen went out with girls of ten or eleven, taking them to cafés to drink chocolate and eat cakes in total silence.

Then there were the 'goldfish'. That's what they called the girls between sixteen and eighteen who were interested in a particular singer or a performance and who dragged their companions along with them. In an aquarium, when the goldfish defecate, they leave behind them a myriad long, transparent threads. A theatre director, speaking about his new performance, told me: 'If the goldfish are not interested, I won't be able to fill the theatre'.

One particular event had disturbed Japan. A girl of twelve had been found cut up in pieces in a wood. They had caught the murderer, a youth of twenty, who had a collection of thousands of videos. Amongst these was one which depicted exactly the same scenario. Of course, as everybody repeated, nothing could be deduced from this fact. But a symptom was clear: young people communicate much less through words. In the contemporary Japanese theatre performances that I saw, there was little speech, only shouting and a technology that spewed out music at full volume.

I asked myself: what should the theatre be searching for in Japan? In Chile or other countries of Latin America, theatre is alive because, with its very presence, it revitalises a hope of union and a commonality of intent. Perhaps in Japan the theatre can become a place where people can whisper their own thoughts and listen to those of others. It could transform itself into a *sanctuary*, a sacred space, where one can take refuge and be protected. Like the churches in Denmark and Sweden where people hardly go any more. However, when a church is invaded by the homeless, or foreigners hide there from the authorities who want to expel them, the police don't intervene although it is within their right to do so.

The theatre can become a *sanctuary*, an asylum for those who thirst for justice, a refuge of freedom, a crypt full of cipher messages for the spectator who visits it.

Statistically these people are few. But what is the value of an individual?

3. 'You are distinguished by what you affirm and what you deny. But what you affirm and deny is just theatre.' (Else Marie Laukvik in Sardinia, 1975)

4. 'The lights of the theatre, its conventions and artistic theories seemed false and anachronistic to me, disguising the grave and brutal evidence of reality. A few moments later, like an optical illusion or a sudden clear-sightedness, those lights seemed instead to be the subterranean glow of a refuge. And I asked myself if the story of the great theatre reformers was not a story of builders of fortresses filled with oxygen.' (Aerial view of Odin Teatret)

5. 'How to pass on, as seeds, the fruits of the actions of a handful of Odin people who will die within a few years but nevertheless cling stubbornly to the small town of Holstebro on the margins of the European empire?' (The members of Odin Teatret on the occasion of its thirtieth anniversary)

6. 'It suffices to remember the old saying that the theatre must be a mirror. The mirror reproduces the image but it also reverses it. What is on the right in real life, is on the left in the mirror. The world can be turned upside down.' (Ulrik Skeel in his room at Odin Teatret)

7. 'You must not limit your presence to this particular moment, to this place, to your present ties, to the questions that others ask you today. Are you therefore apolitical? What is politics? Is it not the art of the possible? You must be 'asocial' in order to realise your own possibilities.' (Iben Nagel Rasmussen in Sardinia, 1975)

II

LABORATORY:
AN UNENDING SCHOOL

Today, at over sixty years of age, I can still do the
acrobatic movements and the strenuous poses of
the woman-warrior in plays such as The Drunken
Beauty *and* The Mountain Fortress ...
In the winter my teacher made me practise dancing
and fighting on short stilts on the ice. At first
I fell all the time, but as I got used to walking with
the stilts on ice, it was easier to do the same
movements on the stage without stilts. When I
practised on the stilts, my feet were covered with
blisters and I suffered great pain. I felt that my
teacher ought not to subject a child of ten to such
a hard ordeal. He ought to show compassion.

Mei Lanfang:
Autobiography

8. *Eugenio Barba working with Iben Nagel Rasmussen, Holstebro 1967.*

TRAINING

This chapter reconstructs Eugenio Barba's theoretical reflections on apprentice-ship. Beginning with the idea of a laboratory as a space for technical research, it ends with ISTA (International School of Theatre Anthropology) and with the idea of the theatre as an unending school, an environment where, through technical principles, one tries to transmit ethical principles.

Training is the transcription of Eugenio Barba's commentary for two films on Odin Teatret, directed by Torgeir Wethal for Italian TV in November 1972. The actors mentioned in the text are: Jens Christensen, Iben Nagel Rasmussen, Tage Larsen, Torgeir Wethal and Else Marie Laukvik.

First published in Materiali sullo spettacolo e sul lavoro dell'Odin Teatret, *Centro per la Sperimentazione e la Ricerca Teatrale, Pontedera 1976.*

Physical Training

During the eight years of Odin Teatret's existence, its actors have trained regularly. Our vision of this training, its forms and aims, have undergone a continuous evolution due to experience, to the contribution of new members and to new needs which have grown up during the work.

At the beginning, the training was composed of a series of exercises taken from mime, ballet, gymnastics, sport - exercises which we knew or which we had reconstructed. Training was collective: everybody did the same exercises at the same tempo and in the same way.

In time, it became clear to us that rhythm varies from person to person. Some have a fast vital rhythm, others a slower one. We began to talk of organic rhythm and by this we meant variation, pulsation as with the heart. From then on the training was based on this rhythm. It became personalised, individual.

Gradually, the exercises which we developed, although remaining the same, changed their meaning. The exercise is like a gate in a slalom through which the actors guide their physical activity, thereby disciplining it.

In our theatre, training has always consisted of an encounter between discipline, that is, the exercise's set form and the surpassing of that set form, which the exercise represents. The motivation for this surpassing is individual, varying from actor to actor, and it is this justification which determines the significance of the training.

At the present time - October 1972 - the training is based on very elementary action-exercises which involve the whole body, making it react totally. The entire body has to think and adapt itself continually to each situation as it arises. The first example is an exercise which demands precision. You have to touch or hit your companion's chest with your foot on a precise spot just above the breastbone so that s/he doesn't get hurt.

(Demonstration: duel with the feet striking the chest)

This exercise serves to inspire confidence. It sounds paradoxical to awaken confidence through an action which frightens and provokes a defensive reaction. But it is a matter of having and inspiring trust in your companion and kicking in such a way that s/he is able to overcome the defensive reflex. The whole body must react, adapt itself, yet work with precision and with all the senses at their sharpest.

This type of exercise, demanding continual self-adaptation, can vary but always requires precision and a cool head. The actors must be carried along by their physical intelligence; it is the entire body which does the thinking and these thoughts are already actions, reactions.

Another exercise involves attempting to strike your companion's neck or ankles with a stick in order to provoke an immediate and precise reaction.

(Demonstration: duel with sticks)

This feeling of trust in your own reflexes, in your own physical intelligence and in your companion becomes apparent through physical actions. But this trust is developed further. In our theatre there are no teachers. The actors themselves have developed their training. Those who have been here longer put their experience at the disposal of the more recent arrivals. Helped by one of the older actors, the younger one begins to assimilate a particular series of exercises. When s/he has mastered these, s/he will be able to personalise them, that is, to adapt them to his/her own rhythm and justification.

First, each exercise is assimilated in a precise way.

(Demonstration: acrobatics)

Once the separate exercises are assimilated and you have mastered them completely, they can be linked, fused together in a series, like a wave of two, three or four exercises, with a different rhythm.

The exercises have now been assimilated. Having complete mastery over them and having linked them together in little waves of three or four, you can now work with them absolutely freely according to your own rhythm.

This series of acrobatic exercises is an example of physical reactions being carried to their extreme consequence. Our body really can fly, can meet the floor as if weightless, without fear. The psychological value of these exercises is enormous. They appear to be very difficult, and for someone who is confronted with them for the first time they may seem quite impossible. However, even after the first day's work, helped patiently by one of the others, you are able to do one or two of these exercises reasonably well. After a month's daily work the new member is able to do almost all of them, not perfectly perhaps, but it does not matter; there is plenty of time ahead. What counts is the knowledge that s/he can succeed; what seemed impossible is within reach if s/he works every day.

In this lies the essential value of the training: daily self-discipline, personalisation of the work, stimulation of and effect on one's companions and milieu.

Now another example of a few exercises which form the basis of the individual work of a group of actors.

(Demonstration)

Training, as we practise it in our theatre, does not teach how to be an actor, how to play a role in the Commedia dell'Arte style or how to interpret a tragic or grotesque part. It doesn't give a sense of being able to do something, that one has acquired certain skills. Training is an encounter with the reality which one has chosen: whatever you do, do it with your whole self. For this reason we talk about training and not learning or apprenticeship. Although all our actors are formed here in our theatre, we are not a theatre school in the usual sense since there are no teachers or study programme. The actors themselves devise and are responsible for their training. But in order to achieve this degree of freedom, there must be self-discipline. And this is why training is a necessity for everyone, irrespective of how long one has been working in the theatre.

Whatever you do, do it with your whole self. It sounds like - and is - a facile and rhetorical phrase. Anybody can say it. But we have only one possibility: to live it, to carry it out in our daily acts. And the training reminds us of this.

***

Vocal Training

The voice, in its logical and its sonorous aspect, is a material force, moving, guiding, moulding, stopping. One can, in fact, talk about vocal actions which provoke an immediate reaction. Now we will demonstrate the voice as an active force.

Using a language that she has invented and which she improvises as she goes along, Iben leads two of her colleagues and tries to make them do what she wants. Her voice acts all the time; it tries to persuade, beg, compel her companions to execute her wishes, while at the same time her voice reacts, i.e. adapts itself to what her companions do. They have their backs to her so that they don't see her. They do nothing, play no role, only react, respond with their entire bodies to her vocal stimulus.

(Demonstration: the voice as an active force)

The voice is a physiological process, and engages the whole organism projecting it into space. The voice is an extension of the body, and gives us the possibility of concrete intervention even at a distance. Like an invisible hand the voice extends out from our body and acts, and our entire body lives and participates in this action. The body is the visible part of the voice and one can see how and where the impulse which will become sound and speech is born. The voice is an invisible body operating in space. There is no separation, no duality of voice and body. There are only actions and reactions which engage our body in its entirety.

Our work has only one aim: to preserve the spontaneous organic reactions of the voice and at the same time stimulate the individual vocal fantasy of each actor.

The working situation is one in which the body and its invisible part, the voice, are constantly adapting themselves, i.e. reacting to stimuli. Here is a demonstration of how the voice reacts to stimuli.

I am going to ask Jens to hold my hand with his voice and let his speech emerge from the part of his body which is nearest my hand. Just that: hold my hand with his voice and answer the movements of my hand; in other words, react to its actions.

(Demonstration: the voice reacting to stimuli)

In the situation we have just shown, the stimulus rebounded as a vocal reaction. The body of the actor who was speaking was totally engaged. The whole body spoke, constantly adapting itself, directed towards the exterior with a very definite point of reference. The rule is this: for precise reactions the stimuli must also be precise - precise in character and precisely situated in space.

I ought now to mention the spoken text. In our daily life when we talk we don't concentrate on the words, we don't interpret the words coldly. Our speech is carried on a wave, the respiratory wave, which may be long or short. If the process is spontaneous, we do not think about the words. Nothing impedes us or restrains us if we have a sense of security; in other words if we are not afraid, if we are not embarrassed, if we do not have to be careful of what we say, or are not speaking in a foreign language in which we are not altogether at home. This sense of security must be recreated within the artificial situation that is the theatrical situation. We must therefore eliminate the objective blocking of the text which can occur if one has continuously to force oneself to remember it. The text must be learnt by heart so perfectly that it flows without the least difficulty as if it were a spontaneous process, allowing the actor, through his/her actions, to reach out in space, oblivious of the words learnt. In reality, even if the words were written by someone else - or if, as in my case now where I am using words which are not my own, nor were invented by me but were passed on to me by a culture and a tradition - these words assume life and presence through my whole being as personal reactions.

What we call stimulus is the starting point which allows the actors to continue freely alone. From this point of departure, the actors themselves select and develop their own images, their own stimuli to which they react. This is the second phase of the work process.

(Vocal improvisation)

That which we call stimulus is a concrete, precise yet suggestive image which appeals to the actors' fantasy. It is a starting point which allows them to take the original image and graft it onto their own fantasy, their own interior universe, thus developing their own images and associations which are vocal reactions. In this way, although the point of departure, the initial image, is given from outside, decided by another, the whole process is personalised and becomes the individual expression of the actor's own universe.

If there are precise stimuli, there are also precise reactions, provided that there are no impediments. Impediments may be objective such as straining to remember the text, or psychological, stemming from a feeling of fear or lack of security. It is essential throughout this whole process to create a feeling of safety around those who are working. The results depend on this.

As I said before, if there are precise stimuli there are also precise reactions. Then a sonorous logic will become apparent, revealing itself through the rhythm, i.e. variations in tone, pauses, intensity, changes in volume, stress on particular parts of the sentences, micro-pauses before certain words and before breathing in, which instead of causing gaps in our speech, sharpen its sense and nerve. This rhythm, this physical and vocal pulsation is a sign that the whole body is alive. It is this pulsation which vibrates the fabric of sounds and meaning which is our body, present in and projected into space.

(Vocal improvisation)

Throughout the entire working process one must resist the temptation to try to obtain original results, to emit strange noises, inarticulate shouts, transforming our vocal reactions into a sonorous magma which may sound dramatic but is strained and artificial. You must forget your own voice and stretch out with all your body towards the stimulus and react to it.

Then the body lives, the voice lives, palpitates, vibrates like a flame, like a ray of sunshine which emanates from our body, illuminating and warming the space around it. From this modest point of departure and through regular work over the years, our own vocal flora springs, with roots that live in and are our body with its experience and longings.

TWO LETTERS

These two letters from Eugenio Barba to his actors focus in a concise way - as two lightning flashes - on the double track which had emerged in Odin Teatret's training during the seventies. The aim is not so much the external face or the technical dimension, but what is concealed behind them. In addition to what one learns on a technical level, it is the discipline with which one struggles that is essential in the training. The recipient of the second letter is Iben Nagel Rasmussen.

The two letters were first published in Il libro dell'Odin *by Ferdinando Taviani, Feltrinelli, Milan 1975.*

Holstebro, 4th February 1973

To my colleagues of *Min Fars Hus* on tour in Copenhagen:

During these last days of work I have often thought of you. When something interesting emerged from the work with the new pupils, I said to myself: if only you were here in Holstebro to share it with me. When the raw material remained just raw material, without the glint of a precious metal, then I felt the lack of your presence for support and advice.

But both these reactions do justice neither to the new pupils nor to you. One must not remain outside, watch the others work or serve as pillars of support.

Justice: you give, we give back in return.

You might want to come to Holstebro to say: this is my daily work as an actor. I do it because ... and say it as an actor says it: with the whole body, with actions.

And the new pupils will answer: we have thought of doing this, because ... and we put it into practice in this way.

Your encounter would place you on the same level, in the work and through the work, where everyone gives and no one is outside because there is no difference between veterans and beginners. If new blood is to flow through the veins of our theatre, it must not be something that is indifferent to you, that does not yet concern you.

Already now, you should feel it as something which gives new life to our common future and work.

Those who want to, may come when they can.

We work from seven in the morning to nine in the evening, also on Saturdays and Sundays.

Come to be present with your whole self, to say: this is how I train, these are my experiences, this is what I am struggling against. Show this through your daily efforts, which we call training. The new pupils will answer in the same way. Perhaps already now their answer will give you something.

Affectionate greetings to you all.

Eugenio Barba

22nd February 1973

To I. - from the director to the actress:

I saw J's and your work last Saturday and Sunday. Something warm entered the black room. Your work embodied something living. I saw what it means not to give in, to grope your way forward and not withdraw, to fight against the solid wall of inertia, the objective difficulties of time and space during the tour, the sensation of being alone, the temptation to let yourself be carried by the tranquil current of the day towards the waiting rapids of the evening's performance, and thereafter to flow peacefully on.

In the past months I have seen how you have matured artistically in your needs, in your strength, in your generosity.

I listen when you speak, when you imagine out loud what will be the work of the future, and I am glad. You have become so independent, that I imagine it is my doing.

Eugenio Barba

WORDS AND PRESENCE

Here, defined in explicit terms, is the vision of training which was already present in the two short letters from Barba to his actors. The training has now become a process of self-definition. Barba brings down to earth 'the myth of technique': the purpose of training is not so much to prepare actors as to form individuals.

First published in The Drama Review, *53, New York 1972. Translated into many languages, it has become one of the main texts for understanding his attitude towards technique and pedagogy.*

Training does not teach how to act, how to be clever; it does not prepare one for creation. Training is a process of self-definition, a process of self-discipline which manifests itself indissolubly through physical reactions. It is not the exercise in itself that counts - for example, bending or somersaults - but the individual's justification for the work which, although perhaps banal or difficult to explain through words, is physiologically perceptible to the observer. This approach, this personal justification decides the meaning of the training, the surpassing of the particular exercises which, in reality, are stereotyped gymnastic movements.

This inner necessity determines the quality of the energy which allows work without a pause, without noticing tiredness, continuing although exhausted and even then going forward without surrendering. This is the self-discipline of which I spoke.

Let us understand each other, it is not by killing oneself with exhaustion that one becomes creative. It is not on command, through force, that one opens oneself to others. Training is not a form of personal asceticism, a malevolent harshness against oneself, a persecution of the body. Training puts one's own intentions to the test, how far one is prepared to pay with one's own person for all that one believes and declares. It is the possibility of bridging the gap between intention and realisation. This daily task, obstinate, patient, often in darkness, sometimes even searching for a meaning, is a concrete factor in the transformation of the actor as an individual and a member of the group. This imperceptible daily transformation of one's way of seeing, approaching and judging the problems of one's own existence and that of others, this sifting of one's own prejudices and doubts - not through gestures and grandiloquent phrases but through the silent daily activity - is reflected in the work which finds new justifications, new reactions: thus one's North is displaced.

***

In the beginning, we had a programme of set exercises that we taught everyone and that everyone had to follow. These were exercises of every kind, taken from ballet, mime, pure gymnastics, Hatha Yoga and acrobatics. We worked out a whole series of physical actions and called this 'biomechanics' after the term used by Meyerhold. We defined biomechanics as a very dynamic reaction to an external stimulus. The exercises were of an acrobatic type and rather violent. However, we had transformed them according to what we imagined the training of the traditional Asian actor might be. Starting from this training as it existed in our imagination, we wanted to achieve a rhythm of work that was intense yet had the same precision and economy of movement, the same suggestiveness and power that we attributed to the Asian actor. For us, biomechanics was not a technically exact historical reconstruction of Meyerhold's exercises and their particular aim: namely, the creation of a social emploi for the actor. We used this term to set our imagination in motion, to stimulate us. What was it like, this biomechanics?

We attempted to re-invent it, to rediscover it in our bodies according to our own justifications. It was the actors who, individually or in collaboration, worked out the map of this territory. Within it also were the 'battles', the fights, the exercises for the reflexes in which the actors had to adapt themselves immediately to a situation, think with their whole body and react with it.

***

In spite of my experience in Asian theatre, especially *kathakali*, I haven't drawn directly from it. I tried to make my actors imagine this theatre of colours and exoticism, acrobatics and religiosity, by appealing to their subjectivity and imagination.

Kathakali, like all Asian theatre, cannot be copied or transplanted. It can only serve as a stimulus, a point of departure. The actors in traditional Asian theatre are immersed in a tradition that they must wholly respect. They are executing a role whose minutest detail has, as in a musical score, been developed by some master in a more or less distant past. As with a pianist or a ballet dancer, their evolution cannot be separated from virtuosity. In western theatre, however, actors are - or should be - creators. Their clash with the text, through their own sensibility and historical experience, opens up a unique and personal universe to their spectators.

This essential difference also determines one's approach to the profession, the preparation, that which is usually called training. Even today, *kathakali* or *kabuki* actors begin their training at the same age as European children who wish to devote themselves to ballet. The psychological and physiological consequences are evident. It is meaningless to go to Japan or India and take exercises from *kabuki* or *kathakali* in order to adapt them passively to the European pedagogical tradition, hoping that our actors might become 'virtuosi' like their Asian colleagues. Let me repeat, it is not the exercises in themselves that are decisive, but one's personal attitude, that inner necessity which incites and motivates the choice of one's profession, justifying it on an emotional level and with a logic that will not allow itself to be trapped by words.

This attitude determines the creation of norms that become almost an artistic or ethical superego in the actor. Similar norms are also to be found in theatre forms based on a purely technical apprenticeship. Here the historical circumstances and the environmental conditions in which the theatre work evolves, influence the development of these norms which are reflected in the technique. For example, the entire training of a young *kabuki* actor takes place in a rarefied atmosphere, without the possibility of contact with actors from other forms, such as *nô* or modern theatre, in a strictly professional hierarchy petrified in family dynasties whose mentality contrasts with the efficient industrial vocation of contemporary Japan.

The same applies to *kathakali*. While the *kabuki* actor is owned by a large impresario firm which places him in various theatres, the *kathakali* actor works on religious ground (the temple courtyard), dedicates his work and his performance to divinities, lives in a very modest way without the prospect ever of becoming a star like his Japanese colleague. These socio-historical circumstances, together with a particular professional tradition which still has great value and prestige for the young would-be actor, are decisive factors in the conception and elaboration of that expressiveness which is codified and so transformed into technique.

***

In the beginning of our activity we too believed in the 'myth of technique', something which it was possible to acquire, to possess, and which would have allowed the actors to master their own body and become conscious of it. So, at this stage, we practised exercises to develop the dilation of the eyes in order to increase their expressiveness. They were exercises which

I had seen in India while studying the training of *kathakali* actors. The expressiveness of the eyes is essential in *kathakali* and the control of their musculature demands several hours of severe training daily for many years. The different nuances each have a precise significance; the way of frowning, the direction of a glance, the degree of opening or closing the lids are codified by tradition and are in fact concepts and images which are immediately comprehensible to the 'expert' spectator. Such control in a European actor would only restrain the organic reactions of the face and transform it into a lifeless mask.

So, at the outset, as in a melting pot in which the most disparate metals fuse, I tried to blend together the most diverse influences, the impressions which for me had been the most fertile: Asian theatre, the experiments of the European Theatre Reform, personal experience from my stay in Poland and with Grotowski. I wanted to adapt all this to my ideal of technical perfection even in the part of the artistic work which we called 'composition', a word which had arrived in our theatre through the Russian and French terminology and Grotowski's interpretation of it. I believed that composition was the capacity of the actor to create signs, to consciously mould the body into a deformation rich in suggestiveness and power of association: the body of the actor as a Rosetta stone and the spectator in the role of Champollion. The aim was to attain wittingly, by cold calculation, that which is warm and which obliges us to believe with all our senses. But I often felt this composition to be imposed, something external which functioned on a theatrical level but lacked the driving force that could perforate the crust of all too obvious meanings. The composition might be rich, striking, throwing the actor into relief, yet it was like a veil which hid from me something that I felt inside myself but didn't have the courage to face, to reveal to myself or others.

In the first period of our existence all the actors did the same exercises together in a common collective rhythm. Then we realised that the rhythm varied for each individual - some have a faster vital rhythm, others a slower one - and we became aware of an organic rhythm. Its perpetual variation, however minute, revealed a wave of organic reactions which engaged the entire body. Training could only be individual.

This faith in technique as a sort of magic power which could render the actor invulnerable, guided us also in the domain of the voice. At the start, we followed the practices of Asian theatre: straightforward imitations of certain timbres of the voice. Using Grotowski's terminology, we called the different tones of voice 'resonators'. In Asian theatre training, the young actor learns entire roles mechanically with all their vocal nuances, timbres, intonations, exclamations: a complete fabric of sounds perfected through tradition and which the actor must repeat precisely in order to gain the appreciation of a critical audience. We too began coldly to find a series of timbres, tones, intonations, and exercised them daily.

This period of calculated work, of pure 'technicality', seemed to confirm that the hypothesis of the actor-virtuoso was right. The effects produced were interesting. But during their work a few actors managed to reach the territory of their own 'vocal flora'. This 'flora' was opened up by stimuli that were striking in their suggestiveness, in their emotional charge, and were not based on logic or a certain intellectuality.

So we discovered the value of personal images for engaging the voice in order to attain one's individual sound universe. We avoided calculated effects or the mechanically placed voice aiming simply for reactions, responses to the image which served as a stimulus. We began to talk of vocal actions. That which for us had once been a postulate - the voice as a physiological process - now became a tangible reality which engaged the entire organism and projected it in space. The voice was a prolongation of the body which, through space, hit, touched, caressed, encircled, pushed, searched far away or close by; an invisible hand which stretched out from the body to act in space or to renounce action. And even this renunciation was spoken by the invisible hand. But in order that the voice might act, it must know *where* the point was toward which it was directed, and *who* or *what* that point was and *why* it was addressing it.

From that moment I ceased to speak of resonators. The actors' bodies resounded, the room resounded, as well as something inside me as I listened, provided the actors really addressed this point in space which, although invisible to my eyes, was concrete to them, perceptible to all their senses, present with physical features.

***

For a long time the 'myth of technique' nourished our work. Then gradually it brought me to a situation of doubt. I had to admit that the argument for technique was a rationalisation, a pragmatic blackmail - if you do this, you obtain that - which I used to make the others accept my way of working and to give it a useful and logical justification. On a personal level - dimly, full of shadows - I felt that under the alibi of a work which the others defined as theatre I was trying to annihilate the actor in my companion, wash him of the character, destroy the theatre in our relationship so that we might meet one another as human beings, as vulnerable companions in arms who have no need to defend themselves, bound closer than brothers by the doubts and illusions of years passed patiently together: not the actor, not the character, but the companion of a long period of my life.

It was no longer a matter of teaching or learning something, of tracing a personal method, of discovering a new technique, of finding an original language, of demystifying oneself or others. Only of not being afraid of one another. Having the courage to approach one another until one becomes transparent, allowing glimpses of the well of one's own experience.

From here stems that reservedness which refuses the presence of strangers during the work. When the time comes for others to be present as spectators, they are witnesses of this human situation that we continue to call theatre, because we have no name for this new frontier beyond which we have little to say to one another in a theatrical language, however perfectly phrased. Virtuosity does not lead to new human relationships. It is not the decisive ferment for a reorientation, a new way of defining oneself vis-à-vis others and overcoming facile self-complacency.

Thus the training transformed itself into a process of self-definition, far removed from any utilitarian justification and guided by individual subjectivity. Each actor gives it a personal meaning. Once again: the exterior forms of the exercises are of no importance. But self-discipline remains.

***

During training one often runs the risk of a sclerosis. This is caused either by the ingenuous attitude which leads one to believe that with training comes creativity, or by the lack of personal justification which brings about the repetition of such exercises as gymnastics. We too have gone through similar periods. Then I succumbed to the temptation to explain, to come up with a sort of training philosophy, Ariadne's thread for my companions lost in the labyrinth of uncertainty. With great loyalty, my companions tried to motivate their own work with my words, my explanations. But something was wrong, something didn't ring true, and in the end a sort of split became apparent between what they were doing and what they wanted to do, or believed they were doing to satisfy me, to meet me. When I realised this, I gave up all explanation.

After working together many hours a day for many years, it is perhaps my presence that speaks rather than my words.

THE PEDAGOGICAL PARADOX:
LEARNING TO LEARN

This text is composed of fragments from six interviews with Eugenio Barba between 1979 and 1989. It shows how, during the sixties and the beginning of the seventies, the search for a technique changes slowly into the search for a pedagogy, a way of handing down one's own experience without suffocating the personal growth of the pupil. This urge motivated the creation and development of ISTA, International School of Theatre Anthropology, which is intended as a laboratory where technical principles from different performance genres are compared.

Barba has made a few changes to the original interviews which are mentioned in the bibliography at the end of this text.

MARIA GRAZIA GREGORI: *People who write about your performances talk about technical perfection or the perfection of the figurative aspect. Do you accept or reject this technical category?*

E. BARBA: You want an answer to a question which springs from diverse problems. When I started out, I had never worked with actors. However I had a few people as points of reference, some of them alive, some dead.

The Odin's first actors were youngsters who had been rejected by a traditional theatre school. I found myself in the position of having to become a teacher and to invent a pedagogy. When one feels insecure one looks to an authority for support. I did this by speaking to my young actors about classical Asian actors, about Stanislavski, Meyerhold and Eisenstein. These artists helped me to demonstrate that we were not a unique case, that there had been a long tradition before us that, following untrodden paths, had achieved results.

In our first phase, the main stimuli were the aspiration to a formal perfection as with Asian actors, the necessity for a methodology as suggested to me by Stanislavski, the research into theatricality which derived from Meyerhold, the care taken with the montage inspired by Eisenstein. But the motivation for this formal and pedagogical pursuit sprang from other personal needs which at that time were expressed through purely theatrical preoccupations.

Through regular work we have arrived at a kind of 'perfection', different from that of traditional theatre. However, if you take the Odin actors and let them perform in a traditional theatre, they will probably become the proverbial fish out of water. This is not because they are not technically prepared, but because they have elaborated a personal way of accomplishing mental and physical actions which, even through the fiction of the theatre, speak in the first person. Not 'the' truth, but 'his' or 'her' truth. Here lies the paradox: the theatre is fiction - you can't say that you want to be sincere. You can only attain a degree of sincerity by means of a sophisticated process which starts out from a fictional situation and carries it to such excess that, in spite of yourself, you reveal yourself. This is the process adopted by our actors: to put into practice their technical knowledge in order to give life to a performance which, by going beyond its own limits, lets us glimpse their personal needs and the needs of the whole group.

M.G. GREGORI: *Developing the paradox still further, we could say that technique is something that actors possess in spite of themselves, and which is a part of their own history.*

E. BARBA: Without doubt. But we realised that actors were 'alive' not because they knew how to do certain things.

Technique is a result, but also a limit. You have to transcend it. But first the limit has to be reached. In the beginning our interest was concentrated on technique. We felt a need to assert ourselves professionally according to the current theatrical categories and thereby overcome the inferiority complex caused by our rejection. Technique has been an objective in our group's biography. Then came the day when we asked ourselves how we could surpass the results we had attained. We realised that Odin Teatret was becoming a model, with the risk for those who were inspired by us of ending like King Midas for whom everything he touched turned to gold - something which glittered but could not nourish.

M.G. GREGORI: *So models should not exist? And yet the Odin is a model for many people.*

E. BARBA: There exists today an autistic attitude or rather the illusion that self-generation is possible. It is essential to have a point of reference with which to measure oneself and to which one can return to reflect. People who are obliged to define themselves in relation to a person with a very strong personality are very fortunate. For some time the shadow of this more mature and expert person will cover their actions. Meyerhold began like this in relation to Stanislavski, Grotowski began in the same way in relation to the shadow of Stanislavski, and I did the same in relation to Grotowski. The duration of this relationship varies, depending on the time necessary to awaken one's own energies. And then there comes a moment when it is important to distance oneself. Now it is absence which accompanies you. It is the time when, left alone to personalise the legacy received, you must invent your own path. The discovery of your own strength may be described in this way: you must surpass your own master by climbing onto his or her shoulders. By so doing, one manifests or denies the ethos which one has learnt.

My point of reference was and is Grotowski. For many years I was considered his pupil. Then, people stopped calling me this, either because they tired of repeating it, or perhaps because they had noticed that something had changed. It is the same with the groups who orientate themselves on Odin Teatret. If they don't give up, sooner or later each of them will find their own path.

The question of pedagogy, or the transmission of experience, is very important for us. In the first years, until '69 or '70, we held seminars in France, Italy, Scandinavia...

FRANCO QUADRI: *If I remember rightly, the seminars took place with theatre groups or communities, at universities ...*

E. BARBA: Also at theatre schools. But mainly universities or else cultural centres and associations. In those days, none of the theatre groups existed which were later regularly to organise courses and seminars both for their own actors and for others. Our first seminars established a normal pedagogical relationship: on the one hand someone who teaches and on the other someone who learns. Our actors presented a series of exercises which constituted their training, at the same time explaining their logic. When we later met again those who had attended our courses, we found ourselves confronted with a parodic repetition, an exterior application, as though the gymnastic - almost contortionist - side of these exercises led to creativity, to those sources from which all impulses, vitality, our very *bios* spring. We realised that this form of transmission didn't work and we stopped teaching.

For many years we asked ourselves how we could pass on our knowledge without causing a block or creating lots of mini-Odins. How could we guide all those who were confronted by our experience to single out that which made sense to them alone, that which was appropriate to their situation? Between '72 and '74 we started a new type of seminar. We did not teach. We only presented our approach to the work, to what we today call our 'group culture', that is to say training as a highly individualised process. But this extremely personal process becomes a socialisation when it encounters the others within the group, according to norms, values and aims shared by all.

HUGO SALAZAR: *Identity, culture and group are concepts that you frequently refer to. Could you explain to me the transition of these concepts from cultural anthropology to theatre anthropology.*

E. BARBA: What interests me in theatre groups is their double need or obsession: on the one hand to define their own values, their own historical-biographical identity which is unique and belongs to the individual; and on the other, how not to reduce apprenticeship to a limited period of schooling, but to transform it into a continuous process of 'learning to learn' in which we expose ourselves to that which is different, whether in our own culture or in others. Interculturality and transculturality are the two poles of our professional identity which indiscriminately includes the *Commedia dell'Arte* and *kathakali*, baroque theatre and *nô*, carneval and indigenous rituals.

GAUTAM DASGUPTA: *How do these observations and experiments of yours apply in your way of doing theatre?*

E. BARBA: I moved in this direction because I was faced with a problem. Over the years, the road which I have followed and the results which seem to be its consequence, have encouraged many young people to approach me. How could I transmit my experience without reducing it to a formula which would kill their autonomy instead of stimulating it? It is the eternal dilemma of how to 'teach without teaching', of how to discover one's own rules without imposing a general rule. The solution consists in a pedagogical process which negates itself and advances via paradoxical digressions.

M.G. GREGORI: *Does not the fact of denying the pedagogical moment also give you the possibility of denying repetitiveness, i.e. crystallisation?*

E. BARBA: Yes, but above all it gives the possibility to deny a certain form of authority. How? The experiences I have lived through have made me indifferent to the rest of the theatrical planet. I am not interested in destroying it, but on the other hand it is of little concern to me. What does matter to me, however, is the path I follow with my companions, deciphering the encounters, the questions, the uncertainties, the results. We must pass on our own experience, but do it in a different way each time. We know how great is the temptation to repeat. Going over what we know gives us a feeling of security, but we avoid exposing ourselves, and renounce every subsequent surprise and discovery. You have to use all your will-power and intelligence to fight against the dark face of a long-lasting pedagogical situation: routine, inertia, entropy.

RICARDO INIESTA: *For many years Odin Teatret concentrated on research and on a pedagogical vision which, later, spread to other continents. In 1979 you founded ISTA (International School of Theatre Anthropology) and in 1980 you organised its first public session in Bonn. In the beginning, the public sessions were held every two or three years. Lately, however, they have become more frequent. What importance does ISTA have for your work?*

E. BARBA: ISTA developed out of the interest that I and a select group of artists and scholars had for pedagogy and the problems concerning performative technique.

On the one hand there are the theatre schools which train actors and integrate them into an existing theatrical context. However, in these schools it would be impossible to nourish visions and acquire the technical tools to create new relationships through theatre. In order to renew and transform theatre, these schools would need, paradoxically, to train 'rebels', that is actors who are not willing to adapt to the present situation. On the other hand, there exists an artistic universe made up of actors and directors who do not come from these schools. What characterises these people and groups is their autodidactic experience, with all the advantages and disadvantages this implies: a greater ingenuity, openness, pragmatism, flexibility. All this, however, often involves a refusal to acknowledge the values of our professional legacy and a lack of conscious confrontation with tradition, with dramatic literature and with the techniques of dramaturgy.

How can one create a didactic situation in which it is possible to transmit a nucleus of essential knowledge without this becoming a static model? How can one succeed in comparing technical experiences within a short space of time, while avoiding the establishment of a school which would inevitably degenerate within a few years? How can one create an environment which shakes up the preconceptions of actors, directors and scholars, stimulating them to find personal solutions to overcome the obstacles which continually arise in their activity on a theoretical, technical and organisational level?

ISTA is an attempt to respond to these questions. It was conceived and organised as a situation offering an optimum of exchange of experience: Eastern/Western, older generation/younger generation, traditional theatre/group theatre, practitioner/theoretician. It gathers together people who feel the need for new impulses or to delve into the subterranean world of the performer's art. ISTA is not just a place where new techniques can be learned. It is a fragile and unstable meeting place where personal needs, curiosity, professional and emotional bonds, as well as an analytical attitude all merge into research and activity.

PIERGIORGIO GIACCHÉ: *Your concept of a school can be read as the final act of a cultural policy that Odin Teatret has always promoted and which has engendered ideas, groups and a whole new theoretical flora. Do you not think that somehow ISTA is involuntarily reinforcing Eugenio Barba as a model rather than a master?*

E. BARBA: I have used the term 'school' for ISTA as a paradox, as a self-provocation. ISTA, however, has never been nor will it ever be organised in the form of courses, lessons, subjects. It is rather the result of continuous changes, groups which come together and break up, programmes that are created from day to day and that can be overturned just as fast. There are no classes, just ephemeral families gathered around the experience of masters of theatre and dance from diverse traditions.

Only because the disorder is conscious and constant can it be perceived to be strictly ordered. But this ordered disorder does not follow the linear phase of a course of learning, but the organic development of the individual paths of each participant.

Any form of transmission of experience risks withering away into a model to be imitated. ISTA's safety valve consists in the fact that it does not concentrate on results which are valid according to a particular aesthetic or style. My task is to set various processes in motion, scrutinising them like an entomologist: on a technical level as a director, and from the point of view of scenic efficacy as a spectator. On other occasions, when I present Odin Teatret's performances, I am showing results, and then there is the danger of involuntarily furnishing models. It should be remembered, however, that I myself started out with a model: Grotowski. You always have to have a concrete starting point which may well be banal, sketchy, rough. What is important is that at the end of your road you meet yourself and not the model.

PIERGIORGIO GIACCHÉ: *With ISTA, the 'school' has in a way become for you a second activity, an experience that can be separated from that of 'doing theatre'. Leaving aside all that you learn from others while you are teaching, how does this school help you and what does it give you from a strictly personal point of view?*

E. BARBA: I have reached an age and a position which would allow me to live off the prestige I have acquired. I am not clear about the reasons which won't let me go along with this choice and which prevent me from accepting what I have accumulated through all these years of work. It is partly because I identify myself with the new generations. Their thirst for knowledge, their desire sometimes to do something so desperate that it bursts out into arbitrary acts, reminds me of my situation as a youngster. I feel an immense desire to be 'alive' and to confront history. My way to remain alive is to stay close to my origins, to take my place amongst the disinherited, the uprooted, the unknowing who want to know, the short-sighted who want to see far.

My choice combines an immeasurable feeling of solidarity (what an inflated word!) as well as a form of lucidity over the risk of being petrified into a monument covered by layers of pigeon droppings.

G. DASGUPTA: *But in various places around the world, and especially in Europe, you are now seen as a Master. Are you pleased with the influence you have?*

E. BARBA: If this influence helps these people to find their autonomy and keep their spirit of revolt alive, then yes. But I feel disheartened when a group, an actor or a director somehow betray this 'aliveness', imitate me, flatly going over to an inert way of doing theatre, forgetting the origin which was the source of their opposition, of their refusal, of the vision which impelled them to create a group.

In the end, theatre is the possibility of shaping your own small revolt, leaving imperceptible traces for those who, by uncovering them, transform them into seeds of life.

Bibliography

Gautam Dasgupta, *Anthropology and Theatre*. Eugenio Barba in *Performing Arts Journal*, Vol. VIII, 3, New York 1984, pp. 8-18.
Piergiorgio Giacché, *A Volterra per imparare a insegnare a imparare* in *Rinascita - Il contemporaneo*, 36, 1981, pp. 24-25.
Maria Grazia Gregori, *Eugenio Barba* in *Il signore della scena*, Feltrinelli, Milan 1979, pp. 215-229.
Ricardo Iniesta, *Eugenio Barba: el teatro es el espectador* in *ADE Teatro*, 45-46, Madrid 1995, pp. 138-141.
Franco Quadri, *Colloquio con Eugenio Barba* in *Il teatro degli anni settanta, invenzione di un teatro diverso*, Einaudi, Turin 1984, pp. 59-60.
Hugo Salazar, *Ilusiones vitales, ilusiones mortales* in *Quehacer*, 56, Lima 1989, pp. 84-90.

THE TRANSMISSION OF A LEGACY

Here Eugenio Barba reflects on apprenticeship, expressing in a complementary manner the two aspects on which it is based: on the one hand the technical side constituted by the training exercises, and on the other the ethical one constituted by the demands of a precise work context. Pedagogy becomes a dialectic between these two poles, directed not only towards the formation of the actor, but also towards the transmission of a legacy. Barba concludes his reflections on apprenticeship by evoking what Odin Teatret, after more than thirty years of work, shelters behind the label of 'theatre-laboratory': the reality of a theatre which is an unending school.

This text originates partly from Exister avant de représenter, *edited by Brunella Eruli in Puck, 7, Les Ardennes 1994, and partly from the preface of* La scuola degli attori *edited by Franco Ruffini, La casa Usher, Florence 1981.*

How do you form an actor?

In all cultures the art of the actor is rooted in variable elements such as individual personality and the performance genre chosen. There is, however, a constant factor which is fundamental: the materiality of the body-mind, that scenic 'presence' which determines the relationship with the spectators. What processes, techniques or principles do actors have to employ to make their actions efficacious with respect to the spectator? Can these be learned? And how?

An Amulet Made of Memory

These questions have gone hand in hand with the formation of the actor in Europe since the time when Stanislavski, Meyerhold and their collaborators invented 'exercises'. These exercises were very different from the ones practised in theatre schools. Actors traditionally trained in fencing, ballet, singing and above all the recitation of fragments of texts from an international repertoire. But the exercises invented by Stanislavski and Meyerhold did not contribute much to the interpretation of a text or the creation of a character. On the contrary, they were elaborate scores, codified down to the last detail, and ends in themselves. Few people understood the point of these exercises which were so far removed from the tasks confronting the actor on stage.

Our century's reformers ascribed a new social objective to the actor. Meyerhold, Copeau, Brecht and Artaud asked themselves about the function or the meaning of theatre in society. To make their visions possible, other technical premises were necessary. Hence their interest in pedagogy. The exercises which they invented are pure form, dynamically evolving webs with no plot, no story. They are small labyrinths through which the actor's body-mind can trace and retrace a path in order to incorporate a paradoxical way of thinking. Thus, the actors distance themselves from their own *daily* way of acting and reacting and enter into the extra-daily acting and reacting of the stage.

Exercises are similar to amulets which the actor wears, not in order to show them off, but to draw from them a special quality of energy from which a second nervous system gradually develops. An exercise is made up of memory: body memory. An exercise becomes memory which acts throughout the entire body.

We see this in the oldest exercises that have been passed on to us, those devised by Meyerhold in which his aim was to teach 'the essence of scenic movement', and which he called 'biomechanics'.

While doing an exercise, the actor is not meant to play a character, but must only concentrate on a humble and irksome task combining precision and a capacity to repeat. Yet repetition, in its fight against automatism, is transformed into personal expression. It is a question of learning to compose and direct a generic 'scenic life', which is the *raison d'être* of a personal technique. One does not establish how to interpret a character, but how to enhance the force of sensorial persuasion of any character.

As Decroux aptly says: first you must exist as an actor, and then perform.

The exercises determine the technical aspect of the apprenticeship. But in the formation of the actor you must also take into consideration another aspect which is complementary to the technical one.

The Invisible Spectator

Young people who decide today to do theatre must be aware of the personal cost their choice entails. Abnegation is indispensable to the profession and above all is necessary to the one who chooses it.

The established system considers theatre as though it had a value in itself. A youngster who is admitted to a theatre school has the possibility later of working in the established theatre. Abracadabra: s/he does theatre and is immediately transformed into the Guardian of Tradition. Actors should only be recognised as such if they are capable of justifying in practice a constant search for meaning and a new value in their art.

The established system, being the expression of an entire culture, has fostered a tendency to be impatient. Right from the start, one waits to be discovered, to arrive, to be acknowledged. The tempering effect of an apprenticeship which lasts for years and years has been lost. Only classical ballet reminds us of how long it takes to incorporate a vast technical patrimony and put it into practice in a personal way. In the world of theatre the propensity to trust one's intuition and inspiration provokes a craving for immediate results that is hardly compatible with the long and laborious preparation necessary for an actor.

I expect from aspiring actors tenacity and doggedness. They must throw away their watches and submit to insane rhythms of work in order to die to the world that has acculturated them and be reborn as actors. They must possess visions and values of their own, and a capacity to dominate technical principles which they put into practice unwittingly. They must live each day as though it was their last, and at the same time, as though they had before them the whole of eternity. Tension guides the apprenticeship: the inexorability of work which renounces the temptation of the short cut and aspires to what is essential, to the detail that at any moment may become the last word, one's testament. But also the elation over the infinite time available to perfect, to delve into the depths, to surprise and uncover oneself.

A theatre school should form actors who master the 'art of bewitchment', the knowledge of how to captivate the senses and induce the reflection of the spectator. It should also convince the student that such mastery is only acquired through an exasperatingly long preparation whose first priority is not to satisfy the tastes of the spectator. From the beginning of their apprenticeship, the aspiring actors should address themselves only to one chosen, invisible and dear spectator. It could be a person whom they have never met, or one long dead who, although from a distant past, converses with them like a benevolent totem. It could be a face, a voice, a look belonging to a future generation.

The actor then becomes provocative because s/he embodies a paradox: s/he acts in the present while addressing spectators who have been or will be, and does not listen to the applause of the present time.

Odin Teatret has survived thirty years because it was founded on this attitude. For a long time we worked in the hostile or indifferent climate of a small provincial town, submerged by financial problems and with so few spectators that they could often be counted on the fingers of one hand. We never doubted that our theatre had a meaning as long as one single spectator felt the necessity to see our performance. In this way we constructed a small world with its own relationships and values, without allowing ourselves to be overwhelmed by the values and the relationships of the world around us.

The Virtue of Fatigue

Theatre schools have always made me feel uneasy, maybe because of the defensive reaction that transforms an inferiority complex into a superiority complex. But even though sufficient time has passed to erase these reactions of defence and inadequacy, theatre schools still make me feel uncomfortable. They are organised just like schools, placing pupils in contact with various teachers who may well be very able, efficient and eager to pass on the best of their experience, but whom the context labels as teachers of this or that subject. I believe that, in theatre, apprenticeship cannot be carried out by teachers. I am convinced it needs masters.

Given that the theatre is undeniably an art of the present, the aspiring actor has to learn to guard against the risk of the ephemeral. This cannot be learned in a theatre school, but with a master. I can immediately recognise an actor or a director who has worked with Decroux: the attitude of solemnity and humour that permeates their extraordinary technical competence makes them stand out as artists who have a totem.

Such masters are rare and their tendency to demand more and more, and to force the defences of the pupil, is condemned by the spirit of our time. Fortunate are those who succeed in finding and being accepted by a master whose demands make them discover the immensity of their own natural wealth. Most people do not feel the need for this constraint. For others, however, it is such a necessity that they invent a master figure whom they can evoke through the words of his or her writings. For some the master is the artistic superego, for others, a 'dear' spectator.

My master was Grotowski. Although we are almost the same age, I owe a great deal to my time spent with him in Opole. At that stage Grotowski was unknown and his position was precarious because the Polish communist authorities did not appreciate his performances. The energy and shrewdness that he summoned up in order to continue doing the theatre he wanted to do, in spite of a hostile context, are for me exemplary.

On the one hand you must have a totem, an artist you have known or who is distant in time, whose example incites you not to give up the climb, hanging on by your nails and your teeth. On the other hand you must favour an organic process, discover your path according to what you are and what you know, having the audacity to cut the umbilical cord that has been nourishing you, and breathe with your own lungs.

Although Grotowski was my master and has had an enormous significance for me, my professional formation is that of an autodidact. When I was young I read all the books I could lay my hands on, in search of advice or a phrase that could give me confidence. I have never lost my veneration for *the book*. I thirst after experience transmitted through words, and the resulting tension which springs from my attempt to decipher them. All the great masters of our century have condensed their wisdom in paradoxes and poetic images which conceal precious technical indications.

Work with my actors, the need to resolve the particular problems of the individual, but at the same time to create problems in order to challenge their strength, day after day, for years and years - that is the thread that runs through my professional biography. To inspire confidence when I myself was uncertain, to carefully weigh words and calculate silences, to seek with determination for the ambiguity which opens up the door to the unexpected, to indicate the road which must become a personal path - this was my daily effort as a director. My young age and inexperience made me believe that it was possible to teach something that was valid for everybody. Time, and above all the actors who have remained with me for decades, have shown me that every individual possesses his own 'jungle' and one penetrates into it with a compass whose 'North' differs from person to person. Theories and methods, especially those that seem coherent and suggestive, encourage discussion, help make comparisons and write books. But the experience of learning, of 'going to school', literally consists in moving one foot after the other without stumbling, and above all without marking time. It is the discovery of a readiness which becomes your destiny and yours alone.

At Odin Teatret we know that endurance and duration are the two secrets of apprenticeship. My actors and I are used to working while tired, forcing our limits. Financial difficulties and the desire to remain alive as a group have left their mark. The climate of silence and concentration of the early years is still the habitual framework of our work. Then, as now, self-discipline reminds us that one false step can bring about the disintegration of the group. When I am preparing a new production, I feel as though I am a part of a group of mountaineers. Each puts his or her own strength to the test, yet is roped to the others. If one falls, the entire group is dragged down.

All this is decided on the first day of apprenticeship.

Theatre as an Unending School
The story of Odin Teatret is characterised by a lasting relationship between me and the handful of actors who founded it more than thirty years ago and who were formed by me. They are still with me and are, in their turn training new actors. They are following different paths from mine, and yet I feel them near.

Some of them want to work only with the same group of people made up of actors and directors from different countries and tendencies. They gather together annually for three or four weeks living at our theatre or in villages around Holstebro. They organise their activity alternating the artistic with the practical - cleaning of the theatre, the preparation of meals, making costumes and props. At the end of their period together they present the results of their work in the form of a public performance or as a barter in the villages or houses which have given them hospitality. They also show the performances that each has created in his or her own country.

Other actors remind me of nomadic bedouins.They travel, visiting groups or individuals in isolated villages or big cities, working with them and carrying out projects together. Here too it is the recurrence, however irregular, that characterises the bond and the exchange.

The younger actors train individually. Every now and then they reassemble under the guidance of an older colleague. Their individual work is shaped into clown scenes and street performances. I watch them go off to kindergartens, town squares, refugee camps, small islands around the coast. They teach amateur groups and schools.

All the Odin actors periodically join the 'flying house' of ISTA amongst masters from other traditions and, together with them, give life to the *Theatrum Mundi* performance.

Twice a year, one of the actors organises an 'Odin Week' at which we welcome fifty or so people to the theatre to introduce them to our world: performances, work demonstrations, film projections, participation in the training, encounters with individual actors or with me.

Every two or three years we throw ourselves head first into Holstebro's *Festuge*. This is a festival in which we bring together more than a hundred of the town's organisations and get them to collaborate: the army with the pacifists, the Lutheran churches with other religious societies, sports associations with the music conservatory. It is an orgy of barters. The spectacularity which is concealed behind daily activities is brought to light without respect for the normal rhythm of day and night.

Odin Teatret has many rooms. In all of them apprenticeship is unending. We have neither a permanent staff of teachers nor set programmes or syllabuses. We have no system of selection or entrance exams. However, the Danish Ministry of Culture considers us to be a pedagogical centre.

Contemplating this diversity, I think back to those five young people who had the bravado to call themselves a 'laboratory'. Before my eyes appears the image of a theatre as an unending school: the exact opposite of a theatre school.

If Odin Teatret has a place in the history of contemporary theatre, it is because a group of people embodied a practice and, by so doing, set an example.

The Odin has existed for 30 years. Herein resides the meaning of our work.

***

How do you form an actor?

Sometimes, while reading a book, I suddenly have the impression that the author has written those pages just for me, hiding a message behind the words that I will be unable to decipher until much later.

The question which guides my work today is not how to form an actor, but how to transmit a legacy.

9. 'There are moments when your condition is stripped bare and is reduced to your craft. But what is your craft reduced to?' (The oldest photograph of Odin Teatret's training, Oslo, October 1964, with Torgeir Wethal and Else Marie Laukvik who are still actors with Odin Teatret today).

10. 'Please, God, give me the strength always to choose the most difficult path.' (Torgeir Wethal, training, 1966)

11. 'The aspiring actors must live each day as though it were their last and, at the same time, as though they had before them the whole of eternity.' (Tage Larsen, training, 1971)

12. 'What you must do, you must do. And don't question, don't question.' (Iben Nagel
Rasmussen, training, 1986)

13(a+b). 'Training is an encounter with the reality which one has chosen: whatever you do, do it with your whole self.' (Training at Odin Teatret in 1983. Above, from left to right: Silvia Ricciardelli, Roberta Carreri, Julia Varley and Francis Pardeilhan; below, Julia Varley.)

14(a+b). 'The question which guides my work today is not how to form an actor, but how to transmit a legacy' (Above, Eugenio Barba with Torgeir Wethal and Else Marie Laukvik in 1972 during rehearsals for My Father's House; below, Eugenio Barba with the Brazilian dancer, Augusto Omolú, during a work demonstration at ISTA, Umeå, 1995.)

15 'Exercises are similar to amulets which the actor wears, not in order to show them off, but to draw from them a special quality of energy from which a second nervous system gradually develops. An exercise is made of memory: body memory.' (Iben Nagel Rasmussen leads the training of the young Odin actors. From left to right: Iben Nagel Rasmussen, Isabel Ubeda, Kai Bredholt and Tina Nielsen, Holstebro, 1996.)

16. 'In the world of theatre one always tries to show off one's own originality, repudiating one's origins, the tradition from which one comes. I never shared such an attitude. I am proud of my origins and of my master, Jerzy Grotowski.' (Jerzy Grotowski and Eugenio Barba, in Holstebro, October 1994, on the occasion of the thirtieth anniversary of Odin Teatret.)

III

TRAVEL : BARTER

I hate travels and explorers.
And yet here I am telling about
my expeditions.

Claude Lévy-Strauss:
Tristes tropiques

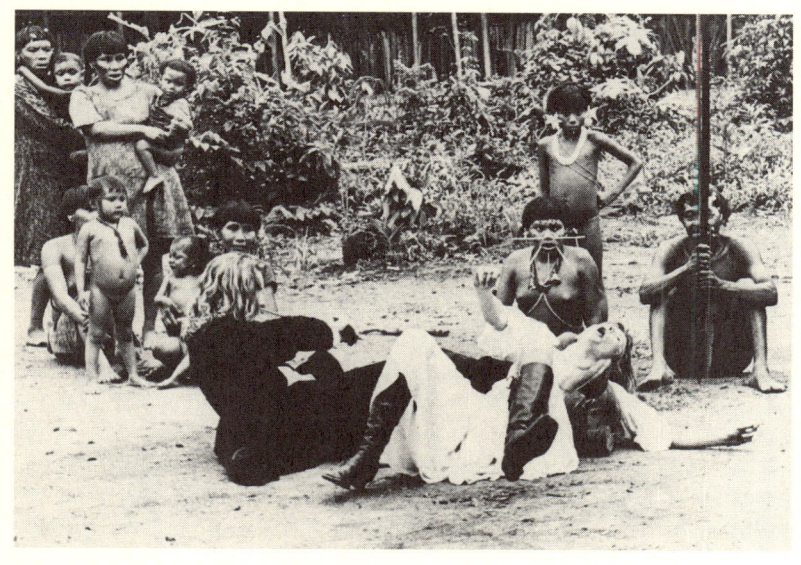

17. *Tage Larsen and Else Marie Laukvik during a barter with a Yanomami tribe in Venezuelan Amazonia in 1976.*

TWO TRIBES

In spring 1974, Odin Teatret left its home in Holstebro and settled for five months in Carpignano, a village of 2,000 inhabitants in southern Italy. This new geographical and cultural environment had a shattering impact on the group, throwing it into many unexpected circumstances. With this sojourn, Odin Teatret began its phase of 'openness', its street performances and the awareness of itself as a micro-culture which could be 'bartered'.

In this interview, recorded in Carpignano by Stig Krabbe Barfoed for Danish Television, Eugenio Barba introduces for the first time the concept of 'barter' to explain Odin Teatret's strategy for coming into contact and establishing an exchange with the local population.

This interview was first published in Biblioteca Teatrale, 10-11, Bulzoni, Rome 1974.

I have been here for a week and seen your activities. Why are you here in Italy? Why can't you do this in Denmark?

We chose the isolated village of Carpignano, on the heel of the Italian peninsula, from which over 800 of the 1800 inhabitants have been forced to emigrate to find work. We wanted to prepare our new production in human, social and geographic surroundings that were out of the ordinary for us. But our stay here confronted us with totally unfamiliar questions: why were we here and how should we define ourselves - strangers and actors - to the population?

After having seen your work here, I still have some doubts. How much of this is altruistic, truly for the people here, and how much is for yourselves?

Your question touches on a central theme: the consequences of one's activity. Take a surgeon, for example, who operates on people because he likes the pay, hopes for fame, or is escaping from a boring wife. If he saves lives, what do his personal motives matter! That which moves Odin Teatret to work in Carpignano is in a sense egoistic. We are here because we find it stimulating being placed in a new situation. But it is the consequences, the results, you should pay attention to. How do the people of Carpignano experience our presence here? Do we represent a stimulus, a strong push that sets a string of processes in motion, allowing the inhabitants to rediscover the common cultural ties which characterise their society and define themselves in relation to us? If the population here responds to Odin Teatret's initiatives with cultural manifestations - dances, songs, improvised scenes, storytelling - then our seemingly egoistic motives will have become a powerful catalyst for a social event.

Yes, but how much do you represent a foreign body here? That is, something that enters, forms an abscess, and then disappears again.

Foreign body is the best term to describe our presence in this southern Italian village. Odin Teatret's actors and the population are poles apart. With their Scandinavian cultural background, their behaviour and way of thinking, with the prejudice of their seeming lack of prejudices, our long-haired actors are totally different from the tightly knit peasant culture and its rigid norms. But it is just this difference, this 'otherness' that has been our point of departure. We do not want to 'teach' anything, nor inform the people here of their social or cultural situation. We do not believe we have a knowledge of something they lack. We are not here to entertain them. On the other hand, we will not bow to the local norms and deny our own experiences, our way of living with its emotional freedom.

Our stay here is built up around the idea of the barter. Imagine two very different tribes, each on their own side of the river. Each tribe can live for itself, talk about the other tribe, praise or slander it. But every time one of them rows over to the other shore it is to exchange something. One does not row over to carry out ethnographic research, to observe the other's way of life, but rather to give and to take: a handful of salt for a scrap of cloth, a bow for a fistful of beads.

The goods we trade are cultural. We began with simple situations where we sang Scandinavian songs, and where the local songs were a natural and organic response. We then widened the barter with fragments of our training which looked like dances, and the people responded with some of their own. Then came our street parades, our theatrical 'siege' of the village and its improvised reaction. The situation began to look like a village get-together with everybody participating.

In any village there are always a few with a gift for entertaining. This was true not just in Carpignano, but in many surrounding villages. People came and asked us to sing, dance or show our newly created clown performance. We asked what they could give in return. They had to find local people, not professionals, who were willing to 'barter' their songs or dances with us. Our own arrival and performance were merely a pretext, a concrete impulse to assemble the population and let it take over, driven by its own cultural premises, creating a situation that does not divide, but binds people closer together. Everybody can join in because they know the songs and dances.

This is the barter. We do not give up our identity, nor do they give up theirs. Both parts go away with more than they brought. And in spite of our diversity, we confront each other, defining ourselves reciprocally through our own cultural backgrounds.

In order to live here you have to present something different from your normal activity in Denmark. You have created a clown show, a type of performance you have never done before.

The situation here is different, both socially and culturally. We do theatre research, and theatre can be many things, even within a single country. It depends on where you are and among which people. Our function in Denmark has been to initiate projects that were generally considered impossible: theatre seminars where the Scandanavian participants could meet personalities from other countries and be confronted with different experiences; the publishing of a theatre magazine in a country which had no other periodicals of this sort; the presentation of performances of some of the most significant artists in Europe, from Dario Fo to Grotowski and Ronconi to Japanese and Balinese theatre. All this corresponds to a theatre laboratory's task in Denmark. We could not bring this type of activity with us to a small Italian village where people had never before seen a play. We had to stop thinking in the usual theatre categories, and ask ourselves: what can we do here? We did not want to spoon-feed these people with theatre, a cultural phenomenon they have lived quite nicely without for centuries. We wanted them to answer us with their own voice, their own language, that which still binds them together and makes them strong, although slowly disintegrating: their culture, a popular culture which does not divide, but unites.

LETTER FROM THE SOUTH OF ITALY

This 'open letter' is Eugenio Barba's reply to a series of questions put to him by the American theatre critic, Jennifer Merin. At the time (autumn 1975), Barba was with Odin Teatret for two months in Ollolai, a village in central Sardinia. Recalling what had happened in Carpignano the previous year, Barba elaborates on the concept of barter as a practice which defines the identity of the group by underlining its differences. Barter is still today one of Odin Teatret's customary activities.

Barba's letter was first published in The Drama Review, *68, New York 1975. It clearly indicates the profound changes which the Odin was undergoing during those years and which caused it to redefine its identity in terms of a group with its own culture.*

Dear Jennifer Merin,

I will try to answer your questions about our work, about its development, about the importance of our experiences in southern Italy, not point by point, but in a continuous statement.

In some cases the answers will be implicit. There are questions which one cannot answer in words, but only through action.

***

Who are you?

Actors.

But is the word 'actor' a real answer, when the question comes from an old woman dressed in black, who speaks only in dialect, in a village in southern Italy? Or from a peasant, or a shepherd?

For them, actor means 'cinema', 'television'. But what does it really mean when we want this word not to refer to institutionalised entertainment, to the television everyone watches, to the respectable theatre that people see from a distance as something refined and difficult, that is loved and studied by only a few enthusiasts?

Where are we actors? In Holstebro and in all the places where we perform before spectators who know why they come to see us. This region of theatre is scattered everywhere, a few thousand people in every city.

But if we venture outside this region, who are we? What do we become in an isolated village in Apulia or Sardinia? What do we have to become in order still to recognise ourselves in this word, 'actor', facing new people whom we can no longer recognise in the word 'spectator'?

One can work for years in a recognisable place, behind a door with 'Theatre' written on it. All that you do there acquires a meaning, not only for you who do it but also for those outside. And there is a significance not only in what you are doing, but also in what you are *not* doing, what you refuse. Your work seems justified in advance. You are distinguished by what you affirm and what you deny. But what you affirm and what you deny is just theatre.

What happens when the door and its sign are knocked down? It can happen that what at first would have been 'facile', 'banal', 'lacking in interest', appears to you now, in areas without theatre, as strangely essential. The choices and the refusals that had clearly defined you while under the protection of the theatre, vanish. If you try to look at yourself in those who surround you and observe you, you become aware that the mirror reflects something nebulous: your manners and features seem to be lost in a mist.

***

So one has to start again from the beginning.
  Who are you?
  Actors.
  But, who are you?
  It is a challenge; if we are actors, if we have chosen this condition, how can we demonstrate it? And again, what does our condition become in these new territories? Will we be like mountebanks who entertain? Like propagandists? Like missionaries? How can we justify the fact of being there, strangers and different, doing what we do?

***

One evening, after about a month in Carpignano (until then we had lived in almost total isolation, concentrating on our work) we decided to visit some friends from the University of Lecce who had come to stay in the same village. We took our musical instruments and left our lodgings.

It was the first time that we had appeared in the village in a compact group with musical instruments and the multicoloured clothing we used in our training. It was also the first time, in so many years of theatre work, that we found ourselves face to face with people in the street. Previously, we had been alone in our work rooms or at our seminars among a few attentive and interested persons.

People immediately began to follow us, asking us to play our instruments. We arrived at our friends' house but they were not in. Without intending it, we found ourselves in the open, in a public square, surrounded by many people waiting for us to do something. We had our backs to the wall and so began to play Scandinavian folk songs mingled with vocal improvisations as used by our actors in their training.

We sang and played for about an hour. And what surprised us most, at the end, was not the long applause of the people around us (what had the Odin actors become: a casual group of musicians?), but the fact that some people said to us: 'Now you must hear our songs'. They began to sing melodies that traditionally accompany the tobacco and olive harvests, about unhappy love and death. From this improvised situation was born our idea of the 'barter'.

What happened in Carpignano recalled a similar situation in the mountains of Sardinia where, about five months previously, we had brought our most recent production, *My Father's House*.

In these isolated localities where theatre had never appeared, the audience of shepherds and peasants reacted in a way which disconcerted us but which we quickly came to understand. It was the same way people in Italian villages reacted at the cinema, commenting on what they saw on the screen. In response to the film, the audience exchanges reactions and ironic or serious comments, while on the screen the images continue to flow by. These were also the reactions of our spectators. Participating in this theatrical situation which was new to them, they expressed their disorientation through comments, noisy exclamations, loud bursts of laughter, and sometimes deep silences.

Despite this enormous clamour, which at first left us perplexed and which was so far from the silence and attitude of the spectators used to the conventions of theatre, there was always applause at the end and then a great desire to ask us questions. They felt they 'had not understood' because - they claimed - they were lacking in 'culture', and they asked us to explain. But often, after the performance, the people seemed animated by a desire to present themselves to us, to do something that corresponded to what they had seen. They began to sing and dance, exhibiting those typical forms of popular culture that are not limited to elaborate verbal language but which, through the whole of their very physical presence, reveal the history and the vision of a community. What had happened in Sardinia after *My Father's House* happened anew in Carpignano, with our songs and the songs in response.

When rumours of a foreign theatre group spread to other localities around Carpignano, young people came and asked us to go to them. We answered frankly that we were not philanthropists, that no one likes to work for nothing, and that we wanted compensation, but not in the form of money. We wanted them to present themselves to us in the same way we presented ourselves to them, with their songs and their dances. These young people often answered that they did not know how to sing, nor did they know the local songs. Sometimes they said that there were no traditions in their locality. We then asked them to seek out the old people, suggesting that they go to the taverns they frequented, and learn songs from them, or else that they invite the old people themselves to come to the village square to sing.

***

When one arrives in a village in southern Italy, in summer, when everyone is out of doors in the evening, it seems split in two: on one side the old, on the other the young. Each group behaves and dresses differently and frequents different places. One realises that the split is not only deep but is felt by both groups as a wound. The old feel the void within them. They live in a place that *has been* but which no longer really *is*. The young live there as strangers, sometimes intolerant, sometimes pointlessly nostalgic for a past way of life that they sense is a possible antidote against the 'values' that flood in from the big cities.

Thus, diverse experiences, almost two eras, two worlds, live a few metres apart from each other, but parallel, without meeting or confronting one another. Parents and children clash in the restricted space of the home, under the suffocating forms of incomprehension found in families. In the villages where we were invited, after we had sung, elderly men and women, whom we would have imagined to be closed in a distant and impenetrable reserve, came forward and sang and danced.

***

But, if the people in the villages presented themselves to us with their dances, how should we, if we had to dance, present ourselves to them? In our group there are Danes, Swedes, Norwegians and Italians. None of us know folk dances, nor feel the need to learn them. Seeing the peasants dance and sing, I became even more aware of how my companions and I belonged to a culture where common ties no longer exist and everyone is individually searching for new ones. By trying to present our folk dances

117

we would have been masking ourselves behind something we did not feel we were, because dance is the unrationalised, uncalculated moment when our biological and social inheritance overwhelms us, transports us, lifts us from the earth, unleashes all our energies.

In what circumstances were the Odin actors overwhelmed, driven by a necessity that was not only a desire to enjoy themselves, but an essential need to be present and to reach out to others? In their work.

The question that had remained open so long ('Who are you?' 'Actors.' But how could we prove it if we did not have a performance?) now found an answer. We would demonstrate it through our training in which the actors seem carried by the wave of their energies, their weight and mass being magnified and transformed into a radiant force.

In this way our 'dances' were born when each actor, driven by the needs that distinguish the individual work, seems to defy the force of gravity. But our actors did not start with the assumption that they wanted to or had to dance. It was a result that came involuntarily and was viewed by others as dance.

We also put on clown shows and parades, improvising our way through the village streets.

We presented ourselves now very differently from in our previous performances. These were the outcome of a very long process in which a group of young people tried to reveal a truth of their own, to crack, to break the skin of clay in which our living body moves and in reality hides itself. To crack it, to break it, and let the flesh, the blood, come to light.

Now in the streets of these villages we had taken on a new skin. Seeing us here again, those who had known us through our productions would have found it hard to recognise us.

***

One reads about actors of three or four centuries ago, reads the descriptions of their performances before aristocratic audiences or in the public squares where the audience is called 'the people'. One reads the description of their dances, of their acrobatics, of their noisy, colourful entrances into the towns where they went to gather up the last spare coins. The descriptions are lively and detailed. They almost succeed in making us hear the sounds, see how the actress made herself provocative and modest at the same time, how one actor made himself appear seductive and yet another moved people and made them laugh. But these actors seem to have no substance. They are two-dimensional figures with a painted face on the front. What lies behind?

The historians were only interested in portraying the theatre, not those who made it. In those times actors were not allowed to think of themselves as artists, and what they did was never called 'culture'. Why did they do this useless thing, theatre? We know: to earn money, to survive. But who were these people who had decided to survive in such a manner? Servants who wanted to become their own masters, and serve only on the planks of the stage? Youngsters who enjoyed adventure? Men caught in the illusion of prolonging their youth, avoiding the roles and rules that govern the life of those doing useful and accepted work? People who fled from fear or shame? Or who were simply born into the roving world of the theatre? Mature women and old men no longer able to live removed from this endless dreariness filled with movement that we call adventure?

The actors of three or four centuries ago are distant figures whom we can describe as we wish. But even if their image is distant, their ambiguity brings them closer to us.

***

Who are you? Actors. But, *who* are you?

It is now almost ten years since I wrote an article called *Waiting for the Revolution*. I spoke of how only a continuous renewal of our awareness and of our personal relationship towards what was happening around us could create a new attitude towards our craft. I said that it is the process that transforms us, that the necessity of this choice of ours must be put to the test through our daily work, with such inhuman demands that only a few persist: those who are animated by an indomitable need, the demons for work who overcome the inertia which contents itself with futile results.

The article concluded: 'It is no longer a question of being a missionary or an original artist, but of being realistic. Our profession gives us the possibility of changing ourselves and thereby changing society. One must not ask: what does theatre mean for the people? This is a demagogic and unfruitful question. But rather: what does the theatre mean for me? The answer, converted into ruthless and uncompromising action, will be revolution in the theatre'.

I have quoted my own writing because later another question followed. It arose naturally in the very life of our group: the revolution in theatre. And afterwards?

***

Odin Teatret has performed often in Italy. We have presented *My Father's House* sixty times during seminars with young people, students or members of small theatre groups. Very often they questioned and doubted that a theatre laboratory, which operates in the Danish welfare state, could function in a society as full of contradictions as Italy.

But what is it that counts? A preconceived form of theatre, or the attitude one has towards one's surroundings, the manner in which one tries to turn one's 'yes' and 'no' into action when confronted with what one hears and sees?

We decided to live for a few months in Italy during a period in which we no longer presented the old production (*My Father's House*) and had not yet produced a new one. A period in which we were only a group of people and not a theatre group touring with a play. And we wanted to go to a place where theatre had never existed and had no meaning. The village where we went to live, Carpignano, was chosen in one of the poorest areas of the south of Italy, where in each family a father, a son, or a brother had emigrated to Switzerland or Germany. A small and isolated village.

My companions and I have always felt uneasy seeing someone trying to be familiar with others who are different: when an adult acts in an infantile way with children, or when students believe themselves to be the same as workers or peasants. We felt ourselves to be different and we lacked the missionary calling to make others accept our truth.

But our truth could be defined only in confrontation with the truth of others. From this encounter with something different we were compelled to reveal the gap between our purposes and what we were capable of achieving through a whole series of reactions of which we were not at first aware.

After we arrived in this village, we did not mingle with the people right away. We lived for three weeks in total isolation in the centre of the village, relying on our safest point, our work. We got up at five in the morning, exactly the same time that the peasants went to work in the fields. Our training was held far from the village, in fields that were deserted yet where we could be seen. We sometimes saw the bronzed and impassive faces of men and women who observed our physical and vocal training. Despite all the questions our disconcerting behaviour provoked, the people felt a logic in it, a necessity and a discipline, the meaning of which escaped them but which was solid in its reality as work.

In isolated places, even if crippled by emigration, reached by television, tempted by the glitter of big cities and their imagined pleasures, there still exist profound rules and taboos which regulate the life of the people. It is foolish to believe that a theatre group can break these taboos and create a condition of liberation and new outlets. If a group seeks to do this, it violates the organism of the community which reacts immediately and rejects it. In Italy, theatre groups have been chased and even stoned from villages where they tried to 'provoke' the population in the illusion of shattering taboos.

A theatre group should not be like those ethnologists who in studying the population seek to camouflage themselves, believing they can be assimilated. It is not the village that should be the object of study but the group. On its arrival, it continues to follow its rules of life, its discipline, the training which is important to each member. It avoids, however, behaving in public in such a way as to offend and trample on rules which are vital to the village. Then it is the theatre group that becomes the object of study for the population. It is no longer the theatre that wants to conquer the village, but the village that wants to seduce the group, and in this attempt reveals the need for theatre, something of which the local people were ignorant before, and which, had it been presented from the outside as a kind of gift, would have been felt as alien, belonging to another planet.

It is through diversity that people meet and define themselves reciprocally, a diversity that for the theatre group involves a life consciously chosen, while for the people of southern Italy it is a hard existential condition from which they cannot escape.

This diversity fascinates. We want to discover it, to measure it against our experience, that which we know, that which makes us secure. But to do this we must face it and expose ourselves. Our stay in southern Italy was to be proof for us that it is not the performance - a result which is limited in time - that counts, but the group's behaviour and vision embodied in the daily work.

During the five months of our stay in Carpignano, 'barter' enlivened the entire region. If we brought our songs, our dances, our parades to a village, the local people were able to give us in exchange something of the same kind; or else a group of them would come to us in Carpignano, or maybe go to another place, where another group had to reciprocate or go elsewhere in their turn. The last three months were a lively 'barter' among peasants, workers and students who went to present themselves reciprocally in the village squares with their own culture.

There was no professional theatre. Yet a theatrical situation existed: a point in time that permitted a gathering together, a net of relationships involving unknown people who made an impact and attracted other people to them.

A small group of foreign actors, seemingly not well grounded in local social and political questions, had destroyed the theatre, but they had brought to light the ore hidden in the mine.

***

But can one go further? Can one transform the barter from a cultural phenomenon into something that will leave a mark on the political and social situation of the place? After many experiences, the 'barter' reminded me of the body of an octopus without tentacles, a little pulsating sack that emits a smoke screen of ink which momentarily seems to change the colour of the water, but then vanishes without trace. How can this little sack be given tentacles capable of clinging to a small piece of rock and breaking it off?

In the following year, in 1975, returning to Carpignano and later moving to the mountains of Sardinia, we tried to make tentacles grow that would take hold and remain after our departure. We demanded not only a barter. We also asked the group that had invited us which problem in their village they most wanted to solve. The answers were many and varied.

Then, as a condition of our presence, we insisted on mobilising more than musicians or people who sang. In Monteiasi, near Taranto, in southern Italy, a group of young people had rented a room at their own expense and had brought some of their own books there with the intention of creating a library for everyone, something that had always been lacking.

When we went to Monteiasi, in addition to the barter, we asked the people who wanted to attend our dances to bring a book. It was paradoxical; why should they come with a book instead of paying with money? What were these written pages, which were alien to them, yet which now permitted them access to the entertainment? It was our desire to support those who wanted to make their village aware of the usefulness of something apparently superfluous. At the end of the evening, the books were brought to the library. That dark little room now stood out clearly in the memory of many who attended. But in doing this, where were we going?

And we who are not missionaries, what did we receive in exchange? How can we, through theatre, have a tangible effect on something which is outside theatre? How can we open a breach - in deed, not in words - in the wall which divides us from others, but at the same time protects us and allows us to live freely?

To do this, we must stay within the domain of our humble craft; things on which we can really make our mark are always much smaller than those we can discuss. Even so, trying always to break out, we run the risk of losing our way.

***

I think of theatre as a body continually losing blood. Each time it descends into the streets and encounters reality, it suffers blows, loses blood from wounds that do not heal. The body of theatre cannot live on its own blood. Its haemophilia requires to be nourished by blood from other bodies. It always needs new blood; it cannot live off itself.

There is a haemophiliac theatre that denies its condition; white as a larva, in its crystal tower, surrounded by authorities and scholars who proclaim it everlasting, and undertake reinvigorating operations through discourses and theories.

But there is a theatre conscious of its haemorrhages, which separates itself from the protective circle of its learned doctors and seems to lose itself in a reality that ignores and degrades it. It bleeds, in collision with this reality that has no use for it.

It is a question of survival. Transfusions irrigate the brain with blood that cannot come from the body of the theatre, but from other bodies, until now ignored and kept at a distance, rejected as questionable and dangerous.

They who treat their haemophilia by flinging themselves against every obstacle, seem to be struck by a new mode of perceiving, of using their own senses, of reflecting. They live a life that they cannot always explain, while learned scholars observe them, disturbed by the fact that a sick man who should have followed the prescription, is nursing himself alone, achieving results like any provincial healer who ought to be rejected in the name of science and good sense.

You are losing blood; and while you refuse to lie immobile in bed, under a canopy, on a catafalque, you have crossed over the frontier into a no man's land: behind you lies the territory of theatre, before you another frontier. You are unaware of what territory you are moving into. You advance cautiously, but obstinately. Sometimes your steps carry you back towards the frontier of theatre, and the scholars and authorities smile, relieved. Sometimes you seem to disappear on the horizon and your fate becomes incomprehensible.

Who are you? A loner who vanishes into the desert or one who, advancing, perhaps even losing himself, finishes by marking a path?

***

In these unknown places, among these uncelebrated people, will the actors lose the drive they seem to possess? Will they lose the intransigent commitment to their own art that seems to give them bearings and which allows them to present themselves to others only through the performance, at the summit of their work and experience?

In our last production it was as if seven young people had abandoned the skin of their being as actors. Like crabs who have lost the shelter of their shells, they were nevertheless able to overcome the panic of being a parcel of white and rosy flesh, at the mercy of pain that could be inflicted at the slightest touch. Their unnatural nudity attracted our looks and made us want to trample on them and to protect our hands. They were shaken by their passions, by the memory of a security now lost, and by a longing for a new one. On their bodies, the slightest quivers and tensions could be distinguished. The interior volcano, seeking to be rid of its fire, made them palpitate as if wanting to burn their frail flesh.

But despite the embarrassment, almost horror these crabs aroused, we felt extremely close to them. Paradoxically strangers in the theatre's familiar landscape, in a group and yet in profound solitude, they moved forward as if they wanted to become human.

***

Dear Jennifer Merin, if you came here now, into the mountains of Sardinia, you would see the actors of the Odin running through the streets and squares, like figures imagined by a bizarre painter. Are they performing for their daily bread and for the applause of the audience, or are they Alvars?

The Hindu Alvars profess that divinity does not exist, that hope does not exist, that all is illusion. In the search for a truth beyond all this, they perform acts disapproved of by society, which make a scandal of them and isolate them. But they are the *fools of God*, and their conflicting passions in search of a unity fall into a realm which society respects: religion.

Within the realm of theatre, the actors present themselves as strolling players, as tightrope-walkers, as grotesque beings, and the people laugh and applaud. But sometimes their laughter freezes, when the players no longer show their virtuosity and almost shamelessly deny the existence of any divinity, deny their profession and seem to go amok, impelled by a will that refuses to be walled in by the applause of the encircling spectators.

Now, in dances and parades, the masks are like crusts on the faces of our actors. Soon, in their new production, they will once again melt the layers with which they have covered themselves.

The mad horse will be left free to fly and fall, pursuing its visions.

ROOTS AND LEAVES

This text was written in the spring of 1975 to present Come! And the Day will be Ours, *a production evoking the encounters and the clashes between the American autochtonous population and the European pioneers during the second half of the nineteenth century. Projected in a context of history and performance, barter becomes a clash of cultures where the implacable logic of progress is corroborated: the weakest is always sacrificed.*

Published first in the programme of Come! And the Day will be Ours, *this text reveals how the Odin productions weave different contents into their plots: the theme being narrated, its historical background and the biographical reality of the group.*

Come! And the Day will be Ours is our fifth production. We started work on it in the spring of 1974 in Holstebro, Denmark, and in Carpignano in southern Italy. The process of its creation was interrupted several times. Twice we had to start all over again.

Six actors are involved: Else Marie Laukvik and Torgeir Wethal have been members of the Odin since it was founded in 1964. Iben Nagel Rasmussen joined immediately after, when we moved from Norway to Denmark; Tage Larsen took part in the whole experience of our preceding play, *My Father's House*; Roberta Carreri joined us when we started work in Carpignano in May 1974. On our return to Holstebro six months later, the present group of actors was completed with the arrival of Tom Fjordefalk.

As with *My Father's House*, we are not able to associate the actors with the names of specific characters. We have identified each one with an object, an instrument or a colour. Respectively: 'the one in white', 'the one with the book', 'the one with the drum', 'the one with the violin', 'the one with the banjo', 'the one with the guitar'.

Inside the circle of the spectators, six people - three men and three women - perform: three who are 'civilized' and three who are 'not civilised'. They meet, seek, push each other back, fight and appropriate each others' belongings.

What is happening is a journey and the description of that journey.

It is the account of a journey, because the images distil, in a theatrical form, something that we have been subjected to, something that we have seen, done or known about: how a culture is wiped out and buried; how anyone who is different disturbs, is rejected, transformed into an object for amusement and destroyed. How treachery is intermingled with defeat, and anxiety and despair with the violence of victory.

It is a journey because all this is not shown, described or explained. The experiences which have taken root in us grow as a testimony, often a cold and detached one.

The performance then becomes for us the border between *representation* and *testimony*. But as with the frontiers of the pioneers, this is not a well defined demarcation line at which you can decide to stop or that you can decide to cross. The frontier is fluid, like the shifting crest of a surging wave.

The performance is a tightly woven net, which we must break through in order to liberate, in an unforeseen moment, fragments of our past and of our experiences. Every evening the actors struggle with this net. Every evening they try to dissolve, to annul the rigorous structure through which they reveal themselves and which makes them into actors and those who surround them into spectators. The resistance that the performance opposes to testimony makes it into an organism which changes form and turns the rehearsed gesture of the actor into one which appears to have the force of an improvised reaction.

It is through the convergence of these opposite forces that our personal experiences can reach others, and be transformed into a social experience: through theatre, its fiction and its artificiality. For this very reason we do not want to abandon ourselves fully to the theatre, to the game of its fiction and the pleasure of its artificiality.

I would be denying the real essence of our work if I spoke of the production as an object that we have created once and for all and of which we knew all the secrets and all its possible directions. Neither the actors nor the director are able to say what the performance is. It is up to the spectator to decide.

The question which we can answer is another one: where does it come from?

I will try to reply with a few points which are related more to our history than to our intentions: a series of fragments from memory.

I

Summer 1976. Now that work on the performance is finished, the images and stories that for months and months have guided us fall like sails abandoned by the wind. Images and stories which were our point of departure. The performance, the point of arrival, no longer seems to contain them.

The leaves, fallen from the branches, mingle with their roots, becoming earth from which a new plant begins to grow. We only vaguely recognise it, and we wonder.

***

Facts reached up to us from the past which we wanted to face: all that happened between the European immigrants and the indigenous populations of America.

Different threads became interwoven during our work, creating new images which astonished us and sometimes perturbed us. There were the experiences of some of us while travelling in Latin America and the Far East; the ten months spent by our group in southern Italy; our own personal experiences of working in a group. For some of us this meant work which had guided us, side by side, through twelve years, out of youth and up to the threshold of maturity. For others, the new arrivals, it meant work which had placed them in the centre of a group of 'veterans', with the problems of integration, the continual risk of feeling left out, even of being impoverished by the richness of the others' experience.

There was also our awareness as a theatre group establishing links, meeting people with whom we had something to exchange, but nevertheless continually living in the isolation, the segregation which the norms of a well organised society impose on whoever wishes to follow a personal path. Our group had felt the tolerant indifference of those who nonchalantly consider you as socially useless, fencing you off in a separate enclosure.

Nevertheless, we do have personal needs, profoundly individual, which could also be defined as unsocial. Why deceive ourselves? Why, instead of considering our true personal motivations, instead of exposing them, driving them on to their maximum incandescence, should we hide them behind a facade of reassuring 'political' or 'social' justifications? If a profound necessity really exists, it leaves its mark, it is contagious, it becomes a social action.

There are people in our society who feel the need to create the cells of a new social body. In small or large groups these different cells appear, struggle to survive, disappear anonymously. A theatre group can be one of these cells. Then we gather together and the theatre becomes the mask behind which the naked face of our dreams and visions is concealed. We still call it theatre. It is judged as theatre. Why give it another name? One word is as good as another.

***

From childhood books, from our adult books, from the commonplaces of our time, other clusters of memories become entwined, other points of reference, which for some may be naive images but for me personally are loaded with a thousand meanings.

Those half-naked savages who, with inhuman cries, slaughter the unarmed and unprotected, terrified me in the books I read as a child, in the films I saw. Thirty years were to pass before the child of those days became aware of what many youngsters today take for granted: that the blankets given away to the savages were infected with cholera, that their womenfolk were herded off to brothels, that the few battles won by them were recorded in history as 'massacres'.

On each page of the chroniclers, biographers and historians are recorded dates, places, heroes, characters from adventure stories.

1867: on November 21, protected by the darkness and the snow, George Armstrong Custer surprises a sleeping Cheyenne encampment on the banks of the Washita river, annihilating it while the military band urges the soldiers on.

1876: on June 25, in broad daylight, George Armstrong Custer and his soldiers are annihilated by the Sioux, Cheyennes and Arapahos.

Crazy Horse, a taciturn man of medium height, had experienced the existence of two realities: one which you share with others, and one which belongs only to you, where horses can dance as though mad. At the age of 35 he was killed by a bayonet in his back. Little Big Man, his best warrior and a young chief who had always refused all compromise with the whites, was beside him, but in the white man's uniform, to hold his hands and prevent him from defending himself.

In a land of active men and women, of pioneers striving for progress and wanting to build a society full of meaning, what meaning could the Indians have?

II

We react emotionally to what happens in the world around us, and attach labels to our reactions. Sometimes these reactions incite us to act. Sometimes they remain inside us and drown in words. We bend like trees in the wind, but we must have roots if we are not to be beaten down.

In the beginning I wanted actors who could work miracles, conscious of their own body, their 'instrument'. This was a misguided way of thinking because the more we are conscious of our body, the more we become blocked. Freedom is forgetting our own person and going beyond ourselves to reach another, feeling secure, without fear.

For us from the Odin, theatre is this reciprocal presence, the relationship we establish between us. Not theories, not methods - just this internal relationship, and a relationship towards others, which changes according to the realities, the conditions and the people we meet.

All this is extremely subjective, some people say. Theatre loses all its objectivity and becomes a group of people who gather together. Why? To carry out a common programme?

It's a nice thought. However, my experience has taught me not to believe in theatre groups that act according to a doctrine common to all their members. I believe in groups made up of strong individualists driven by a profound personal need which they try to placate, and in doing so, they overcome it and encounter the needs of others.

We must shatter our own circle within the theatre. Then shatter the circle of the theatre.

***

In the last few years I have spoken of the theatre as a reservation. And not all reservations are for Indians.

Outside Holstebro stand two large modern buildings, with wide windows and surrounded by green lawns fringed with a well kept hedge. They are rest-homes. Here the old people live, those who are no longer useful and can no longer create with their hands and heads. Human residue. A tiny peaceful reservation similar to many of the others that we have legalised wherever we live and that we, that I, tacitly help to maintain. Places where we keep those who are backward, handicapped, mentally ill, neurotic, psychotic. All who are useless or potentially dangerous.

***

How can we, who are a theatre group, shatter the circle of the theatre without losing our identity and without letting our identity imprison us?

In a village in Guatemala - one of those villages which are often described as 'cut off from the world' - I went into a small church. The entire community was gathered there - men, women, children. The priest was preaching his sermon: 'We are all equal before God, our Father. The man who is rich is not more worthy. The man who knows much is not more worthy. There is no need to learn to read, to become better. Christ was against the Pharisees, those who knew how to read. Christ was also uneducated like you'.

And the tiny Quiche Indians answered him singing the Creed.

***

Come! And the Day will be Ours is not an indignant cry against the politics of deceit practised by the whites against the Indians. It is not moral rage against the attitude embodied in many whites: 'The only good Indian is a dead Indian'. That would be hypocritical. Why use our indignation against something that can no longer be fought, that is already history?

Perhaps it is a reflection, even though contradictory, on the way we destroy each other in the name of values which we believe to be universal, when we encounter whatever is different. Hidden forces, nevertheless well known, determine this confrontation. History reveals to us the ingenious violence hidden behind words such as Altruism, Progress and Truth.

***

In southern Italy, among the people of Salento and Barbagia, we could feel in their daily struggle for survival the remnants of a culture, a tradition, an inheritance which was slowly crumbling, infected by the values of modern times.

Why did I think of a reservation as I watched the old men seated immobile in the shade, the women dressed in black as they hurried by with their burdens, the youngsters dressed in bright colours who paraded up and down the streets of the village like animals in a cage?

I felt that sometime in a not so distant past, in this same place, there had been live roots uniting, nourishing and giving meaning to each daily act. Yet I knew that at the same time hunger was greater, work more exhausting, more children died, and even greater was the disproportion between the few who made heads bow and the many who had to bow them.

But this logic of things known could not silence the other emotional logic: today these villages seemed to be drained of their sap, segregated from the rest of the world, from its rhythm and colours, as though, in order to keep up, they had to disown their own past and drown in an alien future, created by others. To disown their own past like the emigrant, like those who must integrate, losing their own identity. They were 'useless' villages, whose only asset was their meagrely industrialised agriculture.

Useful only as a reservoir of potential workers for distant factories.

***

A reservation, as originally intended by the American government, was a large territory owned entirely by the Indians and administered by them, with no intervention on the part of the whites. Hunger for land caused the breaking of all treaties, until the Indian territory was reduced to such a size that 'reservation' became synonymous with 'confinement', with an underhand attempt to force assimilation: make the red similar to the white.

But who were the thousands of pioneers who pushed the frontier further and further westward, towards a promised land which opened up before their eyes, boundless, waiting only to bear fruit?

Those were the times when in Europe, children were working twelve hours a day in the mines and the mills, the times when the industrial revolution was drawing hundreds of thousands of peasants to the towns where they were forced to sell their own labour and that of their families. Beyond the ocean there was an almost empty continent where it was possible to live in dignity and freedom, from the fruits of one's own work. Why should we be indignant if the freedom of a few thousand nomadic hunters was not respected, people who knew nothing of tilling the soil and whose backward ways hindered the chance of a decent life for millions of disinherited Europeans?

For many Indian tribes, man's model was the bison. Bison were free to roam the prairies, strong, ready to fight and not frightened by any obstacle. In the mating season they danced away all their strength, making the earth tremble, eager to confront any rival. But what does the individual deed of the warrior signify compared with far more important historical concepts and perspectives?

The pioneers are different. They struggle against the forces of nature, against their own limits, with the dignity and the pride of fighters who won't give in, determined to go further. They are useful, efficient, perpetually laborious, avoiding excesses. They go far, so far that by an implacable law of dialectics they transform every value into its opposite: they exclude all who do not organise their lives according to their own values.

We would like to possess clear-cut, unequivocal truths, to be able to say in a performance: this is how things are, or are not. We are attracted by the truths we seek as, in the night, our eyes are attracted by the moon even though it does not shine with its own light and has a hidden face.

***

I watch our latest production. I can hear within me the voice of the 'Indian' and the voice of the 'pioneer'. They come from opposite banks, intermingling, contradicting, conflicting, each tempting with its arguments. The symptoms of a new life merge with the sign of imminent catastrophe.

The mad horse is set free to fly and fall, pursuing its own visions.

III

If you refuse to pretend, if you refuse to play a part, then there is nothing left for you to do but to mirror your experiences, reflect - with all your body - on your own history, on yourself in history.

There are moments when, at the centre of your own madness, you can navigate on the current of your obscure forces, bringing them to the surface, not struggling against them, but showing that it is possible to unleash and guide them, taking them in hand and transforming them into something which uses your 'diversity' as a ford where others can cross to meet you. There are moments when your condition is stripped bare and is reduced to your craft.

But what is your craft reduced to? To a typical example of waste, potlatch, dissipation of energies and goods. Theatre is useless, it does not produce, it does not accumulate. On the contrary, it squanders and is a vast investment of energy for a minimal return. But you are safe in the well-defined and acknowledged circle of the theatre where, amongst colleagues, friends, enemies, critics and spectators, the theatre's value is artificially inflated, protected and over-evaluated. However, if you take your craft to a region without theatre, it then becomes the exercise of a negation, and you appear to repudiate every divinity, every doctrine, even your own profession. You can even now, or perhaps only now, be useful. A usefulness in spite of the waste or because of it.

***

We can live in a world where we know the rules. Or else we can abandon that world and go.

Then what do we meet?

We meet people who do not recognise our currency. You hold in your hand that which, elsewhere, is defined as your art, like an ancient copper coin, rare, altered by time, by the use of generations, corroded by the earth which kept it hidden. The images on its two faces are now an enigma. The coin has now become an object whose value is greater the less it is used. It used to circulate in the markets, in the hands of those who bought and sold. Now it stands on the shelves of coin collectors, or well protected in the glass cases of museums.

You want to take it away from what is apparently its definitive world. You take it back to where it was originally minted as though to restore a fragment of the past to a present which gives it life. But here no one any longer recognises it as something belonging to them. Of course, you should have known. So you can go back, clutching your coin, or else you can stay, and decide to use it, exchange it. But now you know that years of research and specialised catalogues count for nothing, and that its value coincides with what it can be reduced to in material terms: the weight of its copper.

The circle of the theatre can be broken. Your theatre can be used as an object of exchange in a reality without theatre, to confront people whom you wish to meet, whose needs are different to yours. You may not be able to start a dialogue, but you can perhaps approach these diverse needs which are otherwise so distant.

But you must rediscover a new humility. Be a stranger who dances. People will gather around you because you have accepted that you are not the navel of this living organism, that it is not your audience. Yet you must have the same strength, the same inventiveness, the same courage to go forward all the time.

IV

Why deny it?

I watch this performance with a strange uneasiness, as one might watch a child of one's maturity who talks to us not of our future but of our present. Who talks harshly.

Another image, another of the starting points for *Come! And the Day will be Ours*:

Sitting Bull, the shaman, the chief who had inflicted on the United States the greatest defeat of its history, was there in Buffalo Bill's circus. He played the part of the terrifying Indian. Afterwards he signed autographs and sold photographs of himself to the audience.

Buffalo Bill Cody, satisfied, gave him his own trained horse. At the end of the American tour he asked him to go with the circus to Europe, but Sitting Bull refused; he wanted to return to the reservation, the unhealthy poverty-stricken place where the Indian nation had degenerated. Those who had once smoked tobacco as a ritual sign of communion, now alcoholics and in rags, smoked cigarette butts to pass the time, with the same gestures as the whites.

Sitting Bull was buried thanks to the pity of a white soldier, after being killed on the reservation by the Indian police. It was in 1890, when the Ghost Dance should have brought freedom and the reawakening of the dead. The Indians on all the reservations danced at length, danced and danced.

But we do not remember that year for the message of hope of the Indian prophet Wowoka. We remember it for another massacre - the usual women and children and old people - which bears the name of Wounded Knee.

***

I imagine that those who see *Come! And the Day will be Ours* will find in the performance other leaves and other roots, different from the ones I have gathered here. Just as the new tree develops and branches out according to the various saps which course through each actor. The last word does not belong to the director.

After months and months of work, the moment arrives when he must step aside and watch, try to penetrate the web before him, and the meaning of this new presence.

What more can I say?

There are dark forces which blind. And there are dark forces which give insight.

Dark forces are carrying me. I know not where.

DIALOGUE WITH BRECHT

In this text, barter acquires the value of a strategy to question history. While Come! And the Day will be Ours *presented the cruel and dark side of barter,* Brecht's Ashes *is the result of a barter intended as a 'dialogue with the dead'.*

First published in Eugenio Barba's book Il Brecht dell'Odin, *Ubulibri, Milan 1981, this text produced contrasting reactions because of the particular interpretation of Bertolt Brecht's personality and writings.*

Bertolt Brecht is buried in East Berlin, in Dorotheenfriedhof, not far from Hegel's tomb. Erich Engel, Helene Weigel, Hanns Eisler, Elisabeth Hauptmann and Ruth Berlau are also buried there.

How does one have a dialogue with the dead?

Our production *Brecht's Ashes* reveals our longing for an impossible dialogue. We delved into Brecht's life. We read what he wrote for his public, but we also peered into the shadows, and found what he wrote for himself. We empathised with his experiences as an uprooted man, a man in exile. We were confronted with his disenchanted intelligence, his cunning, the shrewd actions which he used to protect what was essential for him: intellectual independence, discerning vision, doubt, an individual voice.

His writing slowly appeared to us not as an immutable body of work, but as his ashes: something which conveys the meaning of a very precise human experience, from which the ambiguity of life and actions still emanates.

'Can this cockpit hold the vasty fields of France?'

Brecht sometimes felt the same discouragement as actors in the past had felt when, confined upon the stage, they looked out on the great events of history which had preceded them and which surrounded them. He found himself doubting that the theatre could chart the dense networks of causes and forces which move human destinies and societies.

Our tiny stage now stands for the squares and crowds of Berlin in the thirties and fifties; the war zones; the concentration camps; the escape routes and refuges where Brecht, bent over his writing desk, received news of friends who had been hung, shot, assassinated or had committed suicide.

Also present is the imaginary China of Me-Ti and Ken-Yeh, a world where reason is dialectically consistent, and therefore resembles a fable.

***

First Meeting with Brecht

My first meeting with Brecht took place in 1961, five years after his death.

When I first went to Poland, my theatrical point of reference was the doctrine of Brechtian theatre. And with this doctrine in mind, I presented myself to the theatre school.

There I happened to meet Tadeusz Kuliszewicz, a graphic artist who had worked with Brecht. He had designed the poster for *The Life of Galileo* in which the delicately drawn figure of Galileo is hunched up, as if closed in his own world. Kuliszewicz gave me a letter of introduction to Helene Weigel, and with this letter in my pocket, I left for Berlin.

It was February, and I arrived from a Warsaw which still bore the scars of war. Reconstruction was proceeding slowly, and in certain areas, at night, there were often outbursts of *joie de vivre*. After their performances, actors ate at the Spatif Club which was open until two in the morning. Vodka, food, and that special post-performance exhilaration made them exuberant. Often they wanted to keep on going after the Spatif closed, and so made their way to the Bristol Hotel, which had the only bar in Warsaw open until dawn. An old woman sat at the entrance, selling paper flowers from a huge basket on her knees. The actors willingly gave her a coin so they could offer an artificial flower to a companion.

During the night, women lit hundreds of little lamps along the ruined walls of the city. In the glow of these small flames one could read the names of the Poles shot by the Germans during the occupation.

Warsaw was sombre and grey, with long queues in front of the food stores. Bulldozers clearing away the ruins were uncovering skeletons which were carried away by the lorry load.

This was the Warsaw from which I travelled to West Berlin and when I saw all its neon, its shops full of flowers and fruit, chocolate and coloured plastic, I suddenly felt sick. And with this sensation of nausea, I entered Socialist East Berlin.

'The Mother' and the Theory

At the end of the performance, I found myself crying. I was at *The Mother*, presented by the Berliner Ensemble. If it is true that at the end of one's life the images of one's most profound experiences pass before one's eyes, I believe that for me among those images will be Helene Weigel with her red flag, in the last scene of *The Mother*.

When I returned to Warsaw I felt uneasy: how could I have let myself be drawn into such sentimentality? How had I fallen into this trap? After a year in Poland I had certainly begun to acquire rather good cynical reflexes. If I had been naive enough to start to cry, what was it, either in the performance or in me, the spectator, that had not worked? What had happened to the *Verfremdung* effect which Brecht had been after and which was so clearly described in his writings?

I was not only embarassed. I was shaken. All my theories became blurred: both theatrical ones and others. Poland acted like a corrosive acid on all that I had believed and imagined.

My Student Residence faced the Square of the Heroes of the Ghetto, which was on a little hill about ten meters high. The ruins here had not been cleared away, just levelled out. On the hill made out of the ruins there was a monument which was visited every day by busloads of East Germans with a Polish guide to explain to them what had happened there.

One of my friends was a promising young party official. 'Trying to change something in this country', he said to me, 'is like sticking your prick in a block of ice. You end up castrated and you don't melt the ice.' What hurt me most was to see him, aware and intelligent, accepting the rules of the game.

Brecht and the theatre were no longer real problems. The real problem was the risk of losing one's bearings.

It was no longer a question of making this or that precise choice, but of being able to survive, gropingly, without becoming part of the ice. And, gropingly, I arrived in Opole where I met Grotowski. He was a young man, only three years older than me, and he became my master. He had been one of the leaders of the Polish Communist Youth when, in March 1956, the workers of Poznan revolted and the students took a stand for Gomulka, who then came to power. For the first time one had the impression that change was possible in a 'socialist' country. But in '57 and '58 what the Poles called the 'salami politics' was introduced: the taking away, slice by slice, of what had been conceded. In 1959, Grotowski gave up politics and started to do theatre.

As soon as we met, I began talking to him about Brecht and his theories. Grotowski was always very polite and listened attentively, smiling in a way that invited me to keep on talking. But after a while I asked myself if it had really been a smile of encouragement.

The Krak

Odin Teatret has very visible masters, against whom we have measured ourselves, with whom we have had a dialogue: Stanislavski, Meyerhold, Eisenstein. Brecht has also been one of our masters, but in a different way, hidden, like in a secret crypt. The parasitic interpretation of his work and the political alibi which his name offered to many filled us with embarrassment. For years, we had a clandestine dialogue with him. But the meaning of his words was difficult to decipher.

I knew that I mustn't search for what Brecht's words meant, but rather for what led him to write them. Then I understood his strange appeal; his faith not in ideals, but in his own actions, however minor, anonymous and apparently senseless; his belief in the value of remaining loyal to one's own identity; and the confidence that our own actions endure, even if the times are dark and no one seems to notice what we are doing. Our actions are like small white pebbles we have left behind and which someone may find long after we have gone.

Between 1933 and 1948 Brecht hardly set foot in the theatre although he never stopped writing, every day, while moving from one country to another. He knew that his plays were not going to be performed, that what he was doing made no immediate political sense. Still, he worked for long hours every day knowing that what he was doing had very little meaning for anyone else. He has been proclaimed the father of engaged, political theatre, but during his life, he had in fact no close contact with workers' movements. Marxist intellectuals reproached him for being a decadent bourgeois intellectual who was flirting with Marxism but who lived in isolation and knew nothing about the working class. And they were right.

During his years of exile in Denmark, Sweden, Finland and the United States, he never entered the political arena. No matter where he went, he had no contact with communist organizations; on the contrary, they often attacked him. In Denmark, where *Round Heads and Pointed Heads* was produced, the left-wing press demolished the play, accusing it of being a coarse and erroneous analysis of the historical and political situation. Few people were interested in his theatre work, apart from some amateur groups. Brecht wrote and wrote.

That is the great lesson to be learned from Brecht: to understand the relationship of an individual with history, and that this relationship is not ephemeral. His way of keeping himself apart, of not participating, of looking on with detachment, as if through a window, is a way of understanding, of keeping a sharp lookout, which seems to be cynical and uncommitted but which is investigating the truth.

From behind a window of Fritz Sternberg's third floor apartment, Brecht watches the crowd on May 1, 1929. Suddenly he sees the people become excited, then scatter as the police fire. Brecht watches the scene without participating in it.

The story of his Berliner Ensemble in East Germany is the story of a great strategy, of the attempt to use the rules of the game without respecting them. A story which also relates how these same rules, used for too long, end up by ensnaring you in their terrible jaws.

In spite of everything, however, the Berliner Ensemble remained a little oasis for East German intellectuals or for those rare western intellectuals who came to visit it. Max Frisch tells how, while Brecht was alive, it was an intellectual adventure to go to East Berlin. Brecht was once again isolating himself, shutting himself up at home where he received only a few people. Helene Weigel was the director of the Berliner Ensemble. Brecht himself had no official title and this made it possible for him to detach himself from his own theatre.

But what was hidden behind the Berliner's velvet seats, behind the images of the huge crystal chandeliers? A hill. And on this hill was a Krak.

There was a period in Palestine when a group of men who had devoted themselves to spiritual undertakings changed themselves into soldier-monks. Roger Buyant, a leper, founded a religious order which gathered together crusaders who had been smitten with leprosy. In order to protect them from discrimination and extermination, he turned the religious order into a military one. And so, on the Lebanese border, the Krak was built, an oasis of security for foreigners travelling through Arab territory.

It was a castle guarded by a handful of leprous knights, so few in number that they were powerless against the forces which surrounded them, but sufficiently strong that their enemies hesitated to attempt to destroy them. It simply wasn't worth the risk.

The Krak knights defeated Nur Edim, resisted Saladin's siege, survived for more than a century. And for all those who had left their homes driven by the need to kneel at an Empty Grave in Jerusalem, for all those wanderers in mortal danger, the Krak was the place where they could find protection, where they could be temporarily sheltered against the danger of being killed or sold as slaves.

Brecht wrote a great deal about how the theatre can become committed, and about the conditions necessary to make it efficient. But there is something he did not write about, which he nevertheless proved: the theatre can be a Krak.

***

Today I realise that Brecht's image was always with me in spirit, even during those years when I believed it to be blurred and faded. Those were the years when I worked with Grotowski and lived the adventure of building a theatrical fortress.

When Grotowski, having abandoned politics, withdrew to Opole, into a tiny theatre no bigger than a stage, and began to work with seven actors, he soon realised that official reactions to his theatre were becoming menacing. His activity did not fit into the habitual categories of the country's cultural politics, since it did not respect the norms which permit the theatre to express and justify itself.

It would actually have been very easy for the communist authorities to silence Grotowski, but there was always a certain doubt, and once again, it wasn't worth the risk. At first the decision to close his theatre lay with the local authorities. But they were unsure; this little theatre had begun to be known outside Poland and, if there were reactions to its closing, the central authorities might become angry. Then the central authorities too realised that Grotowski's theatre had gone so far that now they had to do something about it. But by then his name was too well known outside Poland and prudence was called for in order to avoid unpleasant reactions to his theatre's ultimate closure.

During these years Grotowski was attacked as a formalist and mystic. He did not follow the Ministry of Culture's production plans. When he produced *Kordian and Faustus* in 1962, the audience was not large; the actors were content to perform even for a very few people.

It was like being surrounded and cut off. We felt the ice closing in around us with each passing day as we read the news in the papers, noticed how people greeted us in the street, listened to what the local party officials were saying, and to what they were implying.

The only thing we could do was concentrate on defending this nucleus of life which we did not want to see disappear. I began to travel, to write. I had never written before and I was also rather shy and ill at ease. I had to find the courage to go knocking on unfamiliar doors, on Lévi-Strauss' door for example, just so that, upon seeing me, he could tell me that he was interested in the theatrical experience which I talked to him about. Then I could return to Poland and say: 'Be careful, don't touch this theatre, very important people out there are interested in it'. This was my school, apart from sitting and watching Grotowski at work.

***

In 1978 I was invited to Berlin for the celebration of the anniversary of Brecht's birth. He would have been eighty years old. The cream of the Brechtian intelligentsia was there, the professors who had built themselves university careers writing about Brecht, and who for years had been setting him up as a new orthodoxy. Now they were saying that the Berliner Ensemble had turned into a theatre devoid of meaning, a dusty museum. A new production had just opened at the Berliner, the first version of *The Life of Galileo*, which demonstrated how an intellectual can get his message across in spite of a regime which is trying to muzzle it.

Once again, I felt invaded by emotion, but even more powerful was my astonishment. How had they come to present this production here?

The last scene was glacial and terrible: Galileo is blind and is being spied on and watched over by his daughter. The church has forbidden him to continue his scientific research. In the last moments of the play, when he thinks no one is looking, he reaches under his chair with the rapid gestures of a conspirator, almost with the greedy hands of a thief, and pulls out some papers. He writes rapidly, then immediately hides what he has just written.

The emotion drawing me into the scene was amplified by rage towards all the western intellectuals sitting around me, whispering (as if they couldn't understand what the performance was crying out to them): 'How boring! The Berliner is dying! It's nothing but a museum! They are repeating themselves!'

Seated next to me was a woman about forty years old. We spoke to each other on the way out. She was from Berlin, but had married an Algerian. She talked to me about the years during the war in Algeria when the socialist countries had offered hospitality to Algerian partisans and students. She had fallen in love with one of these young men. But when she decided to marry him and follow him to the now-liberated Algeria, she was summoned to the Communist Youth headquarters, where it was explained to her that her decision to marry an Algerian, and particularly the fact that she was going to abandon Germany in order to follow him to Algeria, was not approved of. The German State had not after all paid for her professional training in order for her then to abandon her country. She could be this young Algerian's girlfriend or even his mistress during his stay in Germany, but she could neither marry nor follow him. She refused to give in. Her last year in Germany, after she had married and was about to leave, was terrible. 'You see', she said to me, 'there was only one place I could go to and feel at home: to the Berliner Ensemble. It was as if the people there did not obey the same rules, didn't behave in the same way as those in the city which surrounded me. It was the only place where there was any oxygen, where you could breathe.'

From the tram taking me back to the hotel, I watched the gloomy shapes of East Berlin's buildings slide by.

The lights of the theatre, its conventions and artistic theories seemed false and anachronistic to me, disguising the grave and brutal evidence of reality. A few moments later, like an optical illusion or a sudden clear-sightedness, those lights seemed instead to be the subterranean glow of a refuge. And I asked myself if the story of the great theatre reformers was not a story of builders of fortresses filled with oxygen.

The Reins and the Horse

There are two images which create the same irresistible associations: Guernica's horse, and the mute cry uttered by Helene Weigel as Mother Courage.

A theatre critic who saw the Berliner Ensemble's *Mother Courage*, said that during the whole performance he had an impression of great emotional earthquakes on which Brecht had imposed a 'crust' of rules in an attempt to control them.

When Brecht returned to Berlin, preceded by swarms of bombers, he began to build the Berliner Ensemble with people who had survived exile, Nazi prisons, concentration camps. The city was completely destroyed after having lived through the enthusiasm and collective fever of Hitler's Germany.

The young people who came to Brecht belonged to that generation of young warriors who had marched off to Russia, singing, certain of victory. They had returned barefoot, their backs broken. One can understand how these young men were not eager to throw themselves into emotivity: they no longer wanted to *let themselves go*.

During his years of exile, Brecht himself had had to fight strenuously against emotion - rage, pain, hopelessness, false dreams and mirages - in order to preserve the lucidity necessary to grasp the course of events, so that they did not drag him down and suffocate him.

When reading Brecht's biography, it is sometimes hard not to disapprove of the way he acted with women, with friends, of his cynicism, his moral nihilism. He was not immoral, but amoral. It was as if blind forces carried him beyond good and evil. They were vital and destructive forces, perhaps of the same 'colour' as those which nourished Dostoyevski.

In his private life, Brecht knew how to control the forces which threatened to destroy him, concealing them behind the mask of a Chinese sage, detached, ironic, always smoking and smiling benignly. It seems almost inconceivable that this man had something in common with the great gambler and mystic who was Dostoyevski.

Brecht sometimes spoke about Dostoyevski with an expeditious, superior air, calling him a 'simpleton', in the tone of an elder brother reproaching his sibling for excessive idealism and sensitivity. One of them knew how to cultivate his vices and passions wisely; the other let himself be dominated by them. One risked being too reasonable, too prudent; the other risked delirium. One chose exile rather than be a traitor; the other chose exile rather than pay his debts.

Yet the two men lived through similar experiences, like two members of the same family. They both suffered being brutally reduced to anonymity after initial success; they both tried to reach the masses, yet were uprooted and faced tragic isolation, one in Siberia, the other through fifteen years of exile. They both confronted their own interior volcanoes, did not deny them, did not hide them, but tried to tame their energies by relying on faith or ideology, against which the ferocious individualism of their lives and the lucid nihilism of their reason, continuously struggled.

***

I spoke about all of this one evening in June 1978, in a lecture at the National Institute of Culture in Lima. There were about thirty people present. A very distinguished looking gentleman in a city suit, who had read widely in philosophy and drove a bulldozer for a living, asked me the meaning of my continual negativity, which never attained the 'negation of negation'. A medical student in sunglasses maintained that art must be pure and not polluted by political engagement. The cultural representative of Communist Youth was there taking notes, and his face became a violent mask when, with a mischievous pleasure, I recalled that Brecht never became a member of the communist party, that he had left Moscow in a hurry, and that Tretiakov, one of his Russian friends, had disappeared during the great purge of the thirties.

Victoria Santa Cruz was also there. A Peruvian, she had been discriminated against because she was black, yet now personified the ideal of her country's cultural tradition: she was the director of the Conjunto Nacional de Folklore. Each evening, in a large theatre, she presented the dances of the blacks from the coast, who abandon themselves in a delirium of rhythm; the dances of the Cuzco Indians, petrified and formal; and those of the *campesinos* who metamorphosed the dances of their former Creole masters.

I walked with Victoria through the centre of Lima. Her words were sometimes obscured by the screams of police sirens converging on the Plaza San Martin where APRA, a Peronist-like party, was dispensing rage and rhetoric, this being the eve of the first political elections in ten years. A few days before, food prices had abruptly doubled and trebled causing a popular revolt, constitutional guarantees had been suspended, a general strike declared, and a curfew imposed.

Victoria's face was luminous under the street lamps. Brecht was her age when he died but she, she seemed hardly more than thirty. I imagined that in her previous incarnations she had been the Queen of Sheba and Casamance, medicine woman and rain witch.

We were walking aimlessly, looking for the most deserted streets, far from the political storm. This too seemed to be a kind of echo of what I had been talking about at the Institute of Culture: Brecht tried to keep as far as possible from the epicentres of history, in order to preserve something which he alone seemed to consider important in the years of solitude and contempt.

Victoria continued her monologue: her father was a simple artisan who soothed his ethnic wound with a great love of culture. He read Molière and Balzac to his children, made them listen to Haydn and Mozart. Victoria and her brother were bored, waiting impatiently for the moment when they could go to their mother who knew the songs of the blacks and danced like every black must dance. 'Not like a slave', says Victoria, 'because the black who manages not to lose his rhythm is never a slave'. Her father, on the other hand, had lost his.

Victoria was seven years old when she found out she was black and that a black could be scorned. For years thereafter, she hated whites. She dreamed the same dream over and over again: she was a station master and when the train arrived, full of people, she shifted the points causing the train to plunge into a deep ravine. The passengers died, each and every one. 'And I gazed at this scene of death without hate and without love, impassive. And so', she continued, 'I was the black they wanted me to be: full of hate. I had actually made myself white.'

For Victoria Santa Cruz, a dancer, there is one essential thing which must be preserved: 'rhythm'. She reminds me of the discovery which had liberated her: you do not *know* your rhythm, you are your rhythm. Rhythm does not belong just to black people, to a single culture. One cannot lock oneself into a sense of superiority, looking for the roots of an identity which makes one different from those one hates and who despise one. Thus she stopped oscillating between hate and fear. 'Rhythm', said Victoria, 'is the *not knowing* which is *knowing*'.

But all that she had been saying during our walk was a kind of reflection on a warning she had given me as soon as we came out of the conference room: 'I recognise you as someone from the same family. I recognise the same violence, which can devour you. You are a Scorpio, whose opposite is the eagle. I feel I must warn you: you are close to your centre, but something is still keeping you from it'. And again: 'Be careful that your violence does not destroy both you and your companions. There is no hate in your violence, yet you both know and do not know what it is'.

I think of Brecht in the middle of an Elizabethan landscape, where the workings of history are revealed amid the corpses. In this immense theatre of war, Brecht is a poet who questions himself, a sage who reflects. No matter where he goes, he refuses to mix in, he continues to use only his own language, his German, which he knows so well how to colour with the accents of Lutheran psalms, with Biblical quotations or echoes from Schiller. Around him, history follows its course, his friends commit suicide, the women he loves die on foreign soil and the victories of the 'Great Housepainter' make his work superfluous.

Victoria was speaking again: 'Know the truth about the obstacle. Only half of it is outside you. The other half is inside. With the help of others, you can overcome the outside half, which then becomes a step to help you climb. But as for the half which remains inside, you must overcome it alone'.

THE PEOPLE OF RITUAL

In this 'open letter' to Richard Schechner, Eugenio Barba reflects on Odin Teatret's activities in its home town. In the nineties, barter becomes the practice of an interculturism. During the Festuge *(a festival organised by Odin Teatret in Holstebro) the barter brings to the forefront its many possibilities, converting a small provincial town into a capital with many cultures in the course of a week. The People of Ritual is the Letter from the South of Italy of the nineties.*

After long sojourns in southern Italy and travels throughout Latin America, facing historical harshness and diversity, Odin Teatret returns home. Thus the chapter on travel becomes a wide detour. The detour is the essence of travel, and we call exiles those who have made the detour into a style of life.

First published in Linea d'ombra, *73, Milan 1992 and then in Eugenio Barba's book* The Paper Canoe, *Routledge, London 1995.*

Holstebro, September 16th, 1991

Dear Richard,

What is most valuable in each one of us cannot make direct contact with others. Inner lives don't communicate with each other. I am not interested in technique. Yet, in order to achieve what interests me most, I must pay attention to essential problems related to technique. What I am searching for lies on the other bank of the river. This is why I am concerned with canoes.

Last night marked the end of the *Festuge* (a Danish word meaning 'week of festivities') in Holstebro, which this year was called 'Culture without frontiers'. In order to emphasise that the absence of frontiers is as much linked to freedom as to fluidity, we merged the nine days and nine nights of activities into one continuous performance event entitled *Vandstier*, Waterways.

The title 'Culture without frontiers', which might seem optimistic, has a malicious undercurrent. When the delineation of borders is lost, identity is threatened. And insecurity over identity leads to rigour, to an exasperated attempt to give oneself a profile by opposing others. Intolerance, xenophobia and racism come out into the open.

On the other hand, frontiers are sheer illusions, and they are sometimes imposed. Then, they lead to suffocation.

During the *Festuge*, a symposium was held on Danish cultural politics. Politicians, administrators, journalists, an anthropologist and a professor of literature spoke. They discussed culture as a means of conquering and safeguarding identity in a Europe which is in the process of abolishing frontiers.

One of the speakers said: 'Look what happens when the contours of a state are obliterated. Look at Yugoslavia, where nobody knows any longer what it means to be a Yugoslav; old divisions, nationalism and ethnic fundamentalism are revived'. Somebody else replied: 'This happens for the very opposite reasons, not because of the loss of a solid profile, but because the profile was artificial. It was a strait jacket, imposed in the name of an abstract ideology to repress a reality which is now exploding. The explosion is violent because the union was violent'.

Something similar has happened in the theatre of this century which is now about to end: the erosion of the definite borders which gave identity to theatre of European origin; the invention of small traditions; the growth of separate cultures.

In order to understand the theatre of the twentieth century, it is necessary to keep in mind that some theatres and groups have functioned, and continue to function, not only as artistic ensembles, but also as tribes. Tribe is the wrong word, though, because it evokes archaic images. It is better to speak of 'theatres which invent small traditions'.

The invention of traditions can lead to sectarianism and ideological intolerance. The theatre has also had its fundamentalist movements (Stanislavskian, Brechtian, Grotowskian). When fundamentalist movements cannot sustain themselves by force, when they are restricted to the use of cultural weapons, they become substantially innocuous and are weakened by their own rigidity; it is enough for fashion to change and they disappear in smoke.

When we think of interculturalism, we have a tendency to think in terms of the cultural divisions we learned in school (Europe, Asia, Africa, popular cultures, the cultures of people studied by anthropologists, Judaism, Islam or Hinduism). We forget, however, that the abstract term 'theatre' refers to non-homogenous phenomena, each with boundaries created by itself and by its context. Limited boundaries sometimes generate a superiority complex; in other cases, they may encourage exchange, create the need to delve below the surface and to venture forth into the different.

You would have enjoyed being here in Holstebro during these days because you like to move in that no man's land between daily life and the organised performance situation, between performance and ritual. We remained in this no man's land for nine days and nine nights, dissolving the theatre into the town and absorbing the reality of the town into the theatre. But mixing with others puts the consistency of one's own borders to the test. It is a way of deepening the differences and of defining oneself. When actors throw themselves into the daily life of a street or a market, they are not blending with the local people, they don't establish a communion with them. They are merely solidifying their own identities, and therefore their own differences. This leads to the possibility of creating a relationship.

The intercultural dimension of the world in which we live is not a conquest, it is a state of danger. When it remains inert, awareness of coexistence with diversity generates indifference. It unleashes rage if the stranger comes too close.

You are familiar with the greyness of Holstebro and with its plastic colours. So you can imagine the surprise of seeing it traversed by two camels, carrying a little fellow in a top hat and his child-double on their backs. But surprise made the passers-by turn their eyes away. For me, this is one of the images of interculturalism when it bursts into the routines of our lives. I am talking about the first morning of the *Festuge*. By the ninth day, things had changed. People were accustomed to no longer being afraid of showing their curiosity and the performers could circulate in the streets and supermarkets, schools, churches and barracks, confident of creating a relationship that went beyond the involuntary spectator's usual limits of acceptance.

The more uniform our panorama seems when seen from afar, the more it resembles an intricate tapestry of minute and diverse cultures when seen close up. Perhaps we should say sub-cultures, if only the word could lose its ring of inferiority.

I wonder whether what I am about to tell you pertains to interculturalism and theatre. I believe it does. Every four hours, in a large car-park on the roof of a supermarket, groups of people united by the same profession, hobby or condition, presented themselves: the archers' and rowers' clubs, the owners of trained Alsatian dogs, of old American cars, music students, motorcycle police, the housewife's association, the fire brigade...

A dozen recruits got down from a military truck and stood to attention - in their underwear. They then demonstrated the elaborate 'dressing' procedures which transform men into soldiers: their daily uniform, their off-duty uniform, parade attire, war gear, with their faces painted black and their helmets covered with leaves, ending up looking like armoured extra-terrestrials, their faces deformed by gas masks. Next to these, a *kathakali* performer, made huge by his costume and crown, was dilating his face with

149

the green and white make-up which turned him into a mythical figure.

Fox-hunters and their buglers arrived, as well as horses from the riding school. Centaurs appeared, those young men in black leather on motor-cycles who intimidate us when they ride through our cities. They roared out their performances to the accompaniment of a violin, at first drowning its sound, and then accentuating it by suddenly switching off their engines. They exhibited their menace, transforming it into vitality and openness. Boys and girls in white pyjamas stopped speaking Danish and shouted in an unfamiliar language, Korean, while they moved according to the martial ballet of *tae-kwondo*.

It was interesting to notice how disconcerted and astonished the spectators were. They must surely have known that these activities went on in Holstebro, just as they probably know that there are men with four wives, or people who burn their dead and eat the soup they make from the ashes. The sub-cultures they saw were recognisable. What wasn't clear to them was the reason why all these people had come out of their shells and were invading the time and space of this car park, day and night, with or without observers, even in the rain.

In the middle of the car park, a fifteen-metre-long wooden ship was being constructed according to the elegant design of an architect; it was not seaworthy (not being possible to build a real ship in only nine days and nine nights). Everything taking place there seemed to be in honour of the ship, without taking the spectators into consideration. The numerous small sub-cultures of Holstebro, once exposed, demonstrated that it was one's next door neighbour who was truly *exotic*.

Here in Holstebro, it starts to get cold around mid-September. On the first few nights of the *Festuge*, there were not many people on the super-market roof. But as time went by, the place became the centre of the town, a sort of secular temple where the long, unsailable ship was slowly taking shape, and where, after this week, there would be nothing left other than the memory of what had been. In this asphalted, open air temple, a ship's bell rang out every half hour, day and night, and *De store Skibe* by Frans Winther was sung. Every four hours, day and night, horses, performers, cars, dogs, soldiers and other representatives of the invisible Holstebro appeared.

It was a lay liturgy, created by the Hotel Pro Forma Theatre from Copenhagen. We from Odin Teatret participated every midnight, with a performance evoking the ghosts of sailors.

On the last day, we carried the long ship to the park and buried it in true Viking style, while a tiny sailing boat drifted up into the sky. The trees in the park were decked with crimson flowers and golden apples. Floating islands caught fire in the middle of the lake, while black-clad Death paddled the Trickster's small boat across its still waters. A mother sat in the boat with her new-born child.

During the entire week, the performers spread out into different parts of the town. At dawn, groups of two or three went to greet the town bakers at their ovens with a short performance. Others would show up, unexpectedly, at birthday parties in people's homes. Some met incoming trains. Others slipped quietly into a meeting of the Town Council, first appearing as jesters and then, like influential monks from the past, admonishing the mayor and the councillors.

There were real performances: by Odin Teatret and by the Italian group, Teatro Tascabile, skillfully performing on stilts an elegant waltz from the time of Anna Karenina. The Teatro Tascabile's actors are also experts in *kathakali,* so expert that they are recognised as such even in India. They danced with their Indian guru, accompanied by his musicians. This theatre comes from Bergamo, an ancient mountain city close to Milan and Bellagio, the town where you organised the colloquium on intercultaralism at the Rockefeller Foundation's villa last February.

In addition to Teatro Tascabile, there was Akadenwa, a group from Aarhus, the second largest city in Denmark. Its performers are members of a mountain climbing club. They give performances climbing the walls of houses, church steeples, town hall towers, tall chimneys. There are no mountains in Denmark.

A Danish mountaineer is, after all, no less strange than a *kathakali* performer who was born and lives in Bergamo. For both, what is important is to find the appropriate context for their professional self-definition. It is said that Harlequin came from Bergamo. But Harlequin, who has become the universal symbol of the fantasy and anarchy of the theatre, was almost certainly invented in France four or five hundred years ago.

There is no *genius loci,* genie of the place, either in theatre or culture. Everything travels, everything drifts away from its original context, and is transplanted. There are no traditions which are inseparably connected to a particular geographical location, language or profession.

What happened this week is something very new to me and my companions from Odin Teatret. Yet it also evokes flavours familiar to us. We have already experienced something similar: the sensation that a metamorphosis is taking place to which we are not yet able to give a name. Seventeen years ago, after ten years of giving performances behind closed doors for a few dozen spectators, we burst out into the streets and squares of southern Italian villages. And from there we then toured much of the planet, bartering theatre. I was about to say: 'we went to central places and to isolated places'. But wherever you fix the point of your compass, that is the centre.

Now we have made a journey in our own home. True travellers know this experience very well: the unknown world is discovered when one returns.

Tomorrow, Odin Teatret's actors will leave for Copenhagen. Essentially, it's no different from touring Poland or Brazil. It takes us just as close and just as far away. This evening, all of us who worked on the *Festuge* gathered in our theatre for a farewell dinner. In these situations, among men and women of our profession, I feel at home regardless of where we are in the world. You also made this point in your essay 'Magnitudes of Performance': performers from distant cultures meet and experience more affinity with each other than with their compatriots.

There is theatre in interculturalism. And there is interculturalism in theatre.

***

Dear Richard, I don't want a country made up of a nation or a town. I don't believe in it. Yet I do need a country. This is why, in simple terms, I do theatre.

I ask myself the question Jean Améry (one of the greatest countryless men of our times) put to himself: 'How much country does a man need?' I have been lucky: my country has expanded. It does not consist of land or geography. It is made up of history, of people.

When talking, one often uses generalisations to speed up the conversation. So I sometimes speak of my interest in Indian theatre and of the contributions Odissi dance has made to ISTA, the International School of Theatre Anthropology. In reality, I do not collaborate with Odissi dance or Indian theatre but with Sanjukta Panigrahi, whom I consider a compatriot. Similarly, thirty years ago, I identified with those children at the Kathakali Kalamandalam in Cheruthuruthy who, before dawn, would burn incense in front of the picture of the school's founder. I have met some of those children years later, as mature men and established performers. They remember me, and I remember them as they were thirty years ago: somewhat frail, with cheeky yet melancholic smiles, their eyes big, enlarged by exercises. Why shouldn't I think of them as compatriots?

Sanjukta is not an 'Indian', she is Sanjukta. After all the years we have been working together, I find it hard to think of her as an Indian. Just as she only rarely, almost as an afterthought, remembers that I am a European.

What would you call this? Interculturalism? Humanism? The culture of work?

It is not only love of the other. It is the need to know oneself.

One night, in Bellagio, I asked you for your definition of interculturalism. You replied that you were not interested in defining it, that you preferred it to remain a gravitational field, an open perspective, a black hole. You were smiling as you said this. It is to this smile which I am now speaking.

The gods have left. We are vessels without a crew, restless vessels carried by obscure currents. And yet, I hold a belief: only by measuring myself against others can I give a meaning to the route and find my identity.

I am interested in a specific intercultural perspective: to explore the pre-expressive level of the performer's behaviour. Sometimes you share my interest. You say that the biologist in you agrees with me, but that the politician in you does not. At times you participate with me in the discovery of this common land that nourishes the roots of diverse performative practices. At others, you shake your head, preferring your favourite study, the description of social interactions.

It is at the performer's 'biological' level, in the domain of impulses and counter-impulses, the *sats* and the physical and vocal score, that my individual research and my individual needs have become political; they interweave with the similarly deep and incommunicable needs of those people who have become my companions. Only by learning how to navigate in these technical waters, whose surface is cold, have they become 'my' actors and I 'their' director. And we have acted together, changing something around us.

When we look around us and compare our craft to the technology of the times, or when we compare our small circle of spectators to mass media audiences, we feel archaic. The theatre seems to us to be a vestige from another time.

If we then compare this vestige to the images of what it used to be, our dismay increases: the ritual is empty.

What is an 'empty ritual'? Is it one that is meaningless, characterised by the absence of values, something which is debased?

Emptiness is absence. But it is also potentiality. It may be the darkness of a crevasse. Or the stillness of a deep lake from which unexpected signs of life emerge.

In the 'stew' of cultures, where old borders creak, disintegrate or become sclerotic, theatre is not a people's ritual.

But it can become the people of ritual.

It cannot remain isolated. But it can be an island.

Every theatre is part of a historical and cultural context from which it cannot escape. Theatre can, however, possess a diversity, an energy of its own by means of which it can translate, in its particular way, the mould of the world it is part of, re-inventing and even inverting it.

We could say that in the theatre the seeds of rebellion, refusal and opposition can be preserved. Perhaps it suffices to remember the old saying that the theatre must be a mirror. But the mirror is not only the performance. The mirror is the whole island: the men and women who cultivate it, their relationships, their boldness. Jan Kott reminded us of this a few years ago when discussing the theatre in relation to one of the recent political upheavals in Europe; the mirror reproduces the image but it also reverses it. What is on the right in real life, is on the left in the mirror. The world can be turned upside down.

In order to realise these possibilities, one has to be able to avoid identifying oneself totally with the present.

The flying houses which I have built with my companions from Odin Teatret and with the people from ISTA are inhabited by ancestors whose presence is invisible but concrete. Every time there is a problem to be dealt with, a difficult step to take, or a new situation to decipher, my thoughts turn to how Brecht behaved, to what Artaud said, to what actors did at the time of the Renaissance or during the Religious Wars. I think of Opole or Moscow, Stanislavski or Grotowski. It is true, those were different times. But our times too are 'different', if we compare them to the times we yearn for.

The present is complex and contradictory. It is enigmatic. Once we look deeply into it, it is difficult to pull our eyes away. We are fascinated by and lose ourselves in the labyrinth of all there is to be seen, pondered and evaluated. Time and generations have not yet eroded the labyrinth to the point of giving it the outline of a landscape. We get entangled as we try to understand, condemn and change the scenery of our present. There is never a moment to raise one's eyes. This is how we tame ourselves to the spirit of our times.

When I was in Opole, Ludwik Flazen used to tell me a story. He would tell it to me, for example, every time I got too worked up about something. One is unable to take one's eyes off something one hates, just as one cannot take them off something one loves. Benvenuto Cellini tells of how, in the streets of Rome, he used to gaze fondly upon his mortal enemy (whom he later killed), devouring him with his eyes, like a lovesick young man staring at a beautiful girl. But it wasn't Cellini's story that Flaszen told me. It was the story of a head and a wall.

A wall was blocking a man's way. He threw himself headfirst against it, determined to knock it down. He hurt his head but kept on. He tried again and again, blinded by the fire of his own rage and pain, banging his head against the wall, banging, banging. Then there was no more resistance. His head had become the wall.

The past is not behind us. It is above us. It is what is left of the vertical dimension.

History, the past that we know, is the tale of the possible. It makes it possible for us to catch a glimpse of the world and the theatre the way it could be. Our dissatisfaction with the present is nourished by this profound dialogue with what was different in the past. This dissatisfaction is what we call our 'spiritual life'.

The dead are the true, diverse interlocutors, Richard. Not macabre corpses, but invisible presences.

The interculturalism which challenges me most is the vertical one.

Eugenio

18. 'We went to central places and to isolated places. But wherever you fix the point of your compass, that is the centre.' (Odin Teatret in Ayacucho, Peru, 1988)

19. 'But if we venture outside the region of the theatre, who are we? What do we become in an isolated village in Apulia or Sardinia?' (Odin Teatret performing in Sardinia, 1975)

20. 'The gods have left. We are vessels without a crew, restless vessels carried by obscure currents. And yet, I hold a belief: only by measuring myself against others can I give a meaning to the route and find my identity.' (Roberta Carreri during a barter in Venezuela, 1976)

21. 'There is theatre in interculturalism. And there is interculturalism in theatre.' (The Brazilian dancer Augusto Omolú and Julia Varley; in the background, from left to right: Frans Winther, Isabel Ubeda, and Tina Nielsen, Salvador, Brazil, 1994.)

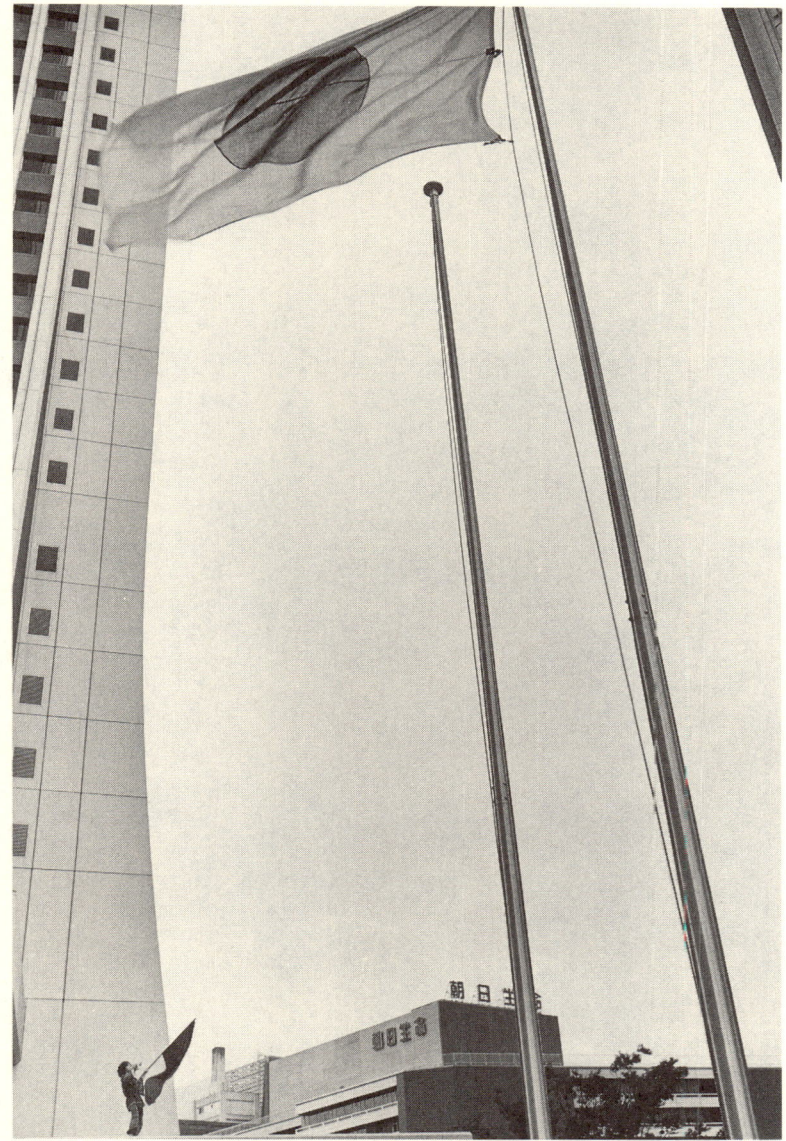

22. 'How can Odin Teatret be an incandescent needle that perforates the glacier of ideas, conventions, criteria and values of its own times, opening for those who come afterwards an invisible tunnel which helps to perceive the other side? What is 'the other side'?' (Odin Teatret in Japan, 1979)

23. 'What immigrant does not dream, momentarily or at length, of abandoning his compatriots, of becoming a citizen of the country s/he is crossing and to which s/he does not belong? Who does not lend an ear to the voices enticing one to the sad peace of self-betrayal?'

(Eugenio Barba leads the march in the desert at the beginning of the performance in honour of Jerzy Grotowski in the archaeological town of Cajamarca, at the end of 'Rencuentro Ayacucho 1988', eighth international meeting of theatre groups, Huampani, Peru)

24. ' Sanjukta is not an "Indian", she is Sanjukta. After all the years we have been working together, I find it hard to think of her as an Indian. Just as she only rarely, almost as an afterthought, remembers that I am a "European". What would you call this? Interculturalism? Humanism? The culture of work? It is not only love of the other. It is the need to know myself.' (Sanjukta Panigrahi and Eugenio Barba during a work demonstration, ISTA, Londrina, 1994)

25. 'True travellers know this experience very well: the unkown world is discovered when one returns home.' (Some Odin actors with the climbers-actors of the Akadenwa group during the Holstebro Festive Week, 1991)

IV

THE WAY OF REFUSAL:
THIRD THEATRE

You must break away from this society,
this state of affairs, and fulfil a total act
of 'heresy'. You must do it quietly,
without screams or tumult, in silence
and secretly, not alone but in groups,
in authentic 'societies', able to build
the most independent and meaningful
life, far from any idea of a phalanstery
or utopistic colony. Here you must learn
above all to govern yourself and to open
yourself justly towards others.
Here you must practise your own craft
according to the norms of the craft itself.
These constitute in themselves the simplest
and most rigorous of moral principles, and
always exclude fraud, prevarication,
charlatanism, the desire for power
and possession. It would not mean absenting
yourself either from the life of your fellows
or from politics in its most serious sense.
It would simply be a non-rhetorical form
of 'global contestation'.

Nicola Chiaromonte:
The Students' Revolt

26. Odin Teatret during a barter in Peru, 1978.

THIRD THEATRE

Here Eugenio Barba formulates the idea of a Third Theatre. Marginality, auto-didactism, the existential and ethical dimension of the craft and a new social vocation seem to him to be the fundamental characteristics of a reality composed of groups who associate themselves neither with traditional nor with avant-guard theatre.

This brief text was intended as an internal document for the participants of the International Encounter on Theatre Research, directed by Barba, during BITEF-Theatre of Nations, Belgrade 1976. However, it quickly assumed the value of a manifesto, becoming a reference point for many groups in Europe and Latin America.

It was first published in International Theatre Information, UNESCO, Paris *1976.*

A theatrical archipelago has been forming during the past few years in several countries. Almost unknown, it is rarely subject to reflection, it is not presented at festivals and critics do not write about it.

It seems to constitute the anonymous extreme of the theatres recognised by the world of culture: on the one hand, the institutionalised theatre, protected and subsidised because of the cultural values that it seems to transmit, appearing as a living image of a creative confrontation with the texts of the past and the present, or even as a 'noble' version of the entertainment business; on the other hand, the avant-garde theatre, experimenting, researching, arduous or iconoclastic, a theatre of changes, in search of a new originality, defended in the name of the necessity to transcend tradition, and open to novelty in the artistic field and within society.

The Third Theatre lives on the fringe, often outside or on the outskirts of the centres and capitals of culture. It is a theatre created by people who define themselves as actors, directors, theatre workers, although they have seldom undergone a traditional theatrical education and therefore are not recognised as professionals.

But they are not amateurs. Their entire day is filled with theatrical experi-ence, sometimes by what they call training, or by the preparation of performances for which they must fight to find spectators.

According to traditional theatre standards, the phenomenon might seem insignificant. But from a sociological point of view, the Third Theatre provides food for thought.

Like islands without contact between themselves, young people in Europe, North and South America, Australia and Asia gather to form theatre groups, determined to survive.

But these groups can only survive on one of two conditions: either by entering the circle of established theatre, accepting the laws of supply and demand, conforming to fashionable tastes, giving way to the preferences of political and cultural ideologists, and adapting themselves to the latest acclaimed results; or by succeeding through continuous work to find their own space, seeking what for them is essential and trying to oblige others to respect this diversity.

Perhaps it is here, in this Third Theatre, that, beyond the *a posteriori* motivations, one can see what constitutes the living matter of the theatre, a remote meaning which attracts new energies to it and which, in spite of everything, keeps it alive in our society.

Different people, in different parts of the world, experience theatre as a bridge, constantly threatened, between the affirmation of their personal needs, and the necessity of extending them into the surrounding reality.

Why do they choose the theatre in particular as a means of change, when we are well aware that other factors determine the reality in which we live? Is it a question of blindness, of self-delusion?

Perhaps for them, theatre is a means to find their own way of being present - which the critics would call 'new expressive forms' - and seeking more human relationships with the purpose of creating a social cell in which intentions, aspirations and personal needs begin to be transformed into actions.

The abstract divisions, made arbitrarily and instituted from on high - various schools, styles, tendencies and other labels which bring order to the recognised theatres - can be of no use here. It is not the styles or the expressive tendencies that count. What seems to characterise the Third Theatre, what appears as a common denominator among such different groups and experiences, is a tension that is difficult to define. It is as if the personal needs - ideals, fears, multiple impulses which would otherwise remain more or less obscure - wanted to be transformed into work, according to an attitude which from the outside is justified as an ethical imperative, not limited to the profession only, but extending through the whole of daily life. But, in the end, these groups are the first to pay the price for their choice.

One cannot dream only in the future, waiting for a total change which seems farther away at each step we take, and which nevertheless gives free rein to alibis and compromises, and to the impotence of waiting.

One wants a new cell to be formed immediately, but without isolating oneself in it.

This is the paradox of the Third Theatre: to submerge oneself, as a group, in the universe of fiction in order to find the courage not to pretend.

THE MUTATION

In this transcription of a speech during the round table on Group Theater in Florence in October 1976, Barba reflects on the transformation that Odin Teatret is undergoing. The Mutation constitutes a key testimony showing how the concept of Third Theatre has its roots in two very recent experiences which have had a profound effect on the Odin: their long stay in southern Italy in 1974 and their encounter with the reality of Latin American theatre in 1976.

The text was first published in Quarta Parete, 3-4, Turin 1977.

We believe that our intentions, when they become actions, take us where we want to go. I cling to the belief that this is so, but my experience makes me shake my head in uncertainty.

The Sea

When I look at the story of the Odin it is clear to me that, in the beginning, my desire to do theatre was founded on contrasting motives.

I wanted to be a director, but was immediately faced with an insurmountable obstacle. I couldn't find work. I had to find a solution, and it was from this struggle that Odin Teatret's particular style of behaviour originated.

Since I am incapable of working fast and achieving immediate results that satisfy me, I had to create a 'smokescreen' together with the actors in order to give the impression that, although producing irregular performances and for few spectators, our group was nonetheless active and present in society. All the time, like a pistol pointed at our temples, we were asked the same question: what is the point of what you are doing?

External necessities have forced us to invent supplementary activities behind which we could protect ourselves and be accepted. These alibi-activities came into being to allow us to concentrate for a year or two on what was essential to us: the preparation of a performance. But the seminars, the publication of books, the presentation of performances from abroad, the sociological surveys, the film clubs or the courses in group dynamics, all these unforeseen activities which were programmed from time to time for the sake of survival, radically changed our way of thinking and doing theatre.

One day we asked ourselves: why are we doing all this? The question arose from a suspicion that something deep down inside us was different. I have difficulty in explaining it, and can do so only in approximate and personal terms.

For years I have lived the situation of the outsider, someone who, in order to preserve his own dignity without bending to abuse or to the constraints of circumstance, has devised a way of attack through theatre for his own defence.

I have lived through this situation of outsider first as an Italian worker in Norway, and then with my Norwegian actors as an unorthodox theatre transplanted in Denmark.

All of us, exiles.

This is one of the wounds that has determined my way of perceiving, of living the reality around me, the relationships that I establish, the stand-points I have taken.

I can only describe what happened to me through a rather primitive image: the theatre as the sea. Theatre people are like fish swimming amongst corals and seaweed with hundreds of other fish, some vividly coloured, others grey, watching out for the bigger ones, heedless of the smaller ones, at ease in those waters, darting hither and thither, moving with the current or struggling against it, occasionally coming up to the surface or diving down into the depths.

Everything that happens in this watery world is studied, appreciated and judged as marine flora and fauna.

Theatre: a multicoloured and silent aquarium.

On the Beach

Personal choices and unforeseen circumstances threw Odin Teatret into another element. Difficult to recognise and hostile, it provoked attacks of asphyxia. In order to breathe, we had to develop other organs. We were no longer in water but in a harsh environment which hurt: on the sand of an endless beach. We realised we were no longer fish elegantly slipping through the water, but clumsily crawling crabs. Ours was an involuntary mutation, not due to originality or whim.

When we retreated to the sea, everybody recognised us: 'Oh! They still know how to swim! But they don't dart about any more as they used to. How ungainly they have become!'

Mutation had caused us to inhabit an uncertain terrain between two distinct worlds: the sea and the land.

Other circumstances have accelerated this process.

One thing gives us a feeling of security and helps us to face any situation: the awareness that we have a profile which makes us recognisable to others. In our case this is the result of our work, the performance. When we went to Carpignano without a performance, our identity as a theatre group melted away. In this tiny village in southern Italy we were just a bunch of people who called themselves actors, yet were not in a position to prove it. So who were we?

It was painful, as though we were suffocating.

We missed the corals, the seaweed and the currents, the vast marine world and its endless depths where the body dilates. We were shipwrecked on an anonymous shore. A solution had to be found, for our very existence was at stake, just as it had been many years before when we had moved from Norway to Denmark.

When I read what theatre historians and critics write, I am aware of the inadequacy of their marine viewpoint when it comes to understanding the crab as it drags itself over terra firma. In their writings and comments I find the same reactions and words of many years ago when our group first started out: what on earth are you doing?

What happened in Carpignano can be judged superficially or studied in depth; there are films and written testimonies. We of the Odin remain indelibly marked by one question: who are we when we leave the aquarium? We are no longer just fish. We are amphibious, we are here and yet elsewhere.

It is the crab's experiences that count. How can I explain them clearly? I am living them; they are what make you shake your heads.

The March of the Crabs

The Carpignano experience put us off balance amongst mountains of sand, new questions, unexpected situations. Another event occurred immediately afterwards: Odin Teatret's first tour to South America, to the Caracas Festival.

I was astonished at the enormous number of theatre groups existing in South America. As I talked with the participants of the festival, I realised that there theatre could not be judged with the criteria usually used for artistic activities. Then I thought of the hundreds and hundreds of theatre groups in Europe too. What is it that makes young people gather in groups and do theatre?

In every large city in South America there is a modern urban nucleus, all glass and steel, intersected by motorways and teeming with activity, cars, shops. Around this hard heart, massive and palpitating, there is a nebulous belt: the 'favelas' of Rio, the 'barrios' of Lima, the 'poblaciones' of Santiago, the 'ranchitos' of Caracas. They are the hovels made of cardboard, huts of corrugated iron or plywood, attached to one another on the slopes encircling the city and collapsing in the rainy season. The one and a half million people who live in Caracas' nebulous belt do not legally exist. They have no address. It is impossible to send a letter or a bunch of flowers to these people.

In Caracas, the Acción Democrática government attempted to carry out a slum clearance programme, moving the inhabitants to better dwellings. It was a failure. The people left the new houses and returned to their rabbit warrens of hovels on the hillsides.

Talking with the actors of the Latin American theatre groups, I discovered that they came from or were fleeing from a particular social stratum and were well aware that the city's expansion was suffocating their needs. I recognised the alternatives: to go underground and take up arms, or else to cauterise the deep wound between the city's hard heart and its nebulous belt through the fiction of theatre.

There was one pressing question for them: who are we Latin Americans? Descendants of the Spanish conquistadors, of the Indios, of the Africans imported as slaves? Are we bastards of all three? Who are we?

In their performances I saw the struggle between the rejection of their Spanish heredity, the idealisation of the indigenous culture and the awareness of the Indios' passivity and indifference to the surrounding reality.

I compared this condition with that of the theatre groups I knew in Europe. I glimpsed a way of rejecting compromise, wear and tear, the inner conflicts deriving from political activity. Theatre as revolt, as a search for identity, as uncertain ground for the cultivation of one's own anger, one's own needs, one's own inadequacy.

Out of these questions and encounters was born the idea of the Third Theatre. I realise that it is not an artistically decipherable phenomenon. It is the fruit of men and women who are confusedly living the mutation from fish to crab, the transition of the theatre as we have known it until now into something like social blasphemy or atheistic prayer, something that we are still unable to name.

On this sandy ground which slides away under our feet, I feel intuitively that the experiences of Odin Teatret encounter the longings and needs of many others.

If Odin Teatret possesses some power of attraction, it is not solely due to artistic results but to something that transcends them. Our mutation appears to appeal to the dreams and necessities of other crabs on their march towards horizons of sand.

THEATRE-CULTURE

Here Eugenio Barba develops further the concept of Third Theatre, injecting into it the idea of an 'asociality' which constitutes the premise of that theatre which, in addition to producing culture, is itself culture.

In spite of the passage of time, Theatre-Culture *remains one of Barba's densest texts and one of the most frequently translated. It was published for the first time in* Arte Nuevo, *Mexico City 1979.*

Occasionally they ask: 'What use are you? What use is your theatre?'

To answer would be to accept the reasoning that only those who produce have a right to exist, and those who do not produce have no function, must be isolated, eliminated, because they are socially *de-functus*: literally, dead.

Those who ask, 'What use are you?', should beware of themselves, of the attitude which makes them deny the value of trees that bear no fruit. The tree that bears no fruit, although ostensibly useless, becomes essential in cities without oxygen.

To produce does not only mean to produce wares, but also relationships between people. This is also true of theatre; it does not only produce performances, cultural products, but also relationships.

He who judges from an aesthetic point of view is merely looking at the theatrical 'ware'.

In order to understand the social value of theatre, it is necessary to look not only at the wares, the performances produced, but also at the relationships established through the producing of performances.

Fear of the Ghetto

The first Third Theatre Encounter took place in Belgrade in 1976.

A modest subsidy intended for conferences, round-tables and debates with critics, experts and directors, enabled me to bring together several theatre groups that I had met in Europe and Latin America. These theatre people, almost always isolated and anonymous, needed a chance to meet, exchanging experiences and working together.

What had seemed a negligible phenomenon, sporadically manifest in various far-off places, showed its profile. An unexpected profile, however, and one that did not seem to fit into our theatrical culture, whether so-called traditional theatre, or the avant-garde. Common traits emerged through a series of negations. Hence, Third Theatre.

It was not important to find a definition for the Third Theatre concept.

What was important was to recognise that there existed a whole set of characteristics which went beyond individual differences and which linked certain groups that were being discriminated against.

Naturally, many people had doubts and reservations about the term Third Theatre. Some felt there was too much ambiguity in this negative definition which created a false unity between differing and contradictory phenomena.

Others dismissed it as being dangerous or mystifying. They saw in it a proposal for a theatre satisfied with its own limits, willingly taking its humble place at the end of the line. A theatre begging for the crumbs of cultural prestige and public funds that, in some countries, are set aside for the development and conservation of Theatrical Art.

They said to me: 'If Third Theatre stands for the ghetto in which we let ourselves be enclosed in order to guarantee ourselves a precarious existence, then we do not recognise ourselves as part of the Third Theatre archipelago'.

***

Third Theatre is a definition that limits itself to recognising the discrimination in which a great many theatre groups live. But it is also the result of a series of questions that I asked myself in order to justify some of my choices and to answer questions others would ask about my work, about its direction and meaning.

It was as though I could distinguish in others around me the symptoms of a disease that I recognised because it affected me as well.

To continue talking about Third Theatre, to attempt to respond to the questions and doubts that the term has raised, means letting oneself be drawn towards another question, a silent one: what meaning does theatre have in my life?

The only way to face the doubts and questions is to answer in the first person. Behind the word theatre I conceal encounters, experiences, moments of illumination, wounds that are my insecure roots. These should not normally be brought out into the open. They should remain disguised as theatre.

***

In the months following the Belgrade Encounter in 1976, the term Third Theatre spread quickly. Not only in polemics and discussions, but also as a fashion. In the province of theatre, fashion often coincides with attention to a problem. Although via a somewhat indirect route, nevertheless a knot of nebulous questions was singled out.

But this knot of questions runs the risk of degenerating into an optimistic image, where light prevails over shadows. Third Theatre does not represent the seed of a renewal, but an ambiguous zone out of which emerge symptoms of mutism and impotence with a need to make themselves heard and develop roots.

One must not deceive oneself; above all, Third Theatre encloses a destructive zone. It is as though theatre's dark face is transforming itself into situations which wrench the usual tools of judgement from our hands.

Does, then, this dark face of the theatre, with all its negations, have a social presence even if it persists in its vocation of refusal, and in spite of the merchants' fashions and the ideologists' optimism?

***

'If Third Theatre stands for the ghetto in which we let ourselves be enclosed in order to guarantee ourselves a precarious existence, then we do not recognise ourselves as part of the Third Theatre archipelago.'

Should we refuse the ghetto?

The Spanish *juderías*, the German *judengasse*, the Italian *ghetti* arose out of discrimination, the violence of the Christian majority against the Jewish minority. They are the physical signs of an intolerance that had not as yet become systematic annihilation.

They were the places where the Jews assembled, sometimes on peremptory order, sometimes to take advantage of some benevolent bishop or prince, or simply as a result of their spontaneous need to live near each other.

These are the origins of the ghetto, a place that limited certain elementary liberties, but allowed the preservation of others: the freedom to follow one's own religious beliefs, to speak one's own language, to live according to one's own norms. The ghetto was a place where one could save one's own identity, defend and hand down the essential values of a culture of which one felt a part.

Should we refuse the ghetto? But on what conditions?

It is possible to leave the ghetto. You need only convert, cover up your own roots, condemn yourself to isolation instead of separation. You need only accept a chronic laceration. You need only accept norms and ways of life that you do not feel are yours and become a *marrano*. Then you are accepted. Outwardly nothing distinguishes the *marranos* from the people of their new environment, even if inwardly they hide other aspirations, other nostalgias, other beliefs.

Perhaps the refusal of the ghetto stems from the fear of being isolated and suffocated in a reality which is separated from what is alive and important in our society.

And yet, consciously or out of ignorance, one forgets that the ghetto has never been separated from what was alive and important in society, in the city that surrounded it. The city's entire economy depended on the ghetto's financiers. The ghetto was the home of philosophers who were in constant confrontation with Christian and Islamic philosophers and theologians. Ghetto physicians were sought out by popes and emperors, its medical schools were secretly attended by Christian students. In the ghetto, Aristotle and Hippocrates were translated, the sciences of linguistics and astronomy were born, marine maps were charted and the nautical instruments used by Bartholomew Diaz, Christopher Columbus and Vasco da Gama were constructed. In the ghettos, in the *juderías*, in the *judengasse* lived Maimonides, jeweller and philosopher, the greatest physician of his time. He was paid in gold by the caliphs and ministers, and treated the poor free of charge, without asking them their religion.

The ghetto was the place in which any Jew, regardless of where he came from - the Orient, the Slavonic lands, distant islands or Africa - could be sure of being received. The separation of the ghetto meant separation from its neighbours. It was not separation from society, from history, from the most significant transformations of the time.

Today, the word ghetto evokes poverty, struggle for survival, pogrom. The ghetto is also the place on which to sharpen one's weapons for condemnation and offence, to plunder and destroy an unarmed supposed enemy. And behind every good intention to abolish all forms of ghetto, there sneeringly lurks the need to abolish every kind of diversity, every minority.

Do the ghettos of which I am speaking in a figurative way exist today or not? If they do exist, what then? Should we remain in the ghetto, with those we feel connected to? Or stay outside?

Anti-Historical Images

There are two questions that seem alike but are not.

The first: what is the social value of a theatre?

The second: what relationships does a theatre establish with the spectators? What influence does it have on them? How does it manage to be influenced by them?

In order to evaluate theatre as a cultural and social phenomenon, one automatically refers to the audience. But the relationships between the actors and the spectators become important only in the second of two phases. The first phase is the most important, when the relationships among those who are doing theatre are established.

The first social phase of theatre takes place internally; it is the way in which different individuals regulate their working relationships and socialise their own needs. The character of this first socialisation determines the theatre group's place and influence in society.

The audience is often an array of faceless ghosts, the Great Beast with the dark countenance, as actors in the past used to call it. The audience attends, then disappears. The performance does not necessarily leave a mark on the person who sees it, nor does the person who sees it necessarily leave a mark on the performer. The only recorded consequences of the encounter between a group of actors and a certain number of people are usually the writings of the critics.

Written words are the only lasting traces of the performance, and give birth to the preconception that the social value of theatre is measured according to what words measure: the audience's judgements and reactions.

Here it seems as if what lasts is important as opposed to the old adage's claim that what is important lasts.

But written testimony is not a testimony of what one has seen, of what one has understood. It is merely a testimony of a way of looking and its conventions. It is, however, a lasting thing and for this very reason imposes its vision.

Actors, obviously, do not write 'reviews' of their spectators, nor do they usually leave behind written testimonies of relationships that occur within the group, of the social dimension of their group.

***

One of the most important phenomena in the history of modern theatre, the Commedia dell'Arte, arose out of the need of a few individuals to come together. They were people who had always practised trades of ill repute: buffoons, charlatans, mountebanks, acrobats and magicians. Or else men and women leading a *disorderly* life, that is, openly breaking society's rules.

These individuals, the first professional actors of modern times, transformed their deviation, their 'asociality', by uniting in groups. They socialised their difference. They 'invented' a new form of theatre, in order to defend themselves. Or rather, their way of defending themselves, of winning a more dignified level of life and the right to be morally and culturally respected, produced as a result a form of theatre that the cultured and uncultured audiences of the time, and later the historians, considered new and original from an artistic point of view.

It was not a new art, however. It was a new micro-culture born out of the collective work of people who, until then, had made their living by making spectacles of themselves, but each one separately.

Theatre historians - starting in the 1700's while the Commedia dell'Arte was still alive - misrepresented this historical process by creating the image of a theatre that had chosen improvisation and gesture instead of words.

From the point of view of the literary audience, the function of the Commedia dell'Arte was to represent the freedom of imagination, the pleasure of a theatrical game liberated from the bondage of verisimilitude.

From the actors' point of view, its function was to force them out of their social confinement, to discover beyond discrimination a form of sociality without having to accept the norms of recognised morality.

***

For most of those who write, read and discuss theatre history, theatre has no backbone.

It is flat, two-dimensional.

This seems normal enough, but in reality it is strange to think that theatre acts only through its surface, that performances constitute its true history.

It is strange because modern thinking compels us to consider social, economic, psychological and physical realities as being driven by deep laws hidden behind the mask of cause and motivation, all the more deceitful as they appear clear and incontrovertible to common sense.

The 'science' of theatre has not yet undergone its Copernican revolution. It seems that individuals are revolving around the immobile stars of theatrical aesthetics and ideologies, instead of these latter revolving around the individuals from whose own history they were generated.

What do you revolve around? Around psychological theatre or biomechanics? Around the Theatre of Cruelty or Epic Theatre?

Brecht, Stanislavski, Meyerhold and Artaud are turned into categories which are used to judge the work of those who follow.

This process hides precisely what these men were: individuals who were isolated or who had to isolate themselves in order to give life to the theatre in a way which corresponded to their own needs and which was different from and unrecognisable to those thinking according to the ideology of the time.

Brecht, in the Germany of the thirties, was accused of being a decadent and bourgeois writer. His Marxism was seen by many militant Marxists as a philosophical and intellectual infatuation that did not involve participation in the revolutionary movement.

The fact that Brecht revolutionised theatre was preached in chorus after his death. But the story of the contradiction that Brecht embodied until the last day of his life, in spite of all the honours that ran the risk of gagging him, almost as much as did his exile, is a story yet to be written.

Just as the true significance of the Berliner Ensemble is a story worth telling. Today those who turned Brecht into a theology in the fifties and sixties in France and Italy, in the United States and Scandinavia, go to East Berlin, to the theatre that Brecht created. They see his productions and those of his collaborators. The rigour, the cold ferocity, the impossibility of speaking openly and the cunning disobedience stamped into Galileo's gestures, are a slap in the face for the spectator. Yet, faced with this, the theologians of Brechtism merely shrug their shoulders: all this has already been seen, they say. At this point, the Berliner is pure museum, just sterile technique.

But what are they seeking in Brecht? The artist's novelty? Or the man's ability to survive historical tempests during which many became traitors and many others perished? The ability to survive, safeguarding his own identity, succeeding, in spite of everything, in speaking out while many mouths were closing or singing along with the crowd, crossing many countries without being a man of any country and keeping the strength to react in a manner rationally adequate to any situation? If it is this, and not the futile 'novelty' of the artist they love in Brecht, then why do they not understand that this *Galileo* which his collaborators are showing us in East Berlin, in 1978, is not *déjà vu*, but rather something which we must scrutinise anew?

***

Stanislavski has been set up on the one hand as a model for the actor of socialist realism. On the other hand, he has become the interpreter of bourgeois individualism. On the pretext of paying attention to social values, metaphysical entities are created and made to enter into conflict. The true historical conflicts are lost and hidden behind simple conflicts of ideas.

Meyerhold's biomechanics is a form of opposition to Stanislavskian *perezhivanye*: so say the handbooks. Meyerhold was not opposing Stanislavski, but his followers that set him up as a system. In the same way, Meyerhold was against what he himself called 'meyerholdism.'

The 'followers of the system' were numerous, but Meyerhold was the true pupil of Stanislavski. He was formed by him and later developed this experience according to his own needs. He, in turn, influenced the master, inspiring his 'method of physical actions'.

When Meyerhold fell into disgrace and was deprived of his work (the first step towards the firing squad, his destiny as a formalist artist) the only one who offered him a theatre was Stanislavski, a moralist never satisfied with himself, who, through theatre conducted a personal, not a private, research throughout his entire life.

Personal, not private research leaves traces. Copeau chose his collaborators according to their human qualities. Little did he care whether they were mediocre actors. Thus began the adventure of the Vieux Colombier and of the Company of the Copiaus. They became excellent actors, moreover, and by the time that this adventure had worn itself out, they had altered the face of French theatre.

***

The Greeks used the same word, *sema*, to mean both 'tomb' and 'sign.' A similar identification is also to be found in the languages of other peoples.

Doctrines, methods, poetics are the tombs and the signs of those individuals who, in the past, ventured down new paths. We can see them as monuments to admire, to comment on and to imitate. Or we can look at them in order to discover, beyond the *sign*, the meaning of a life that has found its own path and travelled it.

The gravediggers and not the pupils, the exploiters and not the admirers, transform these personal paths into convenient highways, monuments to progress, that everyone can and must use.

To avoid being petrified into a theatrical monument during his lifetime, the aged Stanislavski withdraws to his home and gathers around him a group of young people with whom he begins a new research. He dismantles his 'system' giving birth to the 'method of physical actions'.

In order to work undisturbed, to escape political and cultural control, he feigns illness and disinterest in work; one cannot be 'moral' in an immoral society.

This last sentence is Brecht's.

What does it mean to be Stanislavskian or Brechtian? To be the keeper and priest of their tombs, or to be travellers encouraged by their signs?

What does it mean to agree with Brecht? To go along with him when he speaks of *his* technique of alienation, or to confront oneself with him when he speaks of the necessity of retaining one's own identity, of remaining a 'foreigner' in the society one is crossing, of the difficult art of writing the truth without getting one's neck broken?

The Floating Islands

Critics, scholars and theatre artists have for years ignored the simple fact that theatre has lost its character of functional use for a particular social group and a determined community.

In various countries of the world, especially among the younger generations, an unexpected meaning has come to be given to the encounter with theatre: not the need to *receive theatre*, but the need to *do theatre*, to create new relationships, as actor and as spectator.

A theatre is born as the expression of small groups that perhaps present needs and contradictions concerning only a limited number of people. Nevertheless, they exist and are active among us.

These groups do not dream of themselves as being vehicles for great words, for great messages, for great debates, but seek a way to bring the individual into contact with the individual, the different with the different.

Not new contents, but new relationships, often difficult to decipher, take the place of the theatre's usual contents. It is not 'another theatre' that is born. It is other situations that are beginning to be called theatre.

***

Because of certain circumstances, Odin Teatret came to experience some of these situations years ago.

When a group succeeds in arousing discussion about itself, comes under attack, is accused of being useless or counter-productive, often it has already won half its battle.

The strongest discrimination does not occur when one is accused according to precepts. Many groups, many people are reduced to silence even before anyone has begun to discuss whether or not they have the right to speak. The most arduous experiences happen behind closed doors. They can be spoken of only in personal terms.

The struggle to survive determines the choices that follow. For the spectators who judge according to what they see, the results of this struggle appear as a new theatre 'current'.

All the fundamental traits of Odin Teatret (from the actor's technique to the internal organisation, from its ethics to its way of resolving economic problems, and finally to its performances often not based on a written text and destined for a limited number of spectators) are our answer to a situation that seemed to condemn us to impotence.

The solitary situation we were in forced us to start alone and without any experience whatsoever. To the discrimination by the theatrical world was soon added a geographical and linguistic one: in order to survive we had to emigrate from the capital of Norway to a small town in Denmark, far from big cities, far from the critics and the theatre-going public.

We had to succeed in living this situation not as an impairment. We had to find a way of not yielding to the two handicaps that irremediably prohibited us from doing a kind of theatre that, in those years, was recognised and accepted: the handicap of language, that prevented us from expressing ourselves theatrically through texts, and the handicap of our lack of theatrical education.

We had to invent for ourselves both a 'social function' that we didn't seem to have, and a theatrical knowledge of our own. I myself have no professional training. My three years with Grotowski were spent sitting down, observing his work and writing, interested in a conceptual interpretation, with no opportunity for practical experience.

It was repeated year after year that, according to what one normally expects from a theatre, our theatre was of no use, that we were people obsessed by private needs, living 'outside history'.

For a long time Odin Teatret was not recognised as a theatre, but as a group which succeeded in surviving thanks to other cultural activities such as the publication of books and magazines and the organisation of courses and guest performances.

***

The same accusations are today repeated to others who, although justifying their choices with a political and social involvement, are breaking away from big meetings and great assemblies, and gathering in small groups to do theatre.

The groups that I call Third Theatre do not belong to a specific tendency. But they are all discriminated against, personally or culturally, professionally, economically or politically. The masters of writing are the ones who decide the validity of what these groups are doing.

They are thus groups forced into a daily verification of the necessity for an 'anti-historical' obstinacy and persevering, even in isolation, in the search for an answer to their own individual needs.

They are people who, through theatre, pursue the dream of building their own lives.

A theatre of men and women who are different? Of dreamers?

***

What image do we have of a dreamer? A person who leaves the land and takes to the water. But not just to discover or to reach other shores.

Some, although they seem to isolate themselves far out in the water, nevertheless wish to remain close to others. They try to build fragments of land upon the lake. These are the floating islands. The floating islands are not a means of making the vast waters of Texcoco and Titicaca useful and fertile. They are a means of survival.

The floating islands cannot be handed down to one's children; as soon as you cease maintaining it, your field ceases to exist. It is a small, unstable garden that bears fruit, but whose dimensions and whose very existence are conditioned by the currents. It is born out of the need to sink roots. But in an uprooted reality.

***

When the Toltecs saw the Aztecs arriving, few in number and starving, they called them 'the children of nobody', 'those whose faces no one knows'. The Toltecs granted the newcomers a few small islands on Lake Texcoco where they could live. There the many poisonous snakes would soon exterminate them.

Instead, it was the Aztecs who killed and ate the snakes, as had the eagle on the cactus - their vision and their omen.

The Aztecs also built rafts of reeds on which they spread earth and planted seeds. From those floating gardens a village slowly grew, whose name, Mexico-Tenochtitlan, would have a long destiny. Mexico means: 'the city in the centre of the lake of the moon'. This is an optimistic story.

Much further south on the Andean plains of Alto Peru, another tribe, the Uro, built floating islands on Lake Titicaca. The chroniclers of the time of the Conquest had spoken of the Uro as people whose life was little different from that of animals, a life unworthy of being lived.

Years ago, certain anthropologists affirmed that the Uro had disappeared from the face of the earth. But the Uro still survive, cultivating their minute gardens of ephemeral life.

***

There exists no right to be different.

It is moralistic and naive to invoke such a *right*, which is found only in constitutions or in the world of ideas and, at times, not even there.

A right won from whom? Imposed by whom? With what force? If the controlled or open violence of the authorities and of the various majorities cannot grant this right for long, then it is suicide to expose ourselves, with all our aspirations, with all our needs. We run the risk of being defined as 'sinners', 'sick', 'social misfits', 'asocial', and of being treated as such.

We must dig ourselves a trench.

When it was time to sow, many scoffed at what Odin Teatret sowed and the manner in which we did it. They wanted us to sow and cultivate something else. The advice was explicit: follow us where we will lead you and you will be safe in the arms of acceptance. We had to plug our ears, more or less isolate ourselves in order to find the route that was ours and avoid being divided or dragged elsewhere.

Many seasons have passed. Now that it is time to harvest and many recognise that there really is something to harvest, we look around us and it is as though, after the long winter, solitude is now a part of our life.

From the letters I receive, from the visits, from the encounters that I have, I am aware that the meaning of Odin Teatret lies not only in its artistic results. It is in its very existence, in its endurance as a tangible sign that a group of excluded people, from different countries, of different religions, with different languages, in reality a handful of misfits, had the courage to leave the mainland, where the inhabitants seem to be usefully tilling the soil. We brought our own bags of soil on a raft and worked obstinately, without following the mainland's culture, adapting ourselves to the currents that carried us far away.

This is the value of Odin Teatret and other groups, other people who by now have spent almost an entire lifetime sowing on the water.

If in spite of everything one succeeds in carrying on, then paradoxically one's 'asociality' becomes something social. Thus theatre becomes a means of not being alone, of forming a bridge, of creating ties without renouncing one's own dreams.

Theatre also becomes the shrewdness, the trench that protects and hides what we consider essential.

In the years of struggle, in the years of intense activities developed to safeguard the essential, spending energy and imagination simply in order to stay alive, the courage to continue also came from the knowledge that other people, other groups lived in the same conditions as us.

Yet, they too refused to yield and used all their strength and their wits to protect a search that was not merely for theatre.

***

When I try to understand what has happened to the theatrical research of the Sixties, it appears clear to me how it has slowly taken a direction that, in the beginning, none of us foresaw. A deep bond with a specific history, whose ancestors could be Stanislavski, Meyerhold or Brecht, translated our needs into artistic terms, into a reform of 'theatrical language' and expressive means. With time and experience, this bond went beyond the profession, it became an ethical attitude, with a distinct way of perceiving and reacting. Although this attitude represents for many a widening of the confines of theatre, it often seems to us like a refusal of everything in our culture that is called theatre.

I think of Grotowski, of the people of the Living Theatre, of us from Odin Teatret. Many of us, after working for years towards redefining the role of the actor, have sought to obliterate the actor in our colleagues, to abolish the performance. And consequently to abolish the spectator.

I'm speaking of the need to transform theatre into a specific situation that allows one to go beyond the relationships and perceptions that characterise everyday life. For some this means heading towards a dangerous, questionable territory denounceable as 'romantic', 'mystical', 'irrational'.

This conscious search by the person who chooses theatre, not just as a member of an audience, but as a means to attain a different state of experience, is a transcending of the limits of theatre, a convention that is but a few centuries old.

What do we see if we look ingenuously through this ordinary word: theatre?

***

When Leeuwenhoek placed a drop of water under a microscope, he observed with wonder a whole swarm of creatures invisible to the naked eye. Until then, 'life' had been something visible: the horse, the swan, the dolphin, the worm. This new form of life raised many questions: what was the function of these tiny creatures, these 'microbes'? How did they fit into the the 'Order of Nature'? Many important scientists of the time - even Buffon, for example, who had made great progress in the study of natural sciences - called this form of life an 'offence against nature'.

For years microbes were a conversation piece, a curiosity whose existence had no relevance.

But then more became known about them, about their significance in the life process. And how they can be more dangerous than the tiger.

Pueblos, Cimarrones

Sad truths are also solid alibis.

One sad truth has it that when you are few, you can achieve nothing. In the end, you are reduced to being the instruments of those who control big institutions, who have the power to open and close our very sources of sustenance. One is destined to integration, change, or else reduced to inactivity and inefficiency.

The truth of this is easily proved. It is so evident that it is not worth mentioning.

How false it can be is something that can and must be tested.

The uncomfortable truth is that even if we are only a few, we can succeed in shaping the situation that hangs over us and seems to be conditioning us without means of escape.

It is not enough to be different, to use norms and values that are more just, standing by oneself and one's aspirations, however naive and utopian. It is necessary to go through and overcome that which usually brands a marginal group: being a subculture. A theatre which is representative of the 'new culture' of the young, a 'young theatre', is not a value in itself. It is just the theatre of one of the subcultures of our society.

It is necessary to change oneself from a subculture into a culture.

Culture is the capacity to adapt oneself to and modify one's surroundings, to organise and exchange innumerable individual and collective activities, to transmit the collective 'wisdom' gained from different experiences and different technical knowledge.

Only the capacity to reorganise internally all the fundamental aspects that regulate living together allows a group to adapt itself to the outside world without totally depending upon it.

It is necessary to aim for a kind of completeness, a cultural microcosm. Cultural completeness is the opposite of autism; it is the ability to respond continuously, to react in an adequate and appropriate way to changes of situation, without the group being reduced to dead matter, either so rigid that it breaks or so malleable that it can be moulded like wax.

The passage from subculture to group culture is the passage from the state of minority of age to minority of number.

These minorities that present themselves as small pitfalls in the very centre of our society, constitute perhaps the most important cultural change of our years, and not only in theatre.

It is illusory to believe that only big organisms provoke big changes.

***

Discrimination forces theatre groups towards one single choice, other than that of disappearance or betrayal, that is, of transforming themselves into pueblos, in both senses of the word: one's own people, and the physical place where one lives. But being discriminated against or being confined to society's margins do not in themselves constitute culture. Most groups are merely living in a condition of inferiority.

A true, adult culture, even if consisting of a limited number of people, exists when a group is able to confront the surrounding cultures on all levels: from its economical organisation to the use of the products of its labour, from interpersonal relationships to critical reflection on its own conduct.

***

How does one socialise one's own needs, use them, work with them to reach out to others, without hiding behind the supposed answers to the supposed needs of society?

Discussing problems that cannot be solved through discussion is a habit that one must discard.

What sort of theatre does today's society need? Those who do not accept a society and a culture that is imposed upon them, but seek a different society and their own culture, must turn the question around. They must ask what they want from society, through theatre.

***

The nostalgia for the *pueblos*, for a popular culture, rooted in a past shared by generations and generations, is the affliction of the impossible return.

The culture of theatre groups is one without roots. It is the culture of the *cimarrones*, the black slaves who in Brazil, Jamaica, Surinam or Cuba, ran away into the mountains and the jungles, founding tiny communities that sometimes resisted for many years, often even in contact with white plantation owners who were not strong enough to defeat them.

The *cimarrones* had almost completely lost their African culture. They had assimilated many of the cultural characteristics of the whites, from whom they had escaped, and whose world they rejected.

They did not have a culture, they were deprived of roots. Their only root was their very escape.

They had to rebuild a society.

A new identity was born from the fragments of a heterogeneous past, of forgotten or poorly learned languages, of differing crafts and skills and through the solution of concrete problems.

***

The theatre-culture cannot be a defenceless theatre. It would be suicide to treat artistic work and its result, the performance, as secondary problems, as undervalued instruments that do not need to strive for perfection.

Those who wanted to build a new village would look for a site that best allowed for community life, and was at the same time protected by the mountains, the water and the forest.

The performance is our mountain, our water, our forest.

Its ability to impose respect and to fascinate even those who do not accept us, not only permits us to live, but places us out of range.

An Asocial Theatre?
One is not born asocial. One *becomes* asocial.

Another emigration, parallel to the one which sends people in search of bread, is crossing the expanses and the very conscience of our society. It is composed of the willingly or unwillingly 'up-earthed', those uprooted from a country, a religion, an ideology, a class.

Very little unites us in our past, in our history, beyond the fact that different and distant necessities have compelled us to unite.

***

When theatre groups meet, they speak to each other like emigrants. This has occurred every time that we have been able to meet. Time after time, we have experienced the same sense of being hard at work and at the same time of being suspended in mid-air; the same contradictory awareness of having taken our destiny in hand and, consequently, of being at the mercy of forces that we will not be able to dominate when the sea is too stormy for small boats.

Each time we met we felt the same need to give each other something to strengthen our defences for when we again found ourselves alone.

We discovered the same deep and nearly hidden vein of solidarity, with all its ambiguities, divisions, rivalries, enveloped in the grandiose and illusory dreams that haunt us in immigration.

What immigrant does not dream, momentarily or at length, of abandoning his compatriots, of becoming a citizen of the country s/he is crossing and to which s/he does not belong?

Who does not lend an ear to the voices enticing one to the sad peace of self-betrayal?

How often has s/he who renounces these dreams been branded by the same accusation: asocial.

An accusation that is an empty concept.

***

It is never possible to be 'outside society'. One can only diverge from its norms.

The desire to be 'asocial' is sometimes the sign of the deepest commitment to change. It means turning one's head in another direction, seeking something different from the society you wish to refuse. What you refuse becomes the point you use to get your bearings, the 'North' on which you fix your gaze as you depart from it.

This is the march of parallel emigrations which are constantly threatened, often defeated. Each time that you trust too much in dreams, reality engulfs you. But if you succeed in departing, day by day, step by step, with your gaze fixed on what you want *not to be*, supporting your companions and supported by them, one day you will discover with amazement that the society you have left behind is taking an interest in you. It discovers in you the image of a different life. It studies you as the example of a small group, which, while living in the very centre of society, and without detaching itself from it, builds its own culture: a non-destructive microscopic organism, embodying other ways of living together.

Why be afraid of words? To become 'asocial' is to attempt to build your own microscopic 'a-society' in which to try out the *life* you aspire to. It is a concrete way of living together, being concerned with each individual difference; it is not a formless emotivity, not the vague sentimentality of the 'brothers all', of the 'each and every one of us alike'.

***

It makes sense to set oneself apart, not as a big family, but as a small society. It makes sense to choose theatre, a 'useless' job that in time yields objective results which shape relationships between people, their vision of the world, their private behaviour.

You cannot choose ideas in the hope that they will change you. You must choose conditions of life and of work.

You must be 'asocial' if you want to create the opposite of the sociality of injustice.

You must be 'asocial' if you do not want to accept the rules of a game in which you will remain lost and entangled.

You must become 'asocial' if you wish to break at least one of the links in the net and find another space, other relationships on the outside.

You must be 'asocial' if you want to transmit your presence and your actions to those who may tomorrow confront themselves with your experiences, using your tracks as their own point of departure.

You must not limit your presence to this particular moment, to this place, to your present ties, to the questions that others ask you today.

Are you therefore apolitical? What is politics? Is it not the art of the possible?

You must be 'asocial' in order to realise *your own* possibilities.

***

It would be false idealism to consider the reality of theatre groups as an ideal of community life.

These groups are, rather, the result of tensions, of maladjustments, of a divergence that has provoked a lasting anxiety and a sense of suffocation. They are not the islands of Utopia. They are the fragments of a frontier society, the frayed edges of something which is and is not society.

Many feel, as we feel or have felt, that they are slowly slipping into a form of apathy, of impotence. Theatre is the rock onto which we all cling and which makes us social.

From the point of view of those who possess the mastery of words we may resemble mutes who express themselves by way of strange signs, an almost private language of images. From the point of view of mutes, we are mutes who succeed in speaking.

***

Faced with the discomfort or the impossibility of integrating oneself into an inhuman life, some speak positively of marginalization. They speak of their own 'madness' and exalt it as something to be defended.

But marginalization and madness are precisely what we are fighting in order to remain true to our fundamental needs, refusing to be reduced to impotence and silence. The refusal to become domesticated does not mean taking refuge in 'marginalization' and in 'madness'.

It means not becoming *domesticated to* marginalization and *by* madness.

***

Theatre is waste, but it is also a socially accepted activity. It is apparently non-productive, but it justifies group-work. You can project your dreams and your obsessions onto it, giving them a body, reaching out to others without skimming over the surface of a common language.

It is a means to escape the reasoning of the tamers, to break the circle of solitude.

***

To answer in this way would be to answer with the truth. But only one face of the truth.

THE THIRD BANK OF THE RIVER

This is the closing speech at Qosqo '87, the seventh international meeting of theatre groups, which was held in Urubamba, Peru, in October 1987. Barba continues to explore the concept of Third Theatre, exposing in it the possibility of refusal. The asocial attitude of a theatre which seeks its independence is presented here as a form of resistance.

First published in Teatro e storia, *5, Bologna 1988.*

Memory is the spirit which guides our actions. Memory allows us to penetrate under the skin of our times and to trace the manifold paths leading back to our origins, to our first day. Along these paths and at their crossings our ancestors confronted their demons and the demands of their times. These are the cross-roads which we rediscover on reading the classics or history books. Through reflection on these paths we are able to keep the umbilical cord intact with our origins, and glimpse the distant yet clear outline of our identity. Therefore, if you want to blind a person or a people, you must make them lose all ties with their origins, with the secret sense of their memory.

History is often compared to a river, to an impetuous current which sweeps everything along with it. There are those who believe it is possible to escape this current and they build houses on the banks of the river. They think they will be safe. But the river overflows and carries away animals, children, vigorous young men, houses of steel and cement.

Sometimes the historical circumstances seem to conceal the meaning of our path. Then artistic experience helps us to catch sight of the thread which binds us to our origins. That is what happened recently in Brazil when Luis Octavio Burnier and Paulo Dourado told me a version of *The Third Bank of the River,* a story by João Guimarães Rosa. An old man lived with his family near a river. One day he went down to his boat, pushed it into the water and rowed out into the middle of the river where the current was strongest. There he stayed, ceaselessly rowing. He never came back to land. Every day his son took him food and begged him to return home. The father continued obstinately to row against the current. This continued day after day, year after year, until the night of his death. Then at dawn his son took the boat out into the middle of the river to row against the current.

This story was a sort of enlightenment to me. It made visible some of my intuitions and clarified many events that Odin Teatret and I had lived through. As a theatre man, I know that I must dig down as far as the invisible, to what is hidden, down to the subterranean story, to the multiple paths that official or party historians stifle beneath a blanket of words. I know that my obligation is to remember, to fight off the instinct of amnesia common to my society. I know that, anonymously and without rhetoric, every single day I must represent the memory of my times and of the paths trodden. That is the sense my work has for me. I don't want to lose this sense in the exhausting labyrinth of days and years which wear down dreams, illusions, beliefs, energies. I need a thread to guide the continuity and the consistency of my actions, to connect me with my origins.

What is my origin? Who are my ancestors? From a professional point of view I have a totem-ancestor: Stanislavski. Other ancestors of mine are Meyerhold, Vakhtangov, Copeau and Eisenstein. I have an elder brother: Grotowski. What about female ancestors? Who are the women in my origins? Amongst my ancestors I am reminded of Gordon Craig. But why are there no books about his sister Edy? In the final reckoning, she is our ancestor. Group theatre was not created as recently as the sixties, and nor did it come from the Russian and German agit prop theatre of the twenties. It was born at the beginning of the century, started by women struggling for the right to vote: the suffragettes. In order to make a greater impact at their meetings and condense the evidence of their unjust situation, they turned to actresses who, by profession, had experience of public speaking. In this way, theatre groups composed of women were created whose function was not only artistic or aesthetic, but one of giving a different meaning to the relationship we call theatre.

Edy Craig is my ancestor. Her brother became famous for his grandiose visions and his love affairs. But it was she who, with the Pioneer Players in London, persevered in her struggle against the current from before the First World War until 1925.

It is vital we do not forget the heritage of our ancestors. It is this that connects us to the first day and guides us towards transcending our immediate actions and projecting their meaning into the future.

The 'How': Technique

The word representation, which is used as a synonym for performance, contains the idea of double presentation, of a doubling of the actor's presence as a historical being and as a professional. This presence is transformed by the spectator into sensorial experience and mental vision, into feeling and reflection. This 'double presentation' always occurs in a historical context which determines its social effect and artistic value. This context is unique and therefore relative. It cannot be transferred to other

195

places without the representation changing its meaning and altering the most intimate nucleus of the relationship with its spectators.

In order to be more effective in their context, in order to make their historical-biographical identity emerge, actors use forms, manners, behaviour, procedures, guile, distortions, appearances. This is what is called technique and it is characteristic of every actor from all traditions. If we go beyond cultures (north, south, east, west), beyond genres (classical ballet, modern dance, opera, operetta, musicals, text theatre, body theatre, classical, contemporary, commercial, traditional, experimental theatre, etc.), we arrive at *the first day*, at the origins, when presence begins to crystallise into technique, into *how* to become effective with respect to the spectator. We find two points of departure, two paths.

On the first path, the actors use their spontaneity, the behaviour which comes 'naturally' to them, which they have absorbed since their birth in the culture and the social milieu in which they have grown up. Anthropologists define as inculturation this process of passive sensory-motor absorption of the daily behaviour of a given culture. The adaptation of a child to the conduct and life norms of this culture, the conditioning to 'naturalness', permits a gradual and organic transformation which is also growth.

Stanislavski made the most important methodological contribution to this path of scenic spontaneity, or 'inculturation technique'. It consists of a mental process which 'enlivens' the actor's incultured naturalness. By means of the 'magic if', the actors alter their daily behaviour and habitual way of being and embody the character they have to portray. This is also the objective of Brecht's alienation technique or social gesture. Here during the work process, the actor models natural and daily behaviour into extra-daily scenic behaviour with built-in social evidence or subtexts.

Acting technique which uses variations of inculturated patterns is transcultural. The theatre of Oxolatlan, done by isolated indigenous people on a mountain in Mexico, uses a technique which is based on inculturation. It is the same technique found in the Living Theatre of Khardaha on the outskirts of Calcutta, where the actors are farmers, workers or students. There are ways of being an actor in Europe and America, in Asia, Africa or Australia, which are rooted in inculturation technique.

At the same time, it is possible to observe in all cultures another path for actors and dancers: the utilisation of specific body techniques which are different from those used in daily life. Modern and classical ballet dancers, mimes, and performers from traditional Asian theatres have put aside their 'naturalness' and imposed upon themselves another form of scenic behaviour. They have submitted themselves to a process of enforced 'acculturation', imposed from the outside, with ways of standing, walking, stopping, looking, sitting, which are different from the daily ones.

The acculturation technique artificialises, i.e. stylises the actor's behaviour and, just like the inculturation technique, creates another quality of energy. We have all experienced this, while watching a classical Indian or Japanese performer, a modern dancer or a mime. It is fascinating to observe how successful they have been in modifying their 'naturalness', transforming it into lightness, as in classical ballet, or into the vigour of a tree, as in modern dance. The acculturation technique distorts 'natural' appearance and recreates it sensorially in a fresher, more real and surprising way.

On the path of acculturation it is difficult to distinguish the actor from the dancer. This is why, in many traditions, a dancer is also a singer and actor. The accultured performer manifests a quality of energy and a radiation which is presence ready to become dance or theatre according to intention or tradition.

The path of inculturation may also lead to dance based on a richness of variations and shades of daily behaviour and to an essential quality of vocal action, of the spoken word. Both the path of inculturation and that of acculturation make it possible to arrive at the pre-expressive level: presence ready to represent.

However, we must not forget that acculturation is a colonisation, the imposition, even if voluntary, of another kind of presence. Once it has been incorporated, it becomes a 'second naturalness'. We cannot free ourselves of it. Anyone who has worked as a mime or as a classical dancer moves and stops by means of determined dynamic discharges of energy which condition the posture, the use and position of the spinal column, balance. Each detail is codified. Codification means formalisation, precise form which must be respected, a pre-established pattern to be repeated. The dancer and the mime remain captive to these patterns. It is interesting to see them struggle to free themselves from a learned technique and attempt to unlearn what took so many years to master.

The path of acculturation leads to codification, a formalised presence recognisable in a genre: ballet, mime, *kathakali*, *nô*. This formalised presence is necessary for those who wish to express themselves artistically through traditional genres. But for a performer in a contemporary performance who aims to eliminate the boundaries between dance, theatre, song, opera, mime or circus, the most dangerous trap is to develop a formalised presence of a particular genre. It is essential to arrive at a presence which, while respecting the transcultural principles of efficacy found in all performing techniques, permits the construction of a personal technique, of a *presence with personal codification*.

This is the task of the exercises in the training: to leave behind psychology and the preoccupation with giving life to a character, in order to concentrate on the construction of a scenic presence based on a personal codification - a pre-expressive behaviour.

The apprentice can follow the path of inculturation or the path of acculturation. The objective of both paths is totality, the meeting and integration of the complementary pole which at the beginning was not included. Anyone who starts with a 'magic if' or with any other mental process must *materialise this process into scenic presence* which has to be sensorially perceptible to the spectator. And those who have acquired an accultured behaviour must *integrate their mental-emotional universe*. One path is not better than the other. The two paths have the same crevasses into which the performer can fall. On the one hand, there is the risk of empty forms, technical stereotypes, dynamic mannerisms; on the other, the inadequacy of corporal, sensorial, visible impact on the spectator in spite of the performer's social, poetic and psychological intentions.

The process becomes mutilated if it mobilises only mental, inner and invisible energy which does not succeed in merging with the material, visible and physical form, which the spectator perceives. This is what we often miss in the actor using the inculturation technique in that type of theatre whose point of departure has no roots in corporeality. Furthermore, if performers who codify do not connect with their affective logic and with the asymmetrical coherence of their mental behaviour, then they also turn into an amputated being, a gymnastic toy, a circus act, a two dimensional virtuoso. They may perform feats which astonish us with their acrobatic and technical skills, but they will not attain that dimension of which I have been speaking: the genetic memory, the memory of the times, the mythical memory of our ancestors.

The 'Why': the Meaning

Looking back in time, I see the paths which I have trodden, condensed cores of events, books, meetings, voices, accidental sentences, incidents. These help me to explain to myself why I started to do theatre and why I continue to do it. *How* to do theatre is important. But if I am lucky enough to achieve technical competence and objective knowledge to guide me in the construction of the different levels of a performance and its relationships with the spectators, the question comes up again, even more imperatively: *why* do I do it? Because of exhibitionism? For money? In order to gain social prestige? To be someone whom men and women can admire or desire? To escape my condition, my country, my skin, my thoughts? In order to help those who never asked to be helped? To change society?

I know that theatre can radically change something in society if it changes itself, its way of behaving, of thinking about itself, of presenting or representing itself. I know this because the many paths back to my origins demonstrate it. Looking back now, towards my first day, I see Grotowski, my elder brother. I could also call him my father, my grandfather, my totem. It doesn't matter. The essential thing is to recognise the lineage and be proud of it. At his side, I learned certain fundamental principles about how to do theatre. Through him, I intuited a personal meaning of the profession, why I wanted to do theatre.

In the early sixties in Poland, the communist authorities imposed production norms, a pre-established number of performances and openings for each season. It was the quantity which was important, *how many* spectators, *how many* performances. Grotowski did not want to make many new productions a year. He wanted to prepare just one, but well, and present it to a limited number of spectators in order to maximise the communication. He wanted to establish with these few spectators spatial and emotional relationships which constituted an encounter, a dialogue with themselves, a meditation on the times. In order to fulfil his personal necessity, he had to fight against the historical circumstances, to travel back down the paths towards the origins and rediscover, in his ancestor Stanislavski, theatre as a laboratory, as a privileged place for the creation of new relationships. Grotowski's 'poor theatre' was not a technique, *how* to do theatre. It was *why* he was doing it.

In this period - in 1961, 1962 and 1963 - sometimes only three or four people came to his performances. During the three years that I stayed with him, I watched his struggle for only a handful of spectators. It was his resistance, his stubbornness, his rowing against the current which revealed to the theatre of our age another way of being social, taking a stand and being loyal to one's own values.

One of the most moving and ambiguous myths in Western civilisation tells the story of a man who is searching for his origins. On the path towards his identity he kills his father, begets sons/brothers with his mother, brings the plague down upon an entire population. He goes into exile. But someone follows him, an adolescent: Antigone. Years later, when she goes back to her city, Thebans clash with Thebans, brothers enjoy torturing brothers, children carry arms and have learned to slaughter. All is violence and horror: Thebes is the heart of darkness.

During the civil war in which her brothers have killed one another, Antigone takes a stand. She does not defend her uncle Creon and the law of the state which he represents. Neither does she take to the hills to join her brother's army in the war against the state. She knows her role. And she acts in order to be loyal to it. She leaves the city by night and goes to the countryside, takes a handful of dust and scatters it over her brother's corpse for which Creon has forbidden burial. A symbolic ritual, empty and ineffective against horror. But she performs it because of personal necessity, and pays with her own life.

Antigone's handful of dust, Grotowski's handful of spectators: such derisory actions with which to resist the times and row against the currents. But we cannot erase these actions from our memory. They are at the origin and impel us to continue day after day in spite of isolation, lack of consideration, meagre results, danger. This is theatre: an empty and ineffective ritual which we fill with our 'why', our personal necessity. In some countries on our planet it is celebrated amid general indifference. In others it can cost the lives of those who practise it.

I think that the Odin actors and I belong to the same species as the old man who left his family, set off from the bank and, out in the middle of the river, rowed against the current. It would appear that the inhabitants of the banks who laughed at us were right. Twenty-three years have gone by, many wrinkles line our faces, we are turning grey, we feel the exhaustion of the years and of the craft. But now we are no longer alone. Many others are behind our boat, beside us, in front of us. We are a little flotilla in the middle of the river. We are the third bank. The day the river becomes enraged, its waters will sweep us away and, along with us, the stately buildings with their plush seats and bright lights which are there, on the two banks.

At Qosqo '87 I have seen how you have learned to resist. I look at you and I feel a deep pride: you know how to be *un-divided*, individuals who know *how* to be actors and *why*.

I belong to a theatrical family whose grandmothers are Antigone and Edy Craig. This same family has other members who speak different languages, act in different ways, move in different directions, who have never met me and barely catch a glimpse of me through the stories or the example of other theatre groups. It is a family which knows its origins, which is able to recognise its ancestors, its elder siblings, which does not forget its source. This family refuses to collaborate with the society of amnesia and wants to represent the memory of the times, well aware that the memory which can be represented on stage is a symbolic action for a handful of spectators.

That is why in Brazil, when listening to Guimarâes Rosas' story, *The Third Bank of the River*, I intuited the reason for so many years of work. And why, in Belgrade, in 1976, I called Odin Teatret and the other groups by another name, the kind we give to a person dear to us: Third Theatre.

THE HOUSE WITH TWO DOORS

Eugenio Barba tells of his relationship with Latin American theatre and the influence that it has had on his professional biography. He expounds on the concept of Third Theatre, developing an idea which is complementary to that of refusal: the individual search for a meaning.

Written in the Yucatan village of Chicxulub, Mexico, while starting work on Talabot, this text was first published in La escena latinoamericana, 2, Ed. Galerna (Buenos Aires) and Lemcke Verlag (Kiel), 1989.

I have the impression that the whole of my theatre apprenticeship has been a preparation for Latin America.

For a European, Latin American theatre is recognisable and yet unknown, having developed from the same rootstock but with a different history.

The *ethos* which characterises Latin American theatre - i.e. the whole array of social, political, existential, ethical and communal behaviours - should be remembered by all those who, wherever they may be, ask themselves about the meaning of theatre.

The *ethos* is the totality of our actions in answer to this question. It constitutes the third dimension of the theatre. Theatre is often thought of as being two dimensional, as though the only things deserving attention were aesthetics or ideological tendencies, artistic or technical results. The *ethos* is the dimension of profundity which hides the bonds between one's own individual history and History itself.

The two dimensional vision underestimates the value of Latin American theatre, not because of its geographical or cultural distance, but because of the same lack of perspicacity that disregards vast areas of European theatre.

On a Plane Bound for Caracas

'What is the point of doing theatre today in Latin America where social reality is so dramatic, tensions are so acute and tragedies so omni-present?'

These were the sort of discussions we had on a long night-flight to Caracas. The answer seemed obvious and was typical of that form of abstract reasoning which makes judgements easy.

'What a waste to organise a huge international theatre convention! Isn't it a way of closing one's eyes to far more serious problems?'

Odin Teatret and I were part of a small group of actors, directors and authors who had been invited to the Caracas Festival directed by Carlos

Gimenez, and to the ITI conference on the future of theatre in the Third World. It was the spring of 1976.

'The future of theatre in the Third World? Isn't that an example of a luxury problem?'

Behind these rhetorical questions lies the preconception that theatre is food only for people with full bellies.

We talked about carnival which for us Europeans is now almost non-existent. What meaning can the imported art of theatre have in a continent whose rituals, collective festivities and popular celebrations still possess a vigour incommensurably superior to any theatre performance with its handful of spectators?

Once off the plane, that little group of European actors, directors and authors dispersed amidst the frenzy of the Festival. We from the Odin became involved in certain encounters which induced us to stay in Venezuela longer than we had planned.

We met again La Candelaria from Colombia who had previously been our guests in Holstebro in 1973. We saw their performance *Guadalupe - Años sin cuenta* (Guadalupe - Uncounted Years); 'sin cuenta', pronounced as 'cinquenta' (the fifties), as Santiago García and his company explained to us. It was a fragment of unwritten Colombian history, officially censored, and played with an anger and an irony, and with such a professional mastery that the performance which was neither a happy nor an optimistic one, bubbled over with vitality. Not only did it tell a story, but it was also able to evoke the context in which this story found its full meaning.

We met Mario Delgado for the first time, together with his group, Cuatrotablas, from Lima. One morning, in the tiny room belonging to the Venezuelan group, Contradanza, they showed us their latest production: *La noche larga* (The Long Night). It was the first step, they told us, along a new road. They were trying to do theatre which was perhaps less spectacular than what they had been doing up to now, but which corresponded more closely to their dreams and personal obsessions. We had been expecting a self-confessional performance. What we saw was a meditation through images on the clash of cultures in their country. From that moment, a bond was created between us which time has only strengthened.

We met the Teatro Libre de Bahia. Two years later a couple of our actors stayed with them for several months while studying in Brazil.

We also met the Libre Teatro Libre now consisting of only three members of the once large group gathered around Maria Escudero. The

Argentinian Libre Teatro Libre, from Cordoba, had been famous throughout Latin America for the quality of its performances and for its political commitment. Now, these three actors were presenting *El rostro* (The Face) using self-irony to allude to tragedy. They were already on the road to exile.

In Caracas, Carlos Gimenez gave Odin Teatret the opportunity of new experiences by supporting our wish to move outside the confines of the Festival. We bartered performances in the slum areas, in the Barlovento region of negro culture, and in places where anonymous cultural or theatre groups were active.

A film cooperative, Kurare, together with a few anthropologists, took us into the depths of Venezuelan Amazonia, to a Yanomami *shabono*, where we were given a ritual welcome. There we presented our performances, including those which we usually only show in select situations before a limited number of spectators.

'It is a crazy idea', we told the anthropologists when we first heard their proposition. 'Our theatre can't mean anything to the Yanomani. There is no way we can communicate.' They replied: 'Up to now they have only seen missionaries, anthropologists and government employees. We want to show them the unknown face of the white man'.

There theatre encountered ritual. It was the most heart-rending barter: the exponents of a culture which believes in Progress before a community on the brink of its final destruction.

Before arriving in Caracas, I believed myself to be well-informed on Latin American theatre. I subscribed to *Conjunto*, I knew the groups and personalities mentioned in international magazines, and I had seen the performances which came to the European festivals. I believed them to be the numerous exceptions from a theatrical reality of low density. But from the very first encounter with my Latin American colleagues, I realised that the phenomenon which I had thought of as typically European - myriads of groups scattered everywhere, working stubbornly, ignored by the critics and desperate to invent their own theatre - was also widely diffused in Latin America.

There was an astonishing concentration of subterranean theatre. In the same way, the equivalent reality of European groups was invisible to the two dimensional theatre.

I became aware that there existed a third dimension to the theatre, a Third Theatre.

Third Theatre

I began my career at the beginning of the sixties in almost total isolation. Odin Teatret had set up camp outside the walls of the recognised theatre. It was not a position we had chosen; we had been compelled by circumstances. We did not take part in the polemics of the avant-garde against 'traditional theatre'. Occasionally somebody came to visit us. Sometimes we were invited within the walls of theatre and were praised for our diversity.

We felt we belonged to the same mutation which was producing The Living Theatre, Grotowski's Teatr-Laboratorium, the Open Theatre, the Bread and Puppet and the Teatro Campesino. Craig, Stanislavski, Vachtangov, Copeau, Artaud, Meyerhold, Decroux, Brecht, Sulerzhiski and Osterwa spoke to us through their books. They had also placed themselves or had been placed on the outside. In 1968, a great satirical actor from Italy participated in one of our seminars in Holstebro. Dario Fo enjoyed enormous success in commercial circles in his own country but was abandoning the mainstream and positioning himself among the most radical left-wing groups.

During the seventies, the landscape outside the walls of the theatre became more and more populated by people who were not interested in the theatre as it was going on inside the walls. They wanted to form their own groups and do their own theatre. What were they looking for? They didn't have a sophisticated culture. They didn't claim to be avant-garde. Often they had seen performances by The Living Theatre, read Grotowski's book, or seen or heard about Odin Teatret's performances.

A few months after Caracas, in September 1976, UNESCO and BITEF/Theatre of the Nations in Belgrade asked me to organise a conference on 'research' in theatre.

Researching what? New forms? A new language? Or else a new meaning?

The recent memory of Caracas became interwoven with what I knew of European groups. It was no longer a question of Europe or Latin America, but of the massive existence of an unacknowledged level of theatre which did not respect geographical limits.

I invited both European and Latin American groups to Belgrade. The BITEF organisers had never heard of any of them: they did neither 'traditional' nor 'avant-garde' theatre. In the framework of the festival they risked being taken for representatives of a 'minor' or marginal theatre. This they were not. To demonstrate this, we created a collective performance that lasted for a whole day, from dawn to dusk, in the centre of

Belgrade. It was during this conference that I spoke for the first time of Third Theatre.

Third Theatre does not allude to an artistic tendency, a 'school' or a style. *It indicates a way of giving a meaning to theatre.* Since the start of the twentieth century, many people have asked and continue to ask if theatre can have a meaning in the present era. The question seems to me to be wrongly worded. Is it perhaps the theatre which sometimes *possesses* and sometimes *loses* its meaning, just as one possesses and loses money? The problem concerns only us, we who do theatre. The answers must be individual, embodied in actions which belong to us. The pertinent question is: are we in a position to *give a meaning* to what we do?

Research in theatre, is also a search for a meaning. How, otherwise, can we understand the work of groups who are often autodidacts, not blessed with the respect which surrounds whoever enters our art in a recognisable way, groups who often live as emigrants, and who only succeed in imposing their right to exist with difficulty.

After the Caracas Festival of 1976, Latin America became an essential point of orientation for keeping alive my questions on the meaning of doing theatre. So Odin Teatret went to Peru in '78; to Colombia in '83; to Peru, Colombia and Mexico in '84; to Argentina and Uruguay in '85; again to Argentina and Uruguay in '86; and to Argentina, Uruguay, Brazil and Mexico in '87. In addition to these stays of two to three months, with performances and barters, I often travelled alone in Latin America, meeting groups, holding seminars, journeying in order to know and learn. In 1988, in a house outside Chicxulub on the coast of Yucatan, Odin Teatret withdrew for a few months to prepare its production *Talabot.*

A Cuban friend once told me: you are really a Latin American born in exile.

Is there some truth in this compliment? I believe so.

I grew up in the south of Italy. I became an adult in Norway as an immigrant. My theatre formation took place in Poland. The theatre I have founded is Danish. But amidst the groups of Latin America I feel at home.

In Europe and North America theatre-shells prevail: stone buildings and institutions which recruit different artists from time to time according to the demands of the various productions, where directors follow one upon the other, where continuity is maintained through the organisational structure, by statutes, rules and legal recognition. In Latin America it is theatre groups that prevail, created by men and women. This type of theatre fills out almost the whole landscape here. With the exception of a few big cities like Mexico City, Rio de Janeiro, Sao Paolo and Buenos Aires,

Latin American theatre is characterised by groups.

There are as many differences between the Latin American and European groups as there are similarities. In Europe much importance is given to tendencies and fashions. Some see Third Theatre as a trend which is fashionable, a novelty which gets transformed into a 'genre'.

The Latin American theatres have never enjoyed favourable waves of fashion. They are much less affected by its ebb and flow.

If one were to generalise, one could say that Third Theatre in Europe also represents an existential choice, a reaction to surfeit, indifference and artistic overabundance which is unable to transmit a sense of urgency and necessity.

Third Theatre in Latin America is also an existential choice, but one reacting to a state of penury.

In Europe we run the risk of being seduced by an apparent sense of security. We are citizens of welfare democracies. We have to appeal to our historical conscience to keep in mind the sense of precariousness in which we live, not just as theatre professionals.

In Latin America you would have to be blind and deaf to forget it.

Easter 1987

Towards the end of the seventies I received a letter from Bahia Blanca in Argentina. Coral and Dardo Aguirre with their group, Teatro Alianza, told of their work and precariousness, and of the importance for them of Odin Teatret's existence. 'Don't forget us - you who live in a privileged situation.' They were living under the military dictatorship. Their theatre was attacked, they were beaten up, and one of their actresses was kidnapped, raped and killed. Dardo and Coral were imprisoned. They managed to survive the way so many others had done: through exile. They found work as violinists in Turin's symphony orchestra. There they remained for hardly more than a year. In Turin and the rest of Italy there was the 'war against the state' carried out by the Red Brigade and other armed groups. They thought: if we have to live with violence, it's better to be at home.

Coral and Dardo returned clandestinely to Argentina in 1981. In 1986, in Bahia Blanca, with an effort which was something of a miracle, they organised a meeting of theatre groups on the same lines as those which, from '76 on, had taken place in Belgrade, Bergamo, Madrid-Leiketio, Ayacucho (Peru) and Zacatecas (Mexico). They invited groups from Mexico, Chile, Uruguay, Brazil, Argentina and the Mapuche culture as well as European groups including Odin Teatret. When the meeting was over, the Odin went to Buenos Aires to give performances and do barters.

Suddenly some military units revolted. For three days it was feared that the majority of the armed forces would join them. The shadow of the coup was over the country again.

On Easter Sunday we were all at the Plaza de Mayo. Odin Teatret was a part of that crowd. After those three menacing days filled with anxiety, there was a feeling of profound euphoria, almost one of intoxication over living through a historical hour and participating in an act of justice: the triumph of democracy over arms.

The next day we understood from the newspapers that it had all been a deception, a hoax: the victory had taken place on *their* conditions.

Just like that, from one day to the next, everything changed. *Everything could change at any moment.* The surrender had taken place during the exultation of what seemed like victory. Now we had the sensation that our actions were worthless, that we, as individuals, had no weight. For me, the political precariousness in Argentina strengthened my awareness over the vulnerability of my existence in Europe.

How much Fatherland does a Theatre need?

Hans Meyer believed himself to be German. His compatriots told him he was a Jew. He emigrated. The armies and the police of 'his' country caught up with him. He was sent to Auschwitz. He survived and became a writer. He made an anagram of his surname, transforming it into Jean Améry. Now he had a name like the men of Provence, the land of poets and of the mediaeval heretics who were exterminated at the beginning of the thirteenth century by the Catholic armies who made France into a nation.

Jean Améry devoted his writing to remembering. 'All this has really happened, and therefore can happen again.' He repeated this while around him more and more people grumbled impatiently on still hearing about Auschwitz and the tragedies that by now were *definitely* buried. While a few historians had already begun to use scientific methods to demonstrate that nazism had not really been so different from other regimes of the present day, Jean Améry published *An Intellectual in Auschwitz*. In 1978 he committed suicide.

A chapter of his book is entitled: 'How much fatherland does a theatre need?'. The German language has two words for fatherland: *Vaterland* and *Heimat*, the 'mother country' and 'home', that particular place from which one comes. They are, in fact, two realities and not just two different expressions.

In Latin America I have frequently heard it asked: what does it mean to be Argentinian, Peruvian, Colombian, Venezuelan? What does it mean to be Latin American?

How much fatherland do we need? Let's try to be more precise: how much *Vaterland* or how much *Heimat* do we need?

Now let's think in theatre terms.

An awareness of the precariousness or the uncertainty in defining our own cultural identity from a historical viewpoint is a menace to the soul. In many cultures, it is said that the soul is always at risk of flying away. People feel constantly threatened by a 'crisis of presence'. Something similar happens to us; the source of our creativity seems to dry up when it no longer reflects or accepts a history and values with which we can identify ourselves.

Moreover, we want to discover our identity, not just as an individual, but as part of a community. In effect, this discovery means reconstructing and restoring a past which it is possible to call our own and going back over its numerous paths. But in order to go where?

This question confronts us with two problems. Above all it puts us on guard. The path which turns back is only one side of the coin. Alone, the roots guarantee nothing, even when they do not spring from an illusion. The second problem is precisely that of illusion.

It is true, 'vital illusions' do exist. But how and when are they vital? More often illusions are mortal. Many 'ancient traditions', as we nobly call them, are illusions. These are roads bordered by archaeological ruins. They can be an enormous help to us because they preserve traces of the knowledge and wisdom of many generations. But we alone must decide their meaning and direction. And above all, it is not the traditions which choose us, but we who choose them. A Frenchman can become a Muslim and a Korean can be an excellent conductor of European classical music. The fact of being born in a particular land and of particular parentage does not necessarily mean that our identity is to be found in that land and amongst those forefathers.

How much fatherland (*Vaterland*? *Heimat*?) do we need? But also: how much of a capacity for being or becoming foreigners do we need?

What does it mean to be Bolivian, Brazilian, Uruguayan or Latin American? But also: what does it mean not to be only Latin American, Italian or Danish?

I confess to feeling great respect, sometimes great tenderness, always a certain fear when I see a theatre group racing towards the 'traditions of their native land', towards the Incas, the Mayas, the Aztecs, the Indian cultures ... Or in Europe, towards the Basque, Welsh or Sardinian traditions.

Atahualpa del Cioppo and the Tradition-in-life

In the autumn of 1974 a Uruguayan director came to Odin Teatret to study for several months. I was struck by his behaviour: it was that of someone who had met a master. That was how I heard about Atahualpa del Cioppo for the first time. Later I came upon his traces everywhere I went in Latin America. Even before I met him, I associated him mentally with Bertolt Brecht, in part because of the fact of his exile.

I met him ten years later in Mexico. He was over eighty, a nomad who had worked for a long time in many different countries. Even now he travels continuously. In spite of everything he has had to witness, in spite of all those who have turned their backs on him, he will not submit to a distrust in humanity. In spite of the steadfastness of his ideas, he retains a curiosity and openness with regard to the choices of others.

Many masters in India or Japan maintain that tradition doesn't exist: 'I am the tradition; with me it lives and with me it dies'.

Atahualpa del Cioppo is a master because he is a tradition-in-life. He is a testimony to how one can give a meaning and a *Heimat* to one's own theatre.

In 1987 UNESCO organised a conference in Lima on 'Dramaturgy in Latin America and the Caribbean'. One evening the Peruvian guests took the delegates to see a performance in Villa Salvador, the large autonomous *barrio* outside Lima. The self-helping achievements of its inhabitants have won it great international acclaim and a nomination for the Nobel Peace Prize. The barrio stretches out towards the dunes along the coast, its houses built on sand. After the open-air performance on the *arenal*, César Escuza, the director of the group, invited us for a drink. In a voice full of emotion, he turned to the Colombian director, Enrique Buenaventura, and said: 'Our performance is dedicated to you, because your writings and your example have been our masters'.

Masters serve only to help us find our own path and to realise a manifold tradition-in-life.

A House with Two Doors

The search for an identity in Latin American theatre occurs in the relative absence of a theatre which represents continuity with the past.

European theatre possesses several niches. One of these is that of the so-called traditional theatre. It hands down and develops the European theatre of the preceding centuries. The artists and scholars working within this niche refer to Molière or the Commedia dell'Arte, Racine or Shakespeare, Chekhov or Beckett as different representatives, scattered through time, of an uninterrupted theatrical continuity.

This continuity no longer exists in the theatre groups' niche. But whilst European theatre groups are also able to define themselves through that which separates them from the 'traditional theatre', in general the Latin American ones have nothing from which to distance themselves. For this reason they are all, both European and Latin American, similar to and yet different from each other; similar because their conditions of work present analogous characteristics, but diverse because their horizons are different. On one side, in the background, there are the walls of the theatre behind which those who are tired or want to flee may seek shelter. On the other, no such walls exist.

The European groups can define themselves merely by pointing out the theatre they do not do and do not want to do. The Latin American groups are forced to define themselves only on the basis of what they do and what they want to do.

But it is not this that hinders those who do theatre in Latin America in their search for an identity. A more serious problem is the isolation from the house of their ancestors, from the reflections and testimonies of their predecessors.

This does not mean that in Latin America there is a lack of reflection on theatre. On the contrary: suffice it to think of Enrique Buenaventura or Augusto Boal and of their presence in a large section of European theatre too. But a series of circumstances has meant that too many books are lacking. Texts by Dullin, Delsarte, Tairov and Eisenstein, even Stanislavski and Meyerhold, of Appia, Craig, Vaktangov, Copeau or Zeami have not been published or are hard to come by.

Practical and creative work has to be accompanied by a knowledge that takes into account who came before. Conscious of this necessity, Edgar Ceballos, a young director in Mexico City, interrupted the artistic career on which he had just embarked and became a publisher. He struggles against the enforced ignorance which stifles, in the present, the breath of the past. His publishing house, Gaceta/Escenologia, produces the most significant books on theatre history and practice, as well as the magazine *Máscara* which alludes to *The Mask* with which Gordon Craig, in the twenties, attacked the cultural void surrounding performance and its history in Europe. Those were the years when theatre was identified almost exclusively with dramatic texts.

A sound knowledge of our history (ours as theatre people, and not as Latin Americans or Europeans) is all the more necessary in that our creations and our work techniques only survive in time as memory. It is essential that these be linked to a 'professional memory'.

About twenty years ago, when the Comuna Baires began its activities in Buenos Aires, outside every theatre organisation, it started publishing *Teatro 70*, a magazine which, instead of reviewing performances or writing about topical events, devoted itself to the diffusion of theoretical and practical knowledge in theatre work. In the course of these years I have met many colleagues living in Latin America, who have emigrated or are in exile in Europe, and who still remember today how it was this magazine that helped them to discover the possible worlds of the theatre.

Our identity is, on the one hand, individual, deriving from our biography, from the space and time in which we live. On the other hand, it must be a professional identity connecting us to the people of our profession beyond the limits of time and space. It is a question of two poles, each very different to the other, but one cannot exist without the other.

We can think of them as two doors to the same house, doors for entering but also for taking flight when the walls of the house become too suffocating. A poem by Brecht recalls a saying which belongs to the wisdom of exile: be sure that your house always has two doors. It is an allusion to sudden escapes, should the police arrive unexpectedly, and to the obligation to resist. This poem has other implications for those who pursue a meaning in theatre and do not accept the world (including that of the theatre) as it is.

The Long Night

In 1986, at the Montevideo festival, I saw *Lo que está en el aire* (That which is in the air), a performance by the Chilean group Ictus. 'Ictus' means 'fish' in Greek. It was the sign of the Messiah which those who were persecuted used in secret to recognise each other. The fish is also a sign of the life which exists below the surface. *Lo que está en el aire* was a realistic and metaphorical performance showing an oppressive reality and yet, in spite of everything, defending the possibility of hope beyond tragedy.

The Chilean actor and director, Hector Noguera, answered my questions. An explicit one: how is it possible that a dictatorship allows this kind of theatre? And an implicit one: does it have a meaning? He explained to me that their theatre certainly didn't constitute a danger for the regime. And the fact that they were inoffensive didn't threaten the meaning that they gave to their own work. 'We are not doing theatre against the Chilean authorities', he said. 'We are working for a parallel Chile.' It struck me that he was not speaking in terms of time, and thinking of the future, but in terms of space, and thinking of a reality parallel to the existing one and which it was necessary to regard as foreign.

Perhaps that is why the actor, Roberto Parada, refused to cancel a performance in Santiago on the evening when they told him, during the interval, that his son had been murdered by the killers of Acción Pacificadora. At that time, Amnesty International spread the news that members of the Ictus group as well as numerous other theatre people risked death if they did not leave the country. But they remained through *la noche larga*, the long night.

La noche larga was the title of the performance by the Peruvian group, Cuatrotablas, that we had seen in Caracas in 1976 when Latin American theatre burst into the life of Odin Teatret. We were with Cuatrotablas in '78 when they organised a meeting of theatre groups in Ayacucho, in the Andes. The edicts of the military government which had just increased food prices had provoked revolts throughout the country, and a curfew had been imposed. The precariousness exploded. But the Cuatrotablos did not allow it to affect them. The curfew did not suffocate the meeting of Latin American groups, nor the possibility to show their work in the light of day.

Times have changed - but not for the better. Many forms of two dimensional theatre have followed one upon another. Several new roads of research have opened up for me and for Odin Teatret. We founded ISTA (the International School of Theatre Anthropology), and those who believe that life is divided into phases thought that for us of the Odin, the phase of Third Theatre was finished. On the contrary, its meaning has remained intact during all these years. For this reason we were together with Cuatrotablas in Huampani ten years later for a new meeting of Latin American groups in 1988, in a Peru ravaged by civil war and repression.

And every year Odin Teatret goes in search of encounters and barters in Chile or Brazil, Mexico or Uruguay.

Talking of Influences

Some readers may well think that there has been a new influence on Latin American theatre by European culture, this time in the form of 'odinism'. That's how the automatisms of two-dimensional thought function with regard to theatre and its cult of so-called originality.

I first visited Latin America in 1973, but had no contact with theatre. I travelled alone by bus from Cochabamba in Bolivia, across the Andes to the Amazonian jungle, to Iquitos, Leticia, and from there via Barranquilla in the Caribbean to Panama, and again by bus through Central America to Mexico.

Many of my experiences on that trip, the moments of dismay and indignation, re-emerged in Odin Teatret's performance *Come! And the Day will be Ours* which was presented for the first time in Caracas in '76 and told of the meeting between European immigrants and the North American Indians.

During that journey, far away from the theatre, I reflected on the destiny of two Spaniards, Gonzalo Guerrero and Jeronimo de Aguilar. After being shipwrecked on the coast of Yucatan in 1511, they were captured by the Mayas and became integrated into their society, becoming important military leaders. On the arrival of Cortés, Jeronimo de Aguilar was finally reunited with his compatriots and was able to furnish them with vital information about the language and customs of the local populations. Gonzalo Guerrero behaved in a totally opposite way, preferring the second of his homelands and remaining with his Mayan wife and children who became the foundation of a new race. He died from an arquebus shot in 1536, fighting against soldiers who had the same culture and the same roots as himself. Gonzalo Guerrero and Jeronimo de Aguilar represent the two alternatives that spring to mind each time one thinks about the meeting of people from different lands: conquest or assimilation.

And yet who could imagine Odin Teatret as a group that had been assimilated into Latin American theatre? Nevertheless, the people we have met, the theatre groups to whom we have become attached, their history, their performances and their historical and cultural context have marked us deeply and influenced our performances. Just like *Come! And the Day will be Ours*, *The Million* was also interwoven with Latin American memories and experiences. *Brecht's Ashes* was a reflection on recent European history, on an intellectual in exile, but was also nourished by anxieties permeating the Latin American countries. *The Gospel according to Oxyrhyncus* (Oxyrhyncus is the ancient name of the Egyptian city where important Gnostic texts were found) was built up around our reinvention of the popular revolt of the town of Canudo, images of the arid Brazilian *sertão* and its outlaws, visions of Guimarâes Rosa, the meticulous prose of Euclides da Cunha, and the ornate style of *The War of the End of the World* by Vargas Llosa. Other Latin American presences within our theatre are more technical, bound up with the actors' individual work, and are therefore more difficult to define in words. I shall only mention the samba as we saw it re-elaborated by an actor from the Teatro Libre de Bahia, and which inspired our training.

If speaking in terms of 'influence' makes any sense, I should recognise that Odin Teatret has itself been more influenced by its meeting with Latin American theatre than the latter has by us.

But that is a way of thinking which to me is wrong.

Gonzalo Guerrero and Jeronimo de Aguilar are not the only possible alternatives. Through the second door of the house - the professional one - a common identity passes, making it difficult to say what belongs to the one and what to the other, and above all making it impossible to distinguish between something that comes from one's own culture and something coming from the outside. Everything one does in theatre belongs to our professional *Heimat*, the home of theatre people.

The Cuatrotablas had not yet seen our *Come! And the Day will be Ours* when they invited us to their performance in Caracas. They had been working in Lima, we in Holstebro. Their actors were Peruvian and ours were Scandinavian, except for one Italian. Even so, in *La noche larga* we found many elements that echoed parts of our own performance. Two or three of our most original solutions seemed to reflect the originality of the Cuatrotablas. If the circumstances had not made it impossible, anybody would have sworn that either one of us had been inspired by the performance of the other and such had been the influence that whole fragments had been quoted.

When some characteristics of one theatre resemble those of another, critics and experts immediately begin to comment. Words like '*déjà vu*', 'copy', 'influence', 'imitation', 'acculturation' fly around. Sometimes their murmurs become judgements and condemnations. Then the life of theatre is seriously threatened.

There cannot exist a *pure* Latin American, Brazilian, European, Danish, Florentine or Liverpudlian theatre. It is not purity that guarantees individual identity and cultural originality. On the other hand, professional identity has an indelible transcultural character.

While speaking of influences, I would like to say: there's no need to worry if, in the course of events, one leans momentarily for support on someone else. Paths which cross each other cannot avoid separating. Don't worry if you notice similarities. It is all a part of life's flow. Everything that is alive ends up by finding its own way. Don't obstruct the life of the theatre with scarecrows which don't take into account the dimension of *ethos*. Only the dead resemble one another in the end.

THE LEGACY FROM US TO OURSELVES

The concept of Third Theatre was founded on two ideas: refusal and search for a personal meaning. In this text they are articulated in a complementary way. The refusal becomes the premise of one's personal meaning in theatre practice. This complementarity sharpens the concept of Third Theatre and places it in a historical perspective which reveals a professional genealogy.

Published for the first time in La escena latinoamericana, 6, *Buenos Aires 1991, this article has been translated into many languages, becoming one of Eugenio Barba's key texts.*

The Third Theatre suggests a way of shaping our 'why'. It is not a theatrical style, nor an alliance of groups, still less a movement or international association; nor is it a school, an aesthetic, or set of techniques. Nor even is it one of those 'new trends' we associate with the 1970s. Critics and theatre historians may regard it with interest and passion, or choose to ignore it altogether: the Third Theatre continues to exist just the same. The name is a recent invention, the condition which it designates, however, is far from recent.

Louis Jouvet once made an observation which has the echo of an enigma: 'There is a legacy from us to ourselves'. From this, a number of fundamental questions follow: Is the legacy which I built up still in my hands? Can I still recognise its value, or has it been tarnished by the passage of time, by the practice of the trade, or by its attraction to the centre of the planet Theatre?

That enigma and these questions concern the Third Theatre. We could say that they *are* the Third Theatre. They are the expression of everything that escapes the gravitational pull and, like the rings of Saturn, refuses to be flattened out.

Sometimes the force which flattens out is formed by what appears to be wisdom: It no longer makes sense to do theatre, some say. Especially when they live in that second-rate luxury hotel called Europe, and when, after years of work, they look around and contemplate the indifference which surrounds them.

Far away, often beyond the seas, others like them, but in profoundly different contexts, sometimes feel bewildered by the commitment necessary to create theatre when they see the tiny impact it has on social realities which threaten to collapse into barbarism.

'Theatre no longer makes sense.' Who would dare to uphold the contrary?

***

The 'demon of high noon': thus the ancients described that moment of bewilderment which accompanies the achievement of maturity and clarity. Precisely when the sun is at its height and floods everything with a sharp light, one sometimes feels out of place. The legacy of one's initial choices now seems senseless. It is as if the present instant crushed every other set of values. The ancients used to assert that when the demon of high noon passes by, the monk feels that his vocation no longer has any meaning; the knight dreams of the plough; the peasant yearns for a wandering life under arms.

Who would dare to affirm that the act of doing theatre in itself has some meaning? Sometimes it seems to us that all meaning has drained out of the reality of this craft, leaving only dry stones and mud. Perhaps it had some meaning, once, before the modern performance industry, mass culture, and the new myths and rites of the younger generation robbed the practice of theatre of its legitimacy and effectiveness. These are historical events of greater significance than us. That is why we are bewildered; that is why we don't seem able to recapture the motivation which drove us on in the early days of our work. Perhaps we were idealistic in that first phase. Now we feel more mature, but also dried up, and sometimes disillusioned.

This is precisely the moment when we are most likely to be a prey to illusion: the illusion by which things and actions seem to have a meaning in themselves, and that meaning seems to wax and wane for external reasons almost without us noticing it.

Action belongs to us, not its results. Results draw their meaning from context, from the time, from the spectators and their memory.

We cannot define the value of our performances and the message they will carry. Sometimes History with a capital H forges the inner meaning that the results of doing theatre may convey. Slovski tells of an amateur performance for soldiers behind the Russian front line during the First World War. It was Chekhov's *The Proposal,* a satirical and realistic sketch quite without subversive intent. But in the end, when the protagonist flees from his bride's vulgar and oppressive household, all the soldiers in the audience, as if their eyes had suddenly been opened, got up and deserted from the army.

Jan Kott tells how, when news of events at the Twentieth Congress of the Soviet Communist Party was gradually filtering through to Warsaw, they conferred an incisive topicality on what had seemed until then merely an experimental avant-garde piece, *Waiting for Godot,* but which now took on allegorical and political meaning. The same play for the inmates of the San Quentin penitentiary was crude realism.

Of course, these are extreme examples, almost parables. Reality is made up of delicate nuances. Parables serve to remind us of those abstractions which may help to guide us. That is: the results of the action of doing theatre do not belong to us. Only the action itself does. It is our fault if our doing theatre loses its sense in *our* eyes.

It would be foolish to become discouraged by something which has been obvious for almost a century: theatre is an artistic activity in search of meaning. It is, in itself, the archaeological remains of another time.

Into these archaeological remains, which have lost their immediate usefulness, we inject values which change with the times. We may adopt the current values according to the spirit of the time and culture in which we live. Or we may live like the disinherited and discover our legacy ourselves. We may repeat to ourselves that we are not the inheritors of a 'great tradition', but that 'there is a legacy from us to ourselves'.

***

There are people who, when referring to the Third Theatre, mean a fringe, something on the outer limits, the result of deliberate choice or unjust discrimination. This is not what defines us even if it sometimes weighs heavy on our experience. Without a legacy it is not only the child who is disinherited unjustly (or justly), but also the foreigner with bare hands.

When Jouvet spoke of a 'legacy from us to ourselves' he was summing up the sense of many stories which have changed the spirit of twentieth-century theatre. These were stories of individuals, not of institutions. They were stories of foreigners in the theatre.

Who are these foreigners, and what does it mean to say that they are bare-handed?

Recurring again and again in our writings are the names of 'masters' and 'founding fathers' such as Craig, Stanislavski, Copeau, Brecht, Artaud, Meyerhold, Beck, and one or two others. Among those living, Grotowski's name constantly appears. Often we forget, unjustly, names like Joan Littlewood, or the names of those who opened up new directions in the theatre of the southern hemisphere: Atahualpa del Cioppo or Enrique Buenaventura, Vicente Revuelta or Santiago García.

These are artists whose performances have left an indelible mark on the memory of many who saw them. They are original theoreticians and strategists of the theatre. But the roots of their strength lie outside the theatre; they all entered it bringing with them a personal 'longing', recasting it as a new province of a lost spiritual land, either threatened or threatening, different for each one of them: religion, anarchy, revolution, the time of the 'new man', an obscure but tireless individual revolt.

In order to 'invent' a meaning for their own legacy to themselves, each one of them concentrated on specific elements of stage practice, leaving others to one side. They preferred to work in depth in a particular area rather than skate over the whole surface.

If we observe their history with unprejudiced eyes, and free from that kind of idolatry which 'greatness' fosters, we realise that every 'great' figure has laboured under a handicap. They were without the means which those artists who become the favourites of their time enjoy. Some of these handicaps remain hidden under the dust of the past, others emerge with particular clarity. Stanislavski failed to accept himself as an actor; Artaud did not succeed in giving material form to his visions; Brecht could not do without an orthodoxy, nor was he able to come to terms with it in his artistic practice, saturated with individualism and anarchy.

By transforming the 'longing' and the handicaps into signs of differ-ence, these masters became foreigners. They constructed an autonomous meaning for their action of doing theatre. And since they abandoned, or were forced to abandon, some of the defences of theatre, we can speak of them as 'foreigners with bare hands'. In fact, before penetrating into unknown territory, they had not yet acquired sufficient fame to put them on safe ground nor, in abandoning the most common practices, had they substituted more exotic but prestigious techniques for them.

We need to be clear here: the comedians of the Commedia dell'Arte, who spread throughout Europe in the sixteenth and seventeenth centuries, were foreigners, yes, but not bare-handed. Sada Yacco and her actor-dancers, who imported into the West the image of a Japanese theatrical tradition formed on the basis of an intelligent blend of artistic elements, were foreigners, but not bare-handed. And the same could be said of Wagner, Eleonora Duse, Nijinski.

'Foreigners with bare hands': these were not only Stanislavski, but also the young actors of the agit-prop theatres; not only Artaud, but also women's theatre groups struggling for the vote in early twentieth-century England (a Craig excelled here too: the almost unknown sister of the famous inventor of theatre direction). Copeau was a foreigner with bare hands, as were those idealist students in early twentieth-century Russia who, apparently simple amateurs, gave all their time and strength to the theatre, finding there a valid response to the need for ethical rigour and religious attitudes without faith.

The planet Theatre has its outlying zones, its fringe areas, its depressed or divergent regions. They may be far from the centre, but this does not mean they have acquired their own autonomy.

The amateur theatre is deliberately on the fringe when it finds its meaning by mirroring the images and behaviour of 'major' theatre. This does not mean that, among the amateurs at certain times, there have not been extremely innovative 'laboratories'; think of the aristocratic theatre of the eighteenth century, of the performances of Voltaire or Vittorio Alfieri - or Nohant, where George Sand, her family, friends and Frederic Chopin conducted their experiments in the mid-nineteenth century.

The planet Theatre has, in fact, its protected and higher regions, just as it has its areas of discrimination. The theatre of the fairs was one such; the small theatres of the Boulevard du Temple in Paris, in one of which the great Deburau worked, were culturally on the fringe. The Criollo Circus in Argentina seemed 'peripheral', and so did the boundless territory of variety, music hall, and operetta, culturally discredited, but from which the rebellious theatres and the avant-garde drew inspiration, turning their backs on Ibsen, Shakespeare and Sophocles.

The list could be much longer; we could recall the so-called 'popular' theatres, or the many times when the mountebanks, in their wanderings, brought with them the spirit of a theatre of the future. All this constitutes the planet Theatre in whose centre are the monumental edifices of the Comédie Française or of the imperial theatres of pre-Revolutionary Russia, of the Weimar theatre directed by Goethe, or of Wagner's Bayreuth.

But the planet is not everything. We must look beyond the thousand differences which constitute its geography, beyond its centre and fringe zones, and discover the scarcely definable nebula which escapes its gravitational pull and revolves around the planet.

***

We have spoken of the demon of high noon. Let us now turn to Saturn. In olden times, people used to say that artists, intellectuals, and thinkers were 'born under Saturn'. Before becoming a planet, Saturn was a god, the source of talent, melancholy and indolence, closely linked with *Lua Mater* - she, too, a goddess with ambiguous attributes, creator but also destroyer of both good and evil things. Those 'born under Saturn', when subject to moods of melancholy, would hear a whistle in their ears. So it was not only for the sake of expression that images of men and women under the influence of melancholy, like the famous one by Dürer, appear with their head on one side supported by a hand protecting the cheek and ear. A whistle, like some arcane voice, tormented them.

Now, however, Saturn is reduced to being a planet only; it revolves with great velocity on its own axis, and its day lasts ten hours and fourteen minutes. It therefore has a high centripetal force, attracting any mass moving in its space and flattening this against its crust. Which is why the surface of Saturn appears bruised under this relentless hail of meteorites. But what makes this opaque and pitted planet fascinating is its rings, those apparently nebulous concentric circles which escape its gravitational pull.

Thus we return to our point of departure and to the reason which makes Saturn (ex-god and now planet) instructive for our argument. In fact, Saturn's rings are not vapour, or gaseous, shapeless mass; they are made up of innumerable independent solid bodies, some large, some tiny, all moving at their own speed, impelled by their own energy, and with their own cycles of rotation and revolution.

This lack of uniformity, this changing dynamic pattern of tiny diverse worlds and apparent disorder, all give the impression of a nebula. Saturn's rings do not form a compact mass, but are made up of everything that escapes the compact mass of the planet, resisting its force of attraction. But every nucleus, let's not forget, is itself a world in its own right, solid, well-defined, and independent. It follows its own course, in an orbit in connection with others.

The difficulty in understanding what the Third Theatre is, depends on the search for a unitary definition which fixes in one mould the meaning of a theatre reality which is different. But the Third Theatre may be defined precisely by the lack of a unitary meaning. It is the sum of all those theatres which are, each in its own way, constructors of meaning. Each of them defines in an autonomous way the personal meaning of their doing theatre, what Jouvet called 'the legacy from us to ourselves'. But, and this is what is important, each defines its meaning and legacy by embodying them in a precise activity and through a distinct professional identity.

We all attribute a personal, intimate, and private meaning to our own actions, quite independently from the meaning which they take on from an objective standpoint. In just the same way as, in Stanislavskian terms, every text has its sub-text, Saturn's rings are something else: here, that which would elsewhere be sub-text becomes text. The personal and unique motivation for doing theatre is converted into recognisable form. It gives force to autonomous ways of organisation and generates separate identity.

For this reason, those who think that the Third Theatre must have an ideology, a unitary doctrine, something which transforms it into a well-defined artistic movement, a banner to which everyone can rally, are mistaken. This would be like trying to reduce Saturn's rings to a new planet.

What is this yearning for a definition, this search for a category at all costs, a banner to fight under? It is the yearning for something which will endure. A warped way of thinking makes us believe that doctrines are more concrete and durable than biographies.

And yet, when we recall the theatre of the past, it is often the planet's rings that spring to mind rather than the central zones. And almost always, we recall men and women, not movements or banners. It is the history of single individuals that nourishes our artistic memory and provides our craft and our quest with ancestors.

More than the powerful Russian imperial theatres, packed with audiences, the object of constant attention and acclaim by the critics and the spectators who matter, we recall those amateur studios set up by obscure young people, producing few performances, with long rehearsal times and sparse spectators, where Sulerzhitski, Vachtangov, Stanislavski and Meyerhold worked. Performances which received standing ovations, and figured prominently in all the papers, have been blown by the wind from conscious memory, while Gordon Craig in Florence stands out, a solitary worker, determined not to go on with performances, yet an inexhaustible constructor of his own meaning in theatre. Or else there is Artaud, with his wounded soul, whom we now remember as the representative of his time, rather than the famous of the Comédie Française.

Were all these part of the Third Theatre?

When I began to talk about the Third Theatre in 1976 I felt that it was not an aesthetic category, nor simply a sociological category of non-aligned theatre. Today, it is clear to me that the essential character of the Third Theatre is the autonomous construction of a meaning which does not recognise the boundaries assigned to our craft by the surrounding culture.

This search for meaning brings together many theatres and artists of yesterday and today. It matters little what name is given to them, whether they are called 'great' or 'little', 'minor' or 'obscure'. What matters is that they are all related through their flight from the centripetal force of the planet Theatre. Taken together, they constitute an image of theatre which responds in a vital way to the bewilderment and anguish of the demon of high noon: a theatre which does not give in to the last and most dangerous illusion of its 'smallness' - and which from this awareness draws strength and intelligence to transcend itself.

So the Third Theatre has many ancestors. Some were personalities whom history now recognises as of fundamental importance for the quality of our craft; others hid themselves away anonymously behind generalised labels. Thus, concealed behind the term *studijnost*, we fail to discern the faces of those young people already referred to, who created a group of theatrical islands which, in their values and intentions, transcended the limits of conventional theatre in early twentieth-century Russia.

Similarly we can scarcely make out the faces of those who founded the Teatro di Massa (Theatre of the Masses) in Italy after the Second World War. Behind this name there was a highly differentiated reality, substantially analogous with the experiments and experiences of theatre groups in the 1970's: a re-invention of theatre, of its organisation and social context, of its professional qualifications, of its cultural ambitions and dramatic structure, and its methods of communicating technical knowledge. Above all, it was a way in which hundreds of young people used the shell of theatre to build their own personal and political identities, creating relationships that corresponded with their own ideals and dreams.

It lasted only a very few years. Of this last example, Teatro di Massa, almost no trace survives in the written memory that makes up so-called theatre history. I have chosen it precisely because it was apparently evanescent. In that archipelago of theatre islands, great and small, that constitute the ring round the planet Theatre, there are silent regions as well as famous artists. The legacy which each one of us succeeds in establishing for ourselves implies not only the recognition of luminary influences but the rehabilitation of those unjustly forgotten. Among the ancestors of the Third Theatre, we are also influenced by those who are anonymous.

***

The search in the heaven of ideas is one way to discover, as in a mirror, the secrets of our biography. I often use metaphors: the legacy of each one of us to ourselves can never be repeated. One can try to capture its profile in images which others, later, will have to translate into terms of their own professional experiences and lives.

Theatres made of stone which may be identified with the name of an institution represent themselves, not the people who inhabit them. They endure unruffled in time. Their inhabitants of the moment celebrate anniversaries and centenaries nourished by the illusion that this long time-span represents a precious sense of continuity and the valuable asset of tradition and history.

Those theatres which are identified with the relationships between a handful of people - groups, companies or ensembles - disappear much more quickly. Not because their importance weighs light, but because they are not made of stone, are not institutions, but theatre-in-life.

Many groups break up or give up for reasons which are external to them, because of internal disagreements or outworn relationships. Experience teaches that it is extremely difficult for a group to stay together for more than ten years. It is not their disappearance that astounds us. Rather we are more surprised by the survival of some groups, and should reflect on the causes of their longevity. Inventing our own meaning for doing theatre implies the will and capacity to depart from values currently in vogue at the centre of the planet Theatre. It implies the strength to venture out into the nebula, into the orbit of the planet's rings.

But if some do depart from the centre, obeying an inevitable impulse, urged by an artistic and existential longing which renders inadequate for them the practices of the present, others, by contrast, were born far from the bruised surface of the planet. They know only the rings round Saturn, and almost nothing of the imposing planet around which they rotate at different speeds. Sometimes they are attracted and seduced by the planet's consistency and stability, and by the fact that, here, 'meaning' seems established for all time. In vain they aspire to identify with its crust.

The condition of the Third Theatre is, consciously or unconsciously, the search for meaning. But we must not be seduced by the nobility of the language; search for meaning signifies above all a personal discovery of the craft.

It is easy to make the word 'craft' banal, as if it were associated solely with 'technique' and 'routine'. But a craft means something quite different: the patient building up of our own physical, mental, intellectual and emotional relationship with texts and spectators, without conforming to those balanced and proved relationships current at the centre of theatre. This means devising performances which can do without traditional audiences, and which can invent their own spectators. It means knowing how to look for and find money without embodying those values favoured (for economic, ideological or cultural reasons) by those who invest resources in the development of the theatre.

All this is most exclusively craft: the technique of the actor, of the director, dramaturgy, administrative skill. Only in very small part is it idealism and spirit of revolt. To invent one's own meaning, in fact, signifies above all knowing how to seek the means to find it.

It is true: what I have called a 'very small part' is the essential core. However, it concerns that part of our being which is subject to continuous obfuscations, to periods of silence, fatigue, or discouragement. It is a dark sea abounding in fish, which at times appears flooded with light and at others is a source of bewilderment, reduced to the infertile bitterness of salt. One can't go on for long with one's eyes fixed on the stars and one's heart abandoned to the waves. You need the solidly built bridge of a ship.

Everyone ought to be able to translate these metaphors into the concrete reality of a personal language. This, too, is part of the craft. Skill and knowledge enable us to transcend our condition and to become an example which, for a few, is also a legacy.

27. 'How can we shatter the circle of the theatre? Without loosing our identity, since we are a theatre group. Without letting our identity imprison us.' (Tom Fjordefalk in Paris, 1977)

28. 'It is never possible to be "outside society". One can only diverge from its norm.' (Iben Nagel Rasmussen, Tom Fjordefalk, Tage Larsen and Roberta Carreri, Sardinia, 1975)

29. 'Theatre is a means to escape the reasoning of the tamers, to break the circle of solitude. To answer this way would be to answer with the truth. But only one face of the truth.' (Anabasis in Ayacucho, Peru, 1978)

30. *'From the point of view of those who possess the mastery of words, we may resemble mutes who express themselves by way of strange signs, an almost private language of images. From the point of view of mutes, we are mutes who succeed in speaking.' (Else Marie Laukvik and Iben Nagel Rasmussen, Peru, 1978)*

31. *'One sad truth has it that when you are few, you can achieve nothing. It is so evident that it is not worth mentioning. How false it can be is something that can and must be tested.' (Odin Teatret on a visit to Pablo Neruda's house in Isla Negra, Chile, 1988)*

32. 'Time will decide the meaning and value of our actions. But, in fact, time is the others, those who will come after us.' (Eugenio Barba in Peru, 1978)

33. 'I believe that I continue to do theatre because it gives me the chance to meet men and women who do not feel at ease in their condition and keep standing on tiptoe as though, one day, they were going to fly.' (Odin Teatret and Cuatrotablas celebrating their reunion in Peru, 1988)

34. 'This is the paradox of the Third Theatre: to submerge oneself, as a group, in the universe of fiction in order to find the courage not to pretend'. (Iben Nagel Rasmussen and Jan Torp in Carpignano, 1974)

35. *'If Odin Teatret possesses some power of attraction, it is not solely due to artistic results but to something that transcends them. Our mutation appears to appeal to the dream and*

necessities of other crabs on their march towards horizons of sand.' (Odin Teatret in Chicxulub, Yucatan, Mexico, 1988, during the preparation of Talabot)

V

IDENTITY: LEGACY

*I do not work
to compose treatises, but to extend
that island of freedom which I carry
within me. I must solve the problem
of freedom and tyranny in a practical way.
This means that my activity must leave
traces, examples of freedom.*

Jerzy Grotowski:
You are someone's son

36. Iben Nagel Rasmussen in Sardinia, 1975.

THE SHADOW OF ANTIGONE

Address given by Eugenio Barba at the Venice Biennale in 1985 where Odin Teatret presented The Gospel according to Oxyrhyncus. *With this text, the theme of identity first enters into Eugenio Barba's writings, to be further developed in the nineties until it becomes a central theme.*

Referring to the scene in The Gospel according to Oxyrhyncus *in which the Grand Inquisitor tries to erase the shadow of Antigone from the earth, Barba proposes handing down as a legacy one's own shadow, a symbol of refusal which may nourish the spirit of revolt in future generations. Identity is thus seen as the manifestation of one's individuality through refusal.*

First published in Teatro Festival, 2, *Parma 1986.*

We are at *The Gospel according to Oxyrhyncus,* Odin Teatret's latest production. A woman called Antigone has just covered her brother's severed head with a piece of her clothing. His head had been set out as a warning. Her action is interrupted by a man called Jehuda, the Grand Inquisitor, a keeper of the law. He approaches Antigone who prostrates herself. Jehuda, the Grand Inquisitor, draws out of his hat the bunch of flowers hiding the knife he has already used to kill other characters in the performance. He holds the flowers over Antigone's neck. But he does not kill her. Instead he circles around her and, at that moment, the darkness which earlier had blanketed the room is dispelled by the appearance of a golden light, the sun.

Jehuda searches the floor with his knife; he finds Antigone's shadow and starts to scrape at its edges. He outlines the shadow with the dagger and at the same time seems to be trying to efface it.

And so the scene continues, the knife trying to obliterate the shadow and the shadow inexorably advancing.

I worked for a long time to find all the details for this scene, without knowing why. I asked myself all the while: why am I working so much on this scene, why is this scene so essential for me?

On the 8th of August, in Holstebro, I was watching television. For nearly the entire evening, the programmes commemorated the anniversary of a historical event: 40 years earlier, the atom bomb was dropped on Hiroshima. Among other news items was the report that the pilot of the plane which had dropped the second atom bomb on Nagasaki had committed suicide. And then came the customary images, those which by now belong to ... I would not say to our imaginary museum, but to our very real museum which houses the images of our individual-collective memory. Seeing these images again, I realised that I needed to look for yet another. In my library, I took down a book which I had bought in Japan and there I found the explanation for the scene in *The Gospel according to Oxyrhyncus* on which I had worked so much. A postcard bought at the Atomic Museum in Hiroshima shows three steps, the entrance to a bank, on which a shadow had been imprinted. A man was climbing these three granite steps when the bomb exploded and the heat of the deflagration stamped his presence into the stone.

Then I understood why Jehuda persisted in trying to obliterate Antigone's shadow: because it is easy to kill bodies, very easy, but some bodies leave shadows, as if their lives were so loaded with energy that they remain imprinted on history. Even if physically they have vanished, their shadows are there to darken the beautiful landscape.

There are people who have left deep shadows on the history of our profession. And there are many Jehudas who try to erase their shadows. But the shadows remain for those who know how to grasp the meaning of history, for those who want to remember, who do not want to lose the memory.

I have mentioned the beautiful landscape and the shadows which darken it. Since some people think that theatre emanates from literature, let's listen to a playwright, Heiner Müller, one of the most fascinating contemporary writers: 'The sun shines on the beautiful landscape in the time of betrayal. I see bodies in decay and I recognise the ghosts of their youth. I see bodies which are nothing but the landscape of their death.'

Why speak of betrayal? What is betrayed? To betray literally means 'to deliver', 'to hand over' someone or something to someone else. But what is delivered into the hands of others? It could be that one's own shadow is handed over, like the character in Chamisso's novel who entrusted his shadow to that apparently innocuous old man.

What can it mean to deliver one's own shadow to someone else? It means to extinguish, to surrender, to weaken or to suffocate those energies which should imprint one's own presence on the stone, on history.

Not to betray means to refuse, not giving in to the temptations of the spirit of the times. It means being political, in the sense of taking a stand on what happens in the *polis*, the city, using the weapons which belong to the intellectual.

What are the weapons of the intellectual?

Once again I asked myself why the figure of Antigone had for a long time, for three or four years, continually returned to haunt me, like a ghost.

First with *The Story of Oedipus* and then in this other production, *The Gospel according to Oxyrhyncus*. I asked myself: what is Antigone trying to tell me?

Something disturbed me, pitting me against Antigone. 'If you don't agree with Creon's law', I found myself saying to her, 'then don't make your ineffective gesture, don't pretend to bury your brother with nothing but a handful of dust. You go to Creon every day, you see him and speak to him every day. So do as Brutus did. Take a dagger and kill him. Take power yourself in the *polis*, establish the moral norms which are important for you, and see that they are respected. Why this symbolic gesture of burial which accomplishes nothing?'

This is what the blind narrator, a wise old man, says in *The Story of Oedipus*, when he presents the different destinies of the members of Laius' family. He shakes his head sceptically when faced with the ingenuous girl who is trying to change things with her useless gesture.

In *The Gospel according to Oxyrhyncus*, Antigone appears once again. And I could not understand what lay hidden behind her act, what she was trying to say to me personally.

I finally understood it when I asked myself what is the weapon of the intellectual and how can it be used to fight against the law of the city. The weapon is a handful of earth, a useless and symbolic gesture which goes against the majority, against pragmatism, against fashion. That is the intellectual's role: to know that the gesture is useless, symbolic and yet, nevertheless, to make it.

It is a gesture that does not yield to the spirit of the times, a spirit which refuses memory, removes the past believing that all that happened in the sixties and seventies is a vanished Atlantis.

A great sword master in Japan before the Tokugawa period was recognised by his ability to strike a blow to his adversary's neck without removing the head. Everyone thought he had missed. Then the adversary would take a step forward and, at the slightest inclination of the torso, his head would fall to the ground.

I believe that, for the theatre, the experiences of the sixties and seventies, which are no longer in fashion, were a blow dealt to the apparently unitary body of the theatre. Many exult, believing that the body has remained intact, but the generations to come will see its head fall. Something else is hidden in that body, another kind of life flows in the blood, in the arteries, another vision of our profession, which is not only text and scenic embodiment. Again, as Heiner Müller reminds us: we have to accept the decay of the body and try to preserve intact the ghosts of our memory.

Perhaps, with my companions at Odin Teatret, and with all those who are around us, I will succeed in remembering that I must not lose the shadow, the presence, the charge of energy which derives from a single necessity: to refuse. I do not accept the present, I want to remain apart, I want to make performances which are necessary to me, to my companions and to a handful of spectators - not performances which are requested or imposed. I will have strength only so long as I succeed in maintaining this refusal.

I doubt that all those who seek to erase our shadow will succeed in obliterating it. We, and with us Julian Beck, Grotowski, The Bread and Puppet, all group theatre, a certain vision of theatre making, will remain: their shadow, our shadow.

That is the beauty of this period of time: to see which is the stronger, the steel of those who wish to erase our shadow, or us. That is the real challenge of the ice age in which we find ourselves, the glaciation which is slowly mutating all theatrical and cultural life: will we be able to cross the icy landscape, leaving our shadows behind us?

I contemplate with joy the decade to come; it is the decade in which the group of people who have worked with me for so many years, and I myself, will become biologically more than mature. It is the time in which our bodies will begin to become ruins. We will see whether or not we will be able to keep the ghosts of our youth alive in those ruins.

The only hand I hold out, that I would like to be touched and remembered, is towards those people who in ten, twenty years will say: yes, we saw, we have not forgotten, we keep alive the memory of something which happened and which can happen again, differently, but it can happen.

THE PART OF US WHICH LIVES IN EXILE

This text delves deeper into the concept of legacy. 'The part of us which lives in exile' is the space in which the performance succeeds in transcending its ephemeral character. Legacy does not only involve the will to hand down an example, but also the capacity to make the performance grow roots in the memory of the spectator. It is the material dimension of the craft, passed on as a legacy, which allows us 'to negate the theatre through doing it'.

First published in Linea d'ombra, *31, Milan 1988, under the title* Four Spectators.

The Natural Borders

The theatre's nature is ephemeral. What consequences can be drawn from this true yet banal affirmation?

One could dive into the culture of the ephemeral.

One could, on the other hand, oppose the unavoidably transient nature of theatre. This opposition brings us to a discovery of its meaning. It is an attempt to expand the theatre's boundaries, to refuse the predetermined role which it assumes in our culture. In other words, to negate the theatre through doing it.

This implies knowing how to hide the negation in the heart of a work which must above all be 'well-done'. We can transmit the seed of the revolt without naming it, simply by means of technical principles and professional attitudes.

'Ephemeral' means 'that which lasts but one day'. But also 'that which changes from day to day'. The first meaning evokes the image of death; the second, on the other hand, evokes the ever-changing flow which characterises being-in-life.

It is the performance, not the theatre, which lasts only a short time. The theatre is made up of traditions, conventions, institutions and habits which endure throughout time. The weight of this endurance is so heavy that it often prevents life from emerging and replaces it with routine. Routine is another of the theatre's natural boundaries.

To fight against the theatre's ephemeral nature does not mean to protect that which endures: tradition. Nor does it mean to fight for the conservation of performances. The 'electric shadows', as the Chinese called film, do not menace the theatre. They threaten to seduce it. Film and electronics make possible what was unthinkable until this century: performances which can be conserved practically unchanged. And thus they obscure the awareness that the essential dimension of the theatrical performance resists time not by being frozen in a recording but by transforming itself.

The extreme limit of this transformation is found in the memories of the individual spectators.

The Scorpion's Bite

What does it mean to work keeping the spectators in mind, and not the audience? The audience decides on success or failure; that is, something which has to do with breadth. The spectators, in their uniqueness, determine that which has to do with depth and to what extent the performance has taken root in certain individual memories.

There is a part of us which lives in exile, which we or others do not find acceptable or sufficiently important. Certain performances burgeon in this rationally, morally or emotionally exiled region. The spectators do not know how to relate to these performances. Often they do not understand them or do not know how to evaluate them. But they continue to have a dialogue with the memories which these performances have sown deep in their spirit. I say this not as a director but on the basis of my experience as a spectator.

The necessity of distinguishing between audience and spectator derives from the conscious will to exploit an inevitable condition: even though some or many reactions can be unanimous, communion is impossible. Intense relationships can be established, but they are based upon reciprocal estrangement.

This estrangement is not only a source of difficulties but can be exploited as a precious source of theatrical energy. Instead of trying to construct a performance as an organism which speaks to all spectators with the same voice, one can think of it as being composed of many voices which speak together without each voice necessarily speaking to all spectators.

For several years, Odin Teatret's performances have contained fragments (sometimes entire sequences) which are addressed to specific spectators whom we feel are close to us and to whom we speak personally. This does not mean these sequences or fragments must appear incongruous to other spectators. Rather, it has to do with creating a woven fabric of actions which is coherent on the pre-expressive level, precise in its dramatic rhythm, and which contains 'knots' of images that can arouse the attention of every spectator. The action or sequence, which for the majority of spectators is alive but impenetrable, or simply not boring, must, for at least one spectator, contain a clear and central value.

The word 'spectator' does not apply only to those who are gathered around the performance. In part, the actors and director are also spectators: they are active in the composition of the performance; they are not, however, the masters of its meaning.

I have referred to an extreme case. There is a vast gamut of possibilities between this case and its opposite pole, where everything must be equally decodifiable by the maximum number of people. When one is in a position to explore this gamut amply, then one is also in a position to cross barriers of language, of social and cultural divisions, of different levels of education. This happens not because the performance is 'universal' and says something acceptable to everyone, but because at some moments it speaks to all while at others it speaks differently to each individual. The performance dances not only on the level of energy but also on the narrative level. It is its *meaning* which dances, sometimes explicitly, sometimes covertly and secretly, open to the free associations of some spectators, while ambiguous and unrecognisable for others.

The real difficulty does not consist in guaranteeing the presence of multiple voices, but in safeguarding the organic integrity of the performance. There must be a technique which prevents its fragmentation or its degradation into a message which is coded, insensate and inert for those who do not possess the key.

Making it possible for the spectators to decipher a story does not mean making them able to discover the 'real meaning', but implies creating conditions which allow them to ask themselves questions about the meaning. It has to do with uncovering the 'knots' of the story, those points at which the extremes embrace.

There are spectators for whom theatre is essential precisely because it presents them not with solutions but with knots. The performance is the beginning of a longer experience. It is the scorpion's bite which makes one dance.

The dance does not stop when one leaves the theatre. The aesthetic value and the cultural originality of the performance are what make the sting sharp. But its precious poison comes from somewhere else.

The Technique of the Director as Spectator
I continue to do theatre because I can address spectators who seek to be confronted with something which secretly leaves a trace in that part of them living in exile.

But these are merely words if they do not become concretised in precise instructions for theatrical craftsmanship.

During the work on a performance there must be a moment in which the director crosses over to the other side and becomes the spectators' representative. The director must be loyal to them in the same way that s/he must be loyal to the actors. Loyalty to the actors consists essentially in creating conditions which allow them to find a personal meaning in the performance, without being totally subjected to the demands of the spectators. Loyalty to the spectator consists in assuring that each one of them is not patronised by the performance, does not feel treated like a mere number or like 'a part of the audience', but experiences the performance as if it were made *only for him or her*, in order to whisper something personal to each of them individually.

For a director to be loyal to the spectators does not just mean to interest them, to excite them, to entertain them, to move them. It means to master the techniques necessary to break up the unity of the audience on the mental level. In the same way, to be loyal to the actors does not mean to seek success for them, interest from critics, consensus from the theatre milieu.

Many consider the director to be an expert co-ordinator, or a 'protector', or the real author of the performance. For me, the director is rather the person who knows the subatomic reality of theatre and who experiments with ways of breaking the obvious links between actions and their meanings, between actions and reactions, between cause and effect, between actor and spectator. I associate my work with the image of Rabelais' starving dog who persists in biting the bone in the hope of cracking it open and discovering within it *une substantifique mouelle*, a substantial marrow.

This *doggedness* implies hunger, obstinacy and technique.

Let's discuss technique. One could say: 'The director is the first spectator.' Or, 'The director's task is to direct the attention of the spectator through the actor's actions'. But of which spectator are we speaking? The technique exists only when the director can work on de-composing the spectators' possible reactions into certain basic attitudes.

Without a preliminary *de-composition*, there is no orientation in the work, there are no parts which one can then cause to interact and one is unable to proceed by trial and error: no *composition* is possible. The necessity of decomposition is evident when one begins working on the 'materials' of the performance. The process which leads to the final unity - in which it should no longer be possible to distinguish between the different levels and the separate fragments - actually begins with a decomposition into fragments (scenes, sequences, microsequences) and a differentiation between levels (the actions of each individual actor, the relationships, the physical and vocal actions, the time and space of the performance, the visual and sonorous montage). Less evident is the necessity for a similar artisan-like attitude when working on the quality of the relationships with the spectators, guaranteeing for them the plurality of the voices with which the performance can whisper something to each one of them.

When directors affirm that they are the performance's 'first spectator,' they should not identify themselves, their own private identity, with that figure ('the first spectator'). If they do so, the performance runs the risk of becoming arbitrary. Conscious of this danger, directors sometimes mentally construct a spectator-type, a generic image based on the audience which they prefer or most fear. This image does not provide them with a concrete interlocutor who they can profoundly respect.

The technique of the director as spectator is a technique of alienation and identification. It is alienation not only from the 'audience' but also from oneself; and it is identification with the various and precise experiences of spectators which have to do with the various and precise ways the performance succeeds in being-in-life. This technique has a personal nature. Its principles, however, can be communicated and shared.

Four Spectators

It is necessary to assume the reactions of at least three spectators and to know how to imagine a fourth. I call these four 'basic' spectators:
-the child who perceives the actions literally;
-the spectator who thinks s/he doesn't understand but who, nevertheless, dances;
-the director's alter ego;
-the spectator who sees through the performance as if it did not belong to the world of the ephemeral and of fiction.

Every moment of the performance must be justified in the eyes of every one of these four spectators. The director's technique in this essential territory of the work consists in knowing how to identify her/himself first with one, then with another, and with yet another of these spectators, overseeing their reactions, imagining the laughter of the fourth spectator. It is also a question of harmonising the four different spectators so that what permits one of them to react does not block the kinaesthetic or mental reactions of the others.

In this way the director explores the gamut which allows the performance to burgeon in various memories. Each concrete spectator in fact can be thought of as an individual in whom these four 'basic' spectators are combined in differing proportions.

The 'child who perceives the actions literally' cannot be seduced by metaphors, allusions, symbolic images, quotations, abstractions, suggestive texts. S/he observes what is presented, not what is represented. If Hamlet recites 'to be or not to be' the 'literal child' sees a man who is speaking at length, alone, without doing anything interesting.

The second spectator is convinced s/he does not understand the meaning of the performance. We can imagine that s/he might not know the language in which the actors are speaking, or recognise the story. S/he does, however, acknowledge that the work is 'well done', carefully detailed like the handiwork of a master artisan from one of those cultures where no distinction is made between art and craft. Above all, s/he is seduced sensorially by the pre-expressive level of the performance, by the actor's dance of energy, by the rhythm which dilates the space and time of the action. S/he follows the performance kinaesthetically, wide awake because the performance urges her/him to dance although seated.

The spectator who is 'the director's alter ego' is minutely informed about all the contents of the performance, the texts and the events to which it refers, the dramaturgical choices, the biographies of the characters. The performance is for him or her a territory in which traces of the near and remote past give life to new contexts and unexpected relationships. A very personal vision penetrates this living archaeology, passing from the upper strata down to the deepest. S/he must be able to recognise in each fragment, in each detail, in each micro-action, an erratic relic of a uniquely individual knowledge, saturated with information, but endowed with a new energy which elicits unusual mental associations. All that happens here and now, on the stage, must reawaken an inner resonance which is immediately transformed into sound heard for the first time. Only in this way can this third spectator face the events of the performance, passing from recognition to knowledge, from the information on an experience to the *experience of an experience*. S/he must be able to see the performance each evening without becoming bored, as if wandering in a 'dilated mind' which each time causes new questions to surface and provokes a confrontation with an enigma that precludes escape.

These spectators are not pure abstractions but personifications to whom the director must impart precise faces and names. Although they are not real people, the director must be able to identify with them: they are *personae* (masks, roles) which are mentally assumed in order to avoid self-identification and private reactions.

The director concentrates first on one, then on another of these various 'basic' spectators, weaves and tunes their reactions in the same way that s/he weaves and tunes the actions of the actors.

The fourth spectator is nearly mute, smiling at the Maya-veil of the performance. S/he notices that which no one else can see: the embroidery on a character's shirt, hidden underneath a jacket and thus invisible to the eye, which is there because it has a value for the particular actor and the director, and has the same quality as other details which are meant to be seen. S/he notices what the actor does with the left hand while the spectators see only the right hand. S/he notices the 'well-accomplished' work even when it is secret and imperceptible, and recognises if the actor is doing it because of a necessity which goes beyond the demands of the performance.

The fourth spectator is the collaborator who helps us negate the theatre through doing it.

EURASIAN THEATRE

Going beyond all geographical connotations, Barba proposes here the concept of 'Eurasian theatre' understood as a mental category and an active idea within the theatre culture of the twentieth century. The search for identity now appears clearly split into two opposing attitudes: the need to formulate one's own theatre individuality, and the need to transcend it by connecting it to the flow of a 'tradition of traditions'.
First published in The Drama Review, *119, New York 1988.*

The influence of Western theatre on Asian theatre is an acknowledged fact. The important effect that Asian theatre has had and still has on Western theatre practice is equally irrefutable. But there remains an undeniable embarrassment: that these exchanges might be part of the supermarket of cultures.

Dawn
Kathakali and *nô*, onnagata and barong, Rukmini Devi and Mei Lanfang - they were all there, side by side with Stanislavski, Meyerhold, Eisenstein, Grotowski, and Decroux when I started to do theatre. It was not only the memory of their theatrical creations which fascinated me, but above all the detailed artificiality of their creative actor-in-life.

The long nights of *kathakali* gave me a glimpse of the limits which the actor can reach. But it was the dawn which revealed these actors' secret profile to me, at the Kalamandalam school in Cheruthuruty, Kerala. There, young boys, hardly adolescents, monotonously repeating exercises, steps, songs, prayers, and offerings, crystallised their *ethos* through artistic behaviour and an ethical attitude.

I compared our theatre with theirs. Today the very word 'comparison' seems inadequate to me since it separates the two faces of the same reality. I can say that I 'compare' Indian or Balinese, Chinese or Japanese traditions if I compare their epidermises, their diverse conventions, their many different performance styles. But if I consider that which lies beneath those luminous and seductive epidermises and discern the organs which keep them alive, then the poles of the comparison blend into a single profile: that of a Eurasian theatre.

Anti-Tradition
It is possible to consider the theatre in terms of ethnic, national, group, or even individual traditions. But if in doing so one seeks to comprehend

one's own identity, it is also essential to take the opposite and complementary point of view, and think of one's own theatre in a transcultural
dimension, in the flow of a 'tradition of traditions'.

All attempts to create 'anti-traditional' forms of theatre in the West, as
well as in the East, have drawn from the tradition of traditions. Certain
European scholars in the 15th and 16th centuries forsook the performance and festival customs of their cities and villages and rescued the
theatre of Athens and ancient Rome from oblivion. Three centuries later
the avant-garde of the young romantics broke with the classical traditions
and drew inspiration from new, distant theatres: from the 'barbarous'
Elizabethans and the Spaniards in the Siglo de Oro, folk performances,
the Commedia dell'Arte, 'primitive' rituals, medieval mystery plays and
Asian theatre. These are the images that have inspired the revolutions led
by all 'anti-traditional' western theatres in the 20th century. Today,
however, the Asian theatres are no longer approached through tales but
are experienced directly.

Every ethnocentricity has its eccentric pole, which reinforces it and
compensates for it.

Even today, in the Asian countries - here often the value of autochtho-
nous tradition is emphasised as against the diffusion of foreign models
and the erosion of cultural identity - Stanislavski, Brecht, agit-prop, and
'absurd' theatre continue to be means of repudiating scenic traditions
which are inadequate to deal with the conditions imposed by recent
history.

In Asia, this breach with tradition began at the end of the 19th century;
Ibsen's *A Doll's House*, the works of Shaw and Hauptmann, the theatrical
adaptations of Dickens' novels or of *Uncle Tom's Cabin* were presented not
as simple imports of Western models, but as the discovery of a theatre
capable of speaking to the present.

In the meeting between East and West, seduction, imitation, and
exchange are reciprocal. We in the West have often envied the Asians their
theatrical knowledge, which transmits the actor's living work of art from
one generation to another; they have envied our theatre's capacity for
confronting new themes, the way in which it keeps up with the times, and
its flexibility that allows for personal interpretations of traditional texts
which often have the energy of a formal and ideological conquest. On the
one hand, then, stories that are unstable in every aspect but the written;
on the other, a living art, profound, capable of being transmitted, and
involving all the physical and mental levels of actor and spectator, but
anchored in stories and customs which are forever old. On the one hand,

a theatre which is sustained by *logos*. On the other, a theatre which is, above all, *bios*.

Why

Why in the western tradition, as opposed to what happens in Asia, has the actor become specialised: the actor-singer as distinct from the actor-dancer and, in turn, the actor-dancer as distinct from the actor-interpreter?

Why in the West do actors tend to confine themselves within the skin of only one character in each production? Why do they not explore the possibility of creating the context of an entire story, with many characters, with leaps from the general to the particular, from the first to the third person, from the past to the present, from the whole to the part, from persons to things? Why, in the West, does this possibility remain relegated to masters of storytelling or to an exception like Dario Fo, while in the East it is characteristic of every traditional theatre and its actors, both when they act-sing-dance alone and when they are part of a performance in which the roles are shared?

Why do so many forms of Asian theatre deal successfully with that which in the West seems acceptable only in opera, which uses words whose meaning the majority of the spectators cannot understand?

Clearly, from the historical point of view, there are answers to these questions. But they only become professionally useful when they stimulate us to imagine how we can develop our own theatrical identity, by extending the limits which define it against our nature. It is enough to observe from afar, from countries and customs which are distant, or simply different from our own, to discover the latent possibilities of a Eurasian theatre.

Roots

The divergent directions in which Western and Asian theatres have developed provoke a distortion of perception. In the West, because of an automatic ethnocentric reaction, ignorance of Asian theatre is justified by the implication that it deals with experiences that are not directly relevant to us, that are too exotic to be usefully explored. This same distortion of perception idealises, and thus evens out, the multiplicity of Asian theatres or venerates them as sanctuaries.

Defining one's own professional identity implies overcoming ethnocentricity to the point of discovering one's own centre in the tradition of traditions. As I often say, when speaking of Eurasian Theatre, the term 'roots' does not imply a bond which ties us to a place, but an *ethos* which permits us to change places. It represents the force which causes us to change our horizons precisely because it roots us to a centre.

This force is manifest if at least two conditions are present: the need to define one's own tradition for oneself; and the capacity to place this individual or collective tradition in a context which connects it with other, different traditions.

The Performers' Village

ISTA (the International School of Theatre Anthropology) has given me the opportunity to gather together masters of both Asian and Western theatre, to compare the most disparate work methods, and to reach down into a common technical substratum - whether we are working in the West or in the East, in experimental or traditional theatre, mime, ballet or modern dance. This common substratum is the domain of pre-expressivity. It is the level at which the actors engage their own energies according to an extra-daily behaviour, modelling their 'presence' in front of the spectator. At this pre-expressive level, the principles are similar, even though they nurture the enormous expressive differences which exist between one tradition and another, one actor and another. They are *analogous* principles because they are born of similar physical conditions in different contexts. They are not, however, *homologous*, since they do not share a common history. These similar principles often result in a way of thinking which, in spite of different formulations, permits theatre people from the most divergent traditions to communicate with each other.

More than 20 years of work with Odin Teatret has led me, by means of practical solutions, not to take the differences between what is called 'dance' and what is called 'theatre' too much into consideration; not to accept the character as a unit of measure of the performance; not to make the sex of the actor coincide automatically with that of the character; to exploit the sonorous richness of languages, and their emotive force which is capable of transmitting information above and beyond their semantic value. These characteristics of Odin Teatret's dramaturgy and of its actors are equivalent to some of the characteristics of classical Asian forms, but Odin's were born of an autodidactic training, of our situation as foreigners and of our limitations. And this impossibility of being like other theatre people has gradually rendered us loyal to our diversity.

For all these reasons I recognise myself in the culture of a Eurasian theatre today. That is, I belong to the small and recent tradition of a theatre group which has autodidactic origins but grows in a professional 'village' where *kabuki* actors are not regarded as being more remote than

Shakespearean texts, nor the living presence of an Indian dancer less contemporary than the American avant-garde.

Thought-in-Action

It often occurs in this 'village' that the actors (or a single actor) not only analyse a conflict, let themselves be guided by the objectivity of the *logos*, and tell a story, but dance *in it* and *with it* according to the flow of the *bios*. This is not a metaphor; concretely, it means that the actor does not remain yoked to the plot, does not interpret a text, but creates a context, moves around and within the events. At times the actor lets these events carry him, at times he carries them, while at other times he separates himself from them, comments on them, rises above them, attacks them, refuses them, follows new associations or leaps to other stories. The linearity of the narrative is shattered by constantly changing the point of view, anatomising the known reality, and by interweaving objectivity and subjectivity, expositions of facts and reactions to them. Thus the actor embodies the freedom and the leaps of the thinking process, guided by a logic which the spectator cannot immediately recognise.

That which has often created misunderstandings about Asian theatre, has confused it with 'archaic' ritual, or made it appear as perfect but static form, is in fact that which brings it closest to our epoch's most complex concepts of time and space. It does not represent a phenomenology of reality, but a phenomenology of thought. It does not behave as if it belonged to Newton's universe. It corresponds instead to Niels Bohr's subatomic world.

Spectator

Eurasian theatre is necessary today as we move from the 20th into the 21st century. I am not thinking of Asian stories interpreted with a western sensibility, nor am I thinking of techniques to be reproduced, nor of the invention of new codes. It is a fact that the complex codes which seem to make sense of many Asian traditions remain unknown or little known to the majority of spectators in India as well as in China, Japan and Bali.

I am thinking of those few spectators capable of following or accompanying the actor in the dance of thought-in-action.

It is only the western *audience* which is not accustomed to leaping from one character to another in the company of the same actor; which is not accustomed to entering into a relationship with someone whose language it cannot easily decipher; which is not used to a form of physical expression that is neither immediately mimetic nor falls into the conventions of dance.

Beyond the audience there are, in the West as well as in the East, specific *spectators*. They are few, but for them theatre can become a necessity.

For them theatre is a relationship which neither establishes a union nor creates a communion, but ritualises the reciprocal estrangement and the laceration of the social body which are hidden beneath the parchment skin of dead myths and values.

THE STEPS ON THE RIVER BANK

Eugenio Barba's identity has been marked by his experiences as an emigrant and a traveller. These experiences, constantly underlying his reflections and craft, become the traces that lead to the discovery of a professional identity which sinks its roots into the artisan's principles at the foundation of different performance traditions. Within the framework of the 'tradition of traditions', the legacy consists in the capacity to express and hand down an individual identity through a professional one.

This article is an elaboration of several texts, one of which was published in TDR, *Vol. 38, 4, New York 1994, under the title* The Steps on the River Bank.

The poet is sick. He is put ashore in Brindisi and carried on a stretcher over the Apennine mountains to Naples to die (I am talking of Herman Broch's novel *The Death of Virgil*). Just after disembarking from the ship in Brindisi he notices a dark-skinned youth with luminous, impertinent eyes. He thinks he recognises him. Then he realises that he has never seen him before. And yet it is as though he knows him intimately.

During this last journey, Virgil (the wise poet who had also learnt magical and secret arts from the elders of his people, the Etruscans) meditates on what he has achieved during his life.

Poetry?

What purpose was served by telling the story of Aeneas who left a burning city carrying an old man on his shoulders and leading a child by the hand?

When he awakes from his drowsiness, Virgil looks around him and encounters again those luminous and impertinent eyes. The youth continues to follow him, at a distance, laughing, with the swift movements of an intelligent or mischievous child. In the end, just as he is sinking into the last sleep, Virgil realises that the dusky child is himself when he was still far from being the famous and satiated man he has become.

The Road of Dreams

Drammensveien was the third street name I learnt when, in 1954, I left my country, Italy, and settled in Oslo, Norway. The first was Bogstadveien where I had a job in a workshop as a welder; the second was Damfaret where I lived. I later discovered that Drammen was a town about forty kilometres from Oslo and so Drammensveien was simply 'the road to Drammen'. But 'drammen' sounds rather like 'drömmen' which, in Norwegian, means 'dream'.

I had the idea that Drammensveien meant 'the road of dreams' because on the same road was situated the university library where I used to seek refuge every day after work, at about five in the afternoon.

I knew nobody in Oslo, I didn't speak Norwegian and I had no desire to spend my free time in the places where the foreigners met to chat together in their own language. So I went to the library, 'the house of dreams', I found books in Italian and I read.

The Italian books were soon exhausted, so I started on the French ones.

I could not speak French at the time, but I had studied it in school and could read it with some difficulty. I did not choose, but took out books one after another, as I came across them. One day I happened upon a book by Romain Rolland entitled *Ramakrishna*. I discovered that in the last century in Bengal, a peasant's son had become a devotee of Kali and had a series of illuminations. He brought about a revival of religious devotion at a time when Bengal was undergoing an intense philosophical, literary, political and social reawakening inspired by Ram Mohum Roy and three generations of the Tagore family. The last of these, the great poet Rabindranath - winner of the Nobel Prize in 1913 - was about twenty years younger than Ramakrishna.

Ramakrishna had spent most of his life in a temple a few kilometres from Calcutta. Apart from Hinduism, he had experienced other religious forms, causing a scandal when - himself a priest of Kali, the Mother - he had practised Moslem devotion. During another period he immersed himself in the Christian religion. He said that different religions were like people with different languages drawing water from the river: they all used a different word to indicate what was in their pitcher; the pitchers too varied, but their content was the same.

Already agnostic, I was indifferent to religion. I couldn't explain it, but I had an overwhelming desire to go to Dakshineswar, to that temple on the banks of the Ganges which had been built for Ramakrishna by a rich widow of a low cast. I yearned to set foot on those steps which, according to Romain Rolland, Ramakrishna descended every morning to reach the river and perform his ablutions. On the road of dreams, my dream was to go there.

I had no money. In 1955 going to India seemed an impossible dream. The vision of those steps in Dakshineswar which I cradled within me, warmed me in the greyness of the Scandinavian winter.

In the 'house of dreams', a librarian began to talk to me. We became friends. He was a painter. In the mornings he painted and then when the light faded, he earned his living in the library. One day he asked me if I would like to earn a little extra money as a model for a painter friend of his. Thus I found myself in the studio of Willi Midelfart, one of Norway's best known painters. His studio was enormous, the back wall totally covered by books. I had to remain in a pose, but I could talk or read.

I owe most of my intellectual awareness to this elderly, cultured man who had been in Paris in the twenties and Moscow in the thirties. While he painted me he commented, explained, related the book I was reading to other books, other names, other historical events. And I went back to the library, conscious that the books were the bricks of an enigmatic building, a labyrinth whose living thread was hidden underneath the printed words.

One day I spoke of Ramakrishna to Willi and I asked if he knew of him. Of course! And he told me of his disciples, of Vivekananda who had been quite the opposite of Ramakrishna: extrovert, intellectual, committed to action, much travelled in the West. I also told him of my dream. He replied that every year on December 26th he was invited to dinner by Wilhelm Wilhelmsen, the Norwegian shipowner. The names of his ships had a common characteristic: they all began with the letter 'T'. He said he would tell him about me.

On the morning of December 29th Willi phoned me. I was to contact the shipowner's offices because there was a possibility of a job. On January 5th 1956 it was snowing when I boarded a ship, 'Talabot', bound for the East, as engine boy.

The theatre did not enter my mind, did not exist. For me the Orient was strange religions and philosophies.

We passed through Suez and arrived in Aden. I received a parcel. It came from Willi and contained three books. I don't remember the first one. The second was Céline's *Voyage to the Night's End*. The third was *The Human Condition* by Malraux, the description of a revolt in China in 1927 which culminated in a massacre carried out by the troops of Chiang Kai-shek.

That was the other face of the East, the fierce face of history.

The 'Talabot' sailed on to Colombo, Madras, Chittagong. Then Calcutta. One morning, very early, I went to Dakshineswar. I saw the steps. My feet touched them. I too descended them to the river's edge.

Then I went back to the greasy work in the ship's deafening engine room and the seasickness of the return voyage on rough monsoon seas.

This first journey belongs to the subterranean history of the individual, rich in mysteries and enigmatic coincidences, where one cannot apply the criteria used when the history of theatre is told and judged.

A Footnote

I returned to India in 1963 with Judy (later we were to marry). At that time I was working with Grotowski. They were the darkest and most reckless years for his theatre, which was almost unknown and always on the point of being suffocated by censorship. As a foreigner, it was simpler for me to travel abroad, spreading information and establishing contacts which might make it a little less easy for the Polish bureaucracy to eliminate the tiny theatre in Opole.

In June of 1963 the ITI (International Theatre Institute) held its international congress in Warsaw. The Polish hosts had made sure that in the programme of events not even the slightest hint was made of the existence of Grotowski. Grotowski and I discussed how to break this silence. He went with his theatre to Łódz - only a couple of hours away from Warsaw - to perform Marlowe's *Dr. Faustus* which had just had its premiere in Opole. I went to Warsaw and mingled with the delegates of the ITI congress. I succeeded in convincing a number of them to come with me to see *Dr. Faustus*. The performance was a shock for them and the next morning in the congress hall Grotowski's name was on everyone's lips. There was much praise for the Polish authorities for supporting such a theatre. They were astounded but put a good face on it.

Judy worked as a secretary in the ITI and that was how we met. I had told her that I wanted to go back to India, but overland this time. 'I have a car', she said. 'Let's go', I replied. A month later, during the summer holidays, we set out together.

Being used to the space-time of European travel where I could go from one capital to another in a day, India for me was like falling into a bottomless well. Although on the map it seemed only a short jump from the Pakistani border, it took us three days to reach New Delhi. Judy drove the second-hand Land Rover. I didn't know how to drive. I read - perhaps as a counterbalance to the monotony of the Iranian desert - Gibbon's *Decline and Fall of the Roman Empire*.

This time I wanted to learn something professionally useful. I was searching for 'Indian theatre'. In New Delhi, at last, I would be able to get to know it.

The people I approached told me I should meet Ebrahim Alkazi. He was a well-known personality and taught at the National School of Drama. There, to my great surprise, I listened to something that was not so different from what was being taught at the Warsaw theatre school. Ebrahim Alkazi had lived for a long time in Egypt. He had a profound knowledge of British theatre and was making his name as an innovator by introducing the visions of Stanislavski and the Actor's Studio.

Then someone said to me: 'Why don't you go to Bombay? Adi Marzban is there - he is a writer who does some interesting theatre'. More driving, day after day. But also in Bombay, among plays taken from the British tradition and popular theatre, the outlook was not very stimulating for a young man who was impatient and hungry for professional secrets.

Someone else suggested: 'Why don't you go down south? There you will find something that is really unique!'. He assured me that *kathakali* would not disappoint me. He was from Kerala.

And so Judy got back behind the steering wheel. After a seemingly endless journey down through the whole of India, we arrived in Kerala to be faced with the problem of tracing *kathakali*. Finally in Trichur, in a bookshop owned by Kerala's ex-minister of culture, they told us of a school of *kathakali* in a village called Cheruthuruthy.

At last we arrived and were allowed to stay in the local hospital.

I went to the Kathakali Kalamandalam. The teachers were not in the least interested in my presence. I was a burden, and my questions were seen as pedantic and boring, a pure waste of time. Underneath the patina of an elementary courtesy to guests, the teachers made no effort to hide the annoyance they felt towards me. The memory of those weeks at the *kathakali* school still has a bitter flavour, although today I cannot blame the teachers. My prejudices collided with theirs. From my side, I could not help also seeing in the school an image of routine, with the masters seated, beating out the rhythm, in an attitude which to me could either be one of endless patience or of inert resignation. And the students repeated the same handful of exercises *ad infinitum*. Exactly the opposite of what in my imagination during those years I idealised as sacred or necessary theatre.

But something of great importance became deeply engraved in my memory.

The children were admitted to the school at around 9 or 10 years old. They started work at dawn. Still numb from sleep, they began on their own to repeat again and again the laborious (and painful) *kathakali* postures and steps.

They were friendly and curious. They became my companions.

There is an essential difference between the theatre you begin to practise as an adult and that whose apprenticeship begins in childhood. The children are projected into a context which gives them a value, into a tradition which transcends them, and which at first they do not grasp but, little by little, they incorporate. They feel they represent something which is beyond them, a higher meaning.

I thought of myself and my colleagues at the Warsaw theatre school, impatient and full of justifications, with our own confident ways of looking at, explaining and discussing theatre. How difficult it is - I pondered - to love art in oneself and not oneself in art, according to the precepts of Stanislavski, when you start as an adult, already formed.

In Cheruthuruthy the value of the theatre did not lie in what the children may say, believe or dream. It was as though they were carrying on their frail shoulders, sometimes with difficulty, sometimes light-heartedly, the onus of a tradition which they might later interpret and transform, but which was not theirs to dispose of as they wished.

For me *kathakali* was those small boys whose work I followed daily, with whom I chatted, and who answered my complicated questions courteously, or with an embarrassed smile.

There were very few *kathakali* performances at that time of year. During the three weeks of my stay in Cheruthuruthy I only saw a couple, lasting the whole night. I sensed a dilation of time, full of penitence for me, sitting for hours on a rush mat, in that big open space, among mothers and children chattering and eating, hawkers moving around and snoring men. And all the while, on the stage, the actor's flame continued to burn, indifferent to indifference, without any sacred aura.

I came from the experience with Grotowski in Opole where, from 1961, I had participated in the invention of a new theatre identity, trying to restore the sacredness of this art. Yet here, in Kerala, the sacred became calm and serene irreverence. I think that more even than the beauty of the performance, it was my own incapacity to understand that surprised me. Why was I so fascinated when I neither understood the story performed by the actors, nor the meaning of their message? What was it that kept me spellbound in this atmosphere of an Indian railway station which contradicted all my ideas about theatre and its sacredness?

On leaving Cheruthuruty, I wrote this message of thanks:

> The Secretary
> Kalamandalam
> Cheruthuruthy
>
> Dear Sir:
> I had not the occasion, last night at the performance, to thank you for all the kind help you have given me during my stay here. To you, and to the Superintendent, and to all the boys who were so willing to be of service, I would like to express my gratitude and sincerest thanks.

My visit to Kalamandalam has greatly helped me in my studies
and the research material I have collected will surely be of the
greatest assistance to those people working at the Theatre
Laboratory in Poland.
Many thanks once again,
Yours sincerely,
Eugenio Barba

It is a formal note which I had forgotten about until, 10 years ago, I was
surprised to find it on page 147 of Richard Schechner's book *Performative
Circumstances from the Avant Garde to Ramlila*, published in Calcutta by
Seagull Books who, incidentally, have the same emblem as the Moscow
Art Theatre.

Schechner read my words in the school visitors' book when he also
went to the Kathakali Kalamandalam in 1972. He quoted them as a
reminder of how a twenty-seven-year-old Italian passed on the news of the
kathakali exercises to a young Pole of barely thirty - Jerzy Grotowski - who
incorporated them into his actors' training.

That letter of so many years ago is scarcely even a footnote in the
history of theatre research in the second half of the twentieth century, in
the chapter on the beginnings of Grotowski's career, before *The Constant
Prince* and *Apocalypsis cum Figuris*, before the 'poor theatre' and fame. It
could also be a way to introduce the story of Odin Teatret as Eurasian
theatre.

The Legacy
On my return to Europe I wrote about *kathakali* in some French, Italian
and American magazines. Those articles attracted attention and generated
an interest which, throughout the following years, made Cheruthuruthy
into a goal for many theatre people.

But the important thing for me today is that which belongs neither to
kathakali nor to me, and which in quite another context, in forms which
are incomparable, still guides me when I question myself about the
meaning of theatre.

What appears in front of me is not a technical precept or an answer
made up of words, but the touching image of those children who walked
to school at dawn and practised their exercises without the presence of
any teacher. And I repeat to myself the words which for thirty years I have
whispered to my actors: 'What you must do, you must do. And don't
question, don't question'.

Scholars sometimes write about me. They say, among other things, that I like to work with artists from classical Asian theatres. They often refer to my collaboration of more than fifteen years with Sanjukta Panigrahi, the Indian Odissi dancer with whom I founded ISTA, the International School of Theatre Anthropology. They are right. And yet I wonder.

Do I really like to work with performers from other traditions? The real collaboration actually begins when I forget about traditions, about geographical and cultural distance, and all the differences are embodied in the individuality of the person in front of me.

After so many years of working together, I often forget that Sanjukta is Indian, that she dances in the Odissi style, that she excels in this genre. And I believe she sometimes manages to forget that I am European.

Traditions do not exist. Just as ideas and religions do not exist. Only the people embodying them exist. Fidelity to tradition and the desire to preserve its purity, can be powerful guides, when they are personal visions. But they become a burden on others when they turn into orthodoxy. Then the past suffocates the germs of life and the dead bury the living.

I have seen some old photographs of Sanjukta Panigrahi as a child. Underneath the costumes and the dancer's make-up, you can discern the expression that particularly beautiful children often have, who, if they don't encounter something much greater than themselves, risk becoming arrogant. That young girl certainly did not find it easy to obey. For this reason her artistic humility is precious. Those photos of Sanjukta as a child remind me of the ones which I myself took at Cheruthuruthy, depicting the skinny bodies of the *kathakali* pupils doing their exercises.

When I first met Sanjukta Panigrahi, she was already famous. She had founded a style and had made it known outside her own boundaries. But there is something recognisable in those people who have been used to getting up early and working alone, with no one to watch them, no one to rebuke or praise them.

Those who have passed through such an experience which distils the meaning of doing theatre into silent actions, are compatriots, whatever their culture and tradition.

If we call this ethics then we risk turning it into theory or rhetoric.

Looking back, I ask myself what it was that so struck me about Romain Rolland's book on Ramakrishna. The author didn't indulge in powerful images and suggestive language. He didn't oppose the narrowness of scientific reason to the boundless horizons of the spirit. He didn't confront India with Europe, the East with the West. He dealt with the extraordinary experiences of his protagonist with the same vivid concreteness and the same good sense that he applied to the description of nature or the history of modern India. He spoke of the muscles and nerves involved in ecstasy. He showed Vivekananda feeling the muscles of his aspiring pupils before admitting them to spiritual training.

And above all he insisted upon the concept of *realisation*. He denied that there was any point in distinguishing between the real and the ideal. Ramakrishna was a *realiser*, a doer.

In that book there was a primitive photograph accompanied by a note presenting it as an exceptional document. Unwittingly, I have re-evoked this image in some of my productions. The photo showed a few men dressed in white, crouched on the floor against a large window which was covered by a straw blind through which the scorching sun was beating. Ramakrishna was standing in the centre, thin and bearded, like a sick man tottering as he attempts to walk, or one who has had too much to drink. One arm was raised, while the other hand, on a level with the heart, formed the mudra which in dance represents the bee sucking nectar from a flower. Beside him, a robust man was ready to support him.

The scene gives the impression of simple family happiness, a gaiety without festive frills, among people who are able to let themselves go and are not afraid if a companion seems to go too far. Ramakrishna - from what I could make out in the dim light - was laughing. The caption said that the photo portrayed the exact moment when the holy man passed into *samadhi*, ecstasy, during a *kirtan*, a session of religious songs and dances.

This way of representing light through the most humble of actions is what Ramakrishna, the *kathakali* children, Sanjukta and India have all taught me. And I rediscover it in the attention to technical detail and in the visions of the men and women who populate Eurasian theatre.

When I speak of Eurasian theatre I am not thinking of theatres within a geographical space, but of a mental dimension, an *active idea* which has inspired the theatre of our century. This concept includes the experiences which for all artists, whatever their cultural origins, constitute the essential points of reference for their practice: from Ibsen to Zeami, from the Peking Opera to Brecht, from the mime of Decroux to *nô*, from *kabuki* to Meyerhold's bio-mechanics, from Delsarte to *kathakali*, from ballet and modern dance to *butoh*, from Artaud to Bali, from Stanislavski to Natyashastra.

We could say that Eurasian theatre represents a common country: that of our craft, of our professional identity. Or else it is a legacy, that which remains and can be shared equally in the country of transition which is theatre.

Cultural Identity and Professional Identity

The events of our life, when they become dried flowers and fruits, turn into a succession of memories. We may reflect upon our experiences and tell of them in different styles and languages.

My vision of Odin Teatret as Eurasian Theatre, which I have described through a series of anecdotes concerning my contacts with Indians, both dead and alive, could be explained with other words. I could use the terms and the modalities, distant and impartial, with which theory dresses itself. I could talk in terms of Theatre Anthropology. But let us not forget: theory, in Greek, means observation and reflection, as well as succession of images, episodes and ideas.

The field of study of Theatre Anthropology is the technique of the actor/dancer. All who practise a craft belong to their own culture, but also to the culture of the craft itself. They have a cultural identity as well as a professional identity. They can meet 'compatriots' who practise the same profession in other countries. This is why, at one time, the *Wanderlehre*, the 'learning journey' beyond the borders of one's native country, was part of the training of even the most humble artisan.

The theatrical profession is also a country to which we belong, an elective homeland, without geographical borders. Today we accept it as normal that a Mexican philologist should discuss with an Indian philologist, that a Japanese architect shares experiences on an equal basis with a Swedish architect, just as we consider it a form of cultural inadequacy that Chinese medicine and European medicine have not become two complementary aspects of a single body of knowledge. It is not strange that actors and dancers meet within the common borders of their profession. It is strange that it should seem strange.

The notion of identity stems from the Latin *idem* which means that which does not change, that which remains the same. Identity is an axis, a centre, a kernel of values which helps us to orientate ourselves in the face of life's events and obstacles. Actors move within their historical and biographical horizons and the artistic results are relative to their experience, heredity, and vision of the world. It is this relativity which gives each individual his or her uniqueness and difference.

Action, through theatre, is a testimony of and a journey into our own culture. At the same time it takes us into a territory in which all actors meet the same problem: *how* to make their scenic presence efficacious for the spectator.

The professional identity is rooted in this ground, with its different performance genres and styles that correspond to different ways of moulding scenic presence.

This professional identity belongs to a transcultural theatre history built by masters who have preceded us. Therefore actors from Polynesia or Italy can develop their professional identity in relation to the values and experiences of Russian or Chinese, Colombian or Scandinavian masters.

On the one hand our identity is individual, deriving from our life experiences and the place and time in which we live. On the other hand it must be our professional identity that links us to others of our profession far beyond the limits of time and space. It is a question of two poles. The one cannot exist without the other.

Theatre-in-life is nourished by this polarity. On the one hand, there is the question: why do I do theatre? And on the other there must be the capacity for professional exchange with individuals who may be far removed from one's own time or geographic location.

Actors from all traditions use forms, manners, procedures, distortions, paradoxical ways of thinking and behaving - in other words, technique - as a means of attaining scenic efficacy. Looking beyond cultures and performative genres, we find that for every actor the origin is when scenic presence begins to be shaped by technique whose aim is how to make an impact on the spectator.

ISTA is a meeting place for masters of dance and theatre from different genres and cultures. Our aim is to compare the roots of our working methods and to penetrate into a technical foundation which we have in common, whether we are working in theatre in the West or in the East, in the North or in the South, in experimental or traditional theatre, in mime, ballet or modern dance. This common foundation - pre-expressivity - is constituted by technical principles which allow actors and dancers to mould their own energy into the extra-daily behaviour of the scenic fiction.

Some people are perplexed and say: 'How is it possible to study the performers' creative processes without examining their historical and social context? How is it possible to compare various forms of scenic behaviour, and isolate transcultural principles, without taking into consideration the fact that each of the examples belongs to culturally diverse and at times incomparable circumstances?' And they conclude: 'Theatre Anthropology ignores history; it ignores the fact that particular technical procedures have a specific symbolic or ideal meaning in the culture to which they belong; it reduces everything to the materiality of scenic *bios*'.

No, Theatre Anthropology does not ignore, nor does it reduce to ... It concentrates on.

Actors who work in an organised performance situation express their

individuality through profound differences as well as profound common-
alties. It is therefore possible to conduct research of a scientific kind aiming
at singling out transcultural principles which, *on the operative level*, are the
basis of scenic behaviour.

ISTA and Theatre Anthropology are based on this hypothesis.

Tradition and Founders of Traditions

When we speak of culture, that is, of relationships, the subject of identity
is always at the centre of our discourse.

Our ethnic identity has been established by history. We cannot shape it.

Personal identity is formed by each of us on our own, but unconsciously. We call it 'destiny'.

The only profile on which we can work consciously as rational beings
is the profile of our professional identity.

It is possible to construct a professional identity that can grow in contact
with other cultures, also at the intracultural level, allowing for the discovery
and incorporation of that which is different, even in our own culture. For the
European reformers of the twentieth century some of the events belonging to
their history were fundamental for revising their practice: classical Greek
theatre or the Commedia dell'Arte, different types of popular performances
or circus, alive today or extinct, accepted or marginalized manifestations.

It is through exchange, rather than isolation, that a culture can develop
and transform itself organically. The same process applies to actors.
However, in order to make an exchange, you must offer something in
return. Therefore one's historical-biographical identity is fundamental
when confronted with its opposite pole, the meeting with 'otherness', with
that which is different. This does not mean the imposition of one's own
horizon or way of seeing, but rather causes a displacement which makes
it possible to glimpse a territory beyond one's known universe.

Defining one's own professional identity implies overcoming ethnocentricity to the point of discovering one's own centre in the 'tradition of
traditions'. As I often say, when speaking of Eurasian Theatre, the term
'roots' does not imply a bond which ties us to a place, but an *ethos* which
permits us to change places. It represents the force which causes us to
change our horizons precisely because it roots us to a centre.

This force is manifest if at least two conditions are present: the need to
define one's own tradition for oneself; and the capacity to place this
individual or collective tradition in a context which connects it with other,
different traditions.

It is not the traditions that choose us, but rather it is us who choose them. An American can become a Buddhist and a Maori an excellent opera singer.

Traditions preserve and hand down a form, not the sense that gives it life. Each of us must define and reinvent the sense for ourselves. This reinvention expresses a personal, cultural and professional identity.

Traditions stratify and refine the knowledge of successive generations of founders and allow every new artist to begin without being obliged to start from scratch. Traditions are a precious inheritance, spiritual nourishment, roots.

But they are also constraint. There is no identity without a struggle against the constraint of the forms inherited from tradition. Without such a struggle, artistic life collapses. In art, the spark of life is the tension between the rigour of the form and the rebellious detail which shakes it from within, forcing it to assume a new significance, an unrecognisable aspect.

The actor who does not belong to a codified scenic tradition often risks feeling disinherited, rootless and without concrete points of reference to disobey. Those who do not have a tradition, often idealise it and refer to it with a superstitious belief as though it could bestow a meaning on their work.

A spirit of revolt and a longing for a set of values has permeated the theatre of our century from Stanislavski to Grotowski, from Meyerhold to Brecht, from Artaud to Decroux, from Gordon Craig to Isadora Duncan, Jacques Copeau, Martha Graham, Kazuo Ohno. A succession of founders of traditions unfolds across the artificially separated fields of theatre, mime and dance.

At a hasty glance, the distinction between *tradition* and *founders of traditions* is equivalent to that between classical schools and innovators, the orthodox and the rebellious, the Asian actor-dancer hidden beneath a golden costume and the restless and eclectic experiments of contemporary performers. But it is not like that. Even the most rigid tradition only lives on through reinvention by its interpreters. And the more subtle and imperceptible these reinventions seem, the deeper they run.

In daily practice, 'tradition' is the same as 'knowledge', or rather 'technique', a far more humble and effective word. Technique does not define us, but it is the necessary instrument for overcoming the borders which confine us. Technical knowledge allows us to encounter other forms and introduces us to the 'tradition of traditions', to those principles which constantly recur beneath the differences in style, culture and personalities.

The goal is not to identify oneself with a tradition but to build a nucleus of values, a personal identity, both rebellious and loyal to one's own roots. The way to achieve this is always through a minutely detailed practice that constitutes our professional identity. It is competence in one's craft which transforms a condition into a personal vocation and, in the eyes of others, into a destiny which is a legacy and a tradition.

It is for us to decide which history we belong to professionally and who are the ancestors in whose values we recognise ourselves. They may be from distant eras and cultures, but the meaning of their work is the legacy to be safeguarded and transmitted. Each one of us is the offspring of someone's work. Each one of us moves forward, leaving behind a past which we have chosen for ourselves.

37. 'Who are you? A loner who vanishes into the desert or one who, advancing, perhaps losing himself, finishes by marking a path?' (Sanjukta Panigrahi and Eugenio Barba with the ISTA participants, Bologna, 1990)

38. *'How can one resist without becoming only naive or only astute?' (Torgeir Wethal, Carpignano, 1974).*

39. 'It is useless to ask oneself: who will be my heirs? Yet it is essential to remember that there will be heirs.' (Odin Teatret in Venezuela, 1976)

40. 'Know the truth about the obstacle. Only half of it is outside you. The other half is inside. With the help of others, you can overcome the outside half, which then becomes a step to help you climb. But as for the half which remains inside, you must overcome it alone.' (Isabel Ubeda, Tina Nielsen and Jan Ferslev, Kaosmos, 1995)

41. 'When actors throw themselves into the daily life of a street or a market, they are not blending with the local people. They are merely solidifying their own identities, and therefore their own differences.' (Iben Nagel Rasmussen, Peru, 1978)

42. *'How much fatherland do we need? - asked Jean Améry. I have been lucky: my father-land has expanded. It does not consist of land or geography. It is made up of history, of people.' (Eugenio Barba during a rehearsal of* Theatrum Mundi, *ISTA, Bologna, 1990)*

43. 'For theatre people, the intellectual is an ally in the struggle against the dictatorship of the present.' (From left to right: Eugenio Barba, Erik Bentley, Heiner Müller and Ferdinando Taviani who has been Odin Teatret's literary adviser since 1974, at a seminar organised by Odin Teatret in Copenhagen in 1986)

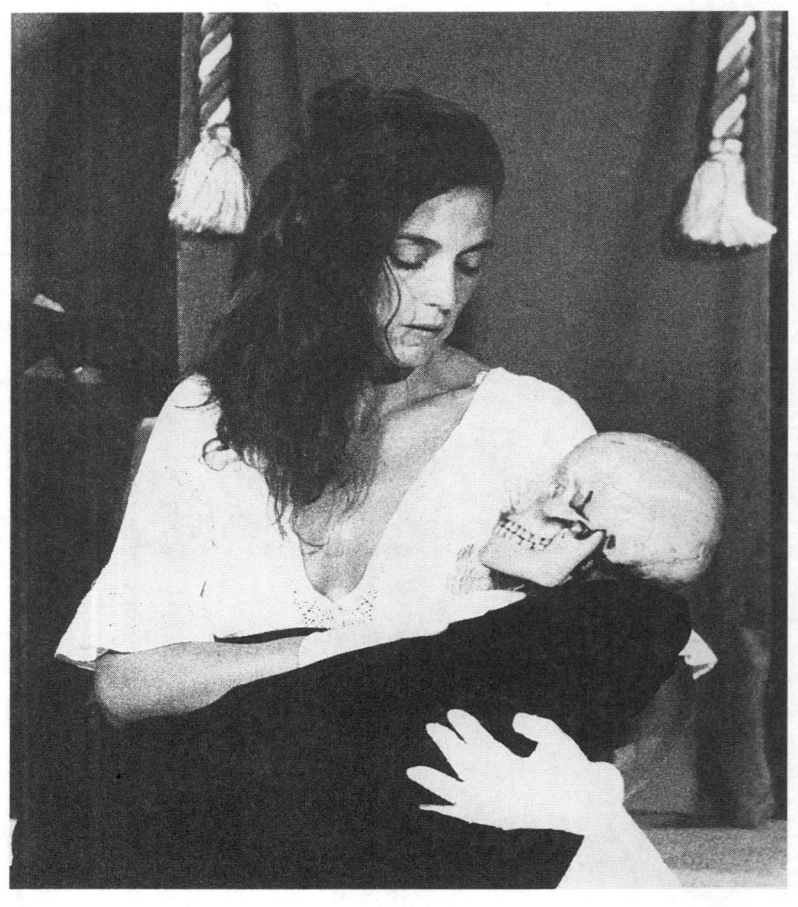

44. *'The legacy, like an occult science, catches its own heirs.'* (*Julia Varley in* The Castle of Holstebro, *1992*)

45. *In the foreground, Iben Nagel Rasmussen; in the background, Tom Fjordefalk and Else Marie Laukvik, Peru, 1978.*

AFTERWORD

SOWING RABBITS WHILE DREAMING OF LIONS

In my work I have always searched for the unexpected. Today I am aware that it blesses me only if I push myself beyond the normal limits of what is considered the legitimate area of research within my craft. After thirty-five years of working with the same nucleus of individuals, do I still have desires or questions? Yes, here are some of them:

How to transform Odin Teatret into the living and metaphorical embodiment of Prince Myshkin, Schweik and Basho?

How to pass on, as seeds, the fruits of the actions of a handful of Odin people who will die within a few years but nevertheless cling stubbornly to the small town of Holstebro on the margins of the European empire?

How to shape the many types of information which impregnate the form of the performer's every action - technical, sensorial, organic, spiritual, sensual, intellectual and archetypal information as well as that concerning the history of the craft and the tradition one has chosen?

How to avoid being taken into consideration by statistics?

How can Odin Teatret be an incandescent needle that perforates the glacier of ideas, conventions, criteria and values of its own times, opening for those who come afterwards an invisible tunnel which helps to perceive the other side?

What is 'the other side'?

How to resist without becoming only naive or only astute?

How to be amphibious, belonging to the theatre element and yet to another?

How to let ourselves be guided by the blind horse within us which gallops on the icy brink of a precipice?

How knowingly to let a performance happen in which 7,000 lions dance on the point of a pin?

How, why, where and for whom do I do theatre?

I often converse with myself. My questions generally concern personal obsessions, halfway between the technique and the ethics of the craft. I have a strong relationship with the times of which I am a part, but I never inquire about its nature. Our times are always a multitude of currents flowing in opposite directions, at different levels and with contrasting rhythms. We can navigate only one current which is sometimes hidden and which we discover through our refusal of the other currents.

Nothing has a meaning or a value in itself. *We* decide what meaning we give to whatever we do. The performance is an 'empty ritual', something which *evokes* a meaning through the care and the precision with which it is carried out but which, by itself, *possesses none.*

The performance always lets us glimpse an uneasiness over a discrepancy. It is the gap between the commitment and the dedication that theatre demands in order to do it well, and the value that it has within the life and times which surround us. It is a work whose products are ephemeral, intended for amusement or at the very most as an art which does not last. But it is a work which has to be accomplished as though it were a matter of life and death.

Copeau, in his old age, used to say that, in the end, theatre seemed to him to be a waste: to be a good actor you need the ingenuity, the zeal, the perseverance and the rigour necessary to be a saint. So why not become a saint?

Four centuries ago a similar question came up in a country lane in Castilla. Sancho Panza asked Don Quixote: if the best one can do is to become a saint, why strive so hard and make such sacrifices to become a knight? Saints and knights are the same, replied Don Quixote.

This paradox is a truth, but is it also an answer?

What does it mean to be a saint if one does not believe in the demands imposed by a religion?

Do I want to be a saint? Certainly not.

Do my actors want to be saints perhaps? They would laugh at such a proposition.

Do our spectators expect it of us? I don't think so.

However, if being a saint implies selfishness to the point of self-denial, blasphemy to the point of discovering, in spite of ourselves, what is sacred; if it means being an unbeliever towards all masters, even those who teach and practise the way of unbelieving, would we then be able to recognise ourselves in this mysterious word, this paradox?

What does it mean to be an unbeliever with respect to one's own times, one's own work and oneself? Can one be loyal and yet an unbeliever?

I cannot answer questions of this sort with concepts. I will therefore try with a story.

There was once a peasant who decided one day to sow his field with lions instead of beans.

'What is the point of cultivating lions?' asked his neighbours.

'At harvest time you will understand', replied the peasant.

Spring came but in the field no lions grew, only rabbits.

The neighbours laughed: 'He has no beans, but instead he has rabbits which devour everything that grows in the field.'

The man was not discouraged. The next year he sowed lions again. And once more he harvested rabbits. Again everybody laughed.

As the years passed, it was no longer funny. It seemed normal that while everyone else in the village planted useful or edible crops, there was one eccentric who sowed lions and harvested rabbits.

When the peasant died, his son inherited the field and he too sowed lions. The neighbours started laughing again: 'Who does he think he is!' And the laughter turned to mockery when the harvest was of rabbits.

Then the son understood that it was time to stop. So he planted beans.

His neighbours looked at him with scorn. Shaking their heads, they pronounced judgement: 'His father, he was a man! He sowed lions.'

I have often spoken of theatre as of a haemophiliac body losing blood as it collides with reality, as a ghetto of freedom, a floating island, a fortress filled with oxygen, a canoe rowing against the current and yet remaining on the same spot like the third bank of a river; of theatre as a house with two doors, one for entering and one for flight; of theatre as the people of an empty ritual; of theatre as a ship of stone which can take us on a journey through the experiences of the individual and of history; of theatre as a wall which obliges us to stand on tiptoe to see beyond it; of theatre as barter, potlatch, waste, emigration.

These are metaphors which suggest a craft which is valid only if it transcends itself and searches for its value by striving to liberate itself from its function merely as performance.

I have tried to explain all this while speaking of third theatre, of an asocial theatre, of the way of refusal, of the legacy from us to ourselves and the necessity to escape from the spirit of the times.

I think that the meaning and the subtext of all I have said is distilled into the story of the peasant who sowed lions and harvested rabbits.

Where do I stand in relation to my times? I have resisted their seduction for more than thirty-five years, eating rabbits. Mostly roasted or in a stew, with olives and garlic, as is the custom in my native village.

46. 'Looking back for a moment I think: what a long preparation! I ask myself: for what? And I answer recalling a sarcastic saying: it takes sixty years to make a man, and when he is finished, he isn't good for anything but dying.' (Julia Varley with her character, Mr. Peanut, Salvador, Brazil, 1994)

APPENDIX

....

THE DARK LEGEND

A catalogue of Odin Teatret's productions
by Ferdinando Taviani

Dark is a way
and light is a place
Vincent Gaeta

The political dimension of theatre resides in the tension between what the performance *says* and what it *does*, between its *contents* and its *efficacy*.

Of course Eugenio Barba and Odin Teatret are not explicitly political. But do they have a policy?

I have often thought that the secret of Odin Teatret is its paradoxical way of thinking. But it is easy to think in paradoxical terms. To act in a paradoxical way, however, is difficult. Is this its secret? I believe that 'to act in a paradoxical way' and to 'have a policy' are two different ways of expressing the same thing. Very few theatres know how to have a policy.

Among the paradoxes of political action, two are more difficult than the others. Both are extremes, different in their paths yet identical in their orientation. One is utopia, while the other has been formulated as follows: 'pessimism of the intellect and optimism of the will'.

This definition is usually attributed to Antonio Gramsci, the founder of the Italian Communist Party. Some say that it goes back further. It is of no importance. What matters is what it indicates: a behaviour which is the exact opposite of normal behaviour, where the intellect serves to console, to fill the will with hope that will enable us to be active in changing the world around it.

Odin Teatret's performances embody the second of the two paradoxes of political action. They expose a 'dark legend' which is then contrasted with and contradicted by an optimistic dilation of scenic life. What they show and narrate is not encouraging. It is what Eugenio Barba and the Odin consider to be true, not what they consider to be good. But in telling their dark truths, they create a live and deep bond between themselves and the spectators. They present disillusioned and pessimistic visions to the point of being nihilistic or misanthropic, yet with a wasting of energy, with an excess of care for the minutest detail, with the incandescence and the sensuality of love.

This dialectic between the 'dark legend' and optimism often pushes the spectators off balance, lifting them towards a contemplation of themselves, of their surroundings, of their own times, and of the way in which they take a stand.

1. Ornitofilene (The Bird-Lovers), 1965.

Created in Oslo, during the first months of Odin Teatret's existence, in the total isolation of a nuclear bomb shelter.

51 performances from October 1965 to March 1966.

Actors: Anne Trine Grimnes, Else Marie Laukvik, Tor Sannum, Torgeir Wethal.

Text by Jens Bjørneboe.

Adaptation and direction: Eugenio Barba.

Language: Norwegian.

Number of spectators: 120.

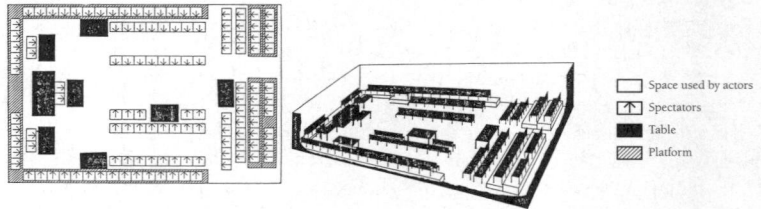

Space used by actors
Spectators
Table
Platform

In a village in southern Italy, one of the local leaders recognises, amongst a group of wealthy German tourists, some of the Nazi occupiers who had once oppressed, tortured and killed many of the villagers. The performance is centred on a story full of mocking irony uncovered by Jens Bjørneboe in the early sixties, those 'glorious years' of the economic boom. The Germans are rich and opposed to violence. The Italians are poor and ferocious: they revel in the slaughter of the migrant birds which fly over their sun-scorched, rocky coast. These are cooked and eaten in their thousands, each bird no more than a mouthful, but delicious. The Germans declare: 'You must stop your hunting. We will build a tourist paradise here in your village. You will be well-off. But no civilised foreigner will want to come to a place where there is so much useless killing'. These are the years when foreign tourism explodes, especially amongst the Germans, becoming one of the most important industries in Italy. It is also the time when, in Europe, ecology starts to become a popular religion. The ex-torturers and ex-occupiers now come to bring well-being and to defend (bird) life. Their ex-victims, as poor as ever, resist the new order in the name of their own independence and dignity, and want to continue to plunder nature. In the end the people of the village choose progress, modernisation and well-being, whatever the source. The daughter of the village leader commits suicide: 'Those who loved me have abandoned me. Now I shall see how alone one is in death'. Her father laughs mockingly and, turning to the spectators, announces: 'Your children!'.

This is the first of many suicides to be encountered in the twenty-one productions of the 'dark legend'.

47. *The daughter of the village leader:* 'Those who loved me have abandoned me. Now I shall see how alone one is in death'. (Else Marie Laukvik)

2. Kaspariana, 1967.

Created in Holstebro, during the first few months after the Odin emigrated from Norway.

74 performances from September 1966 to February 1968.

Actors: Jan Erik Bergström, Anna Trine Grimnes, Lars Göran Kjellstedt, Else Marie Laukvik, Iben Nagel Rasmussen, Dan Nielsen, Torgeir Wethal.

Text by Ole Sarvig.

Adaptation and direction: Eugenio Barba.

The actors speak different Scandinavian languages, according to their nationalities.

Number of spectators: 60.

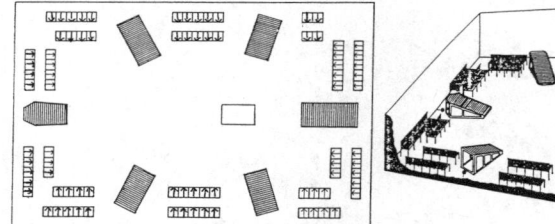 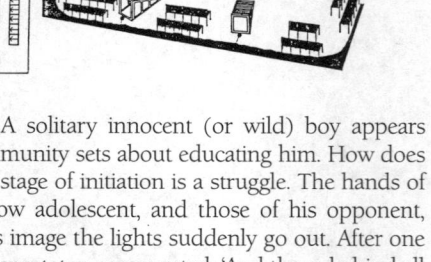

A square in Nuremberg at dawn. A solitary innocent (or wild) boy appears amongst the people. The entire community sets about educating him. How does one become... a real man? The final stage of initiation is a struggle. The hands of the solitary boy, Kaspar Hauser, now adolescent, and those of his opponent, stretch out to grab a knife. With this image the lights suddenly go out. After one performance, Martin Berg, a Danish spectator, commented: 'And there, behind all this, are the faces of the other spectators opposite me, looking into my face as I look into theirs, and the eyes I see before me are so moved that I believe I understand what they see'.

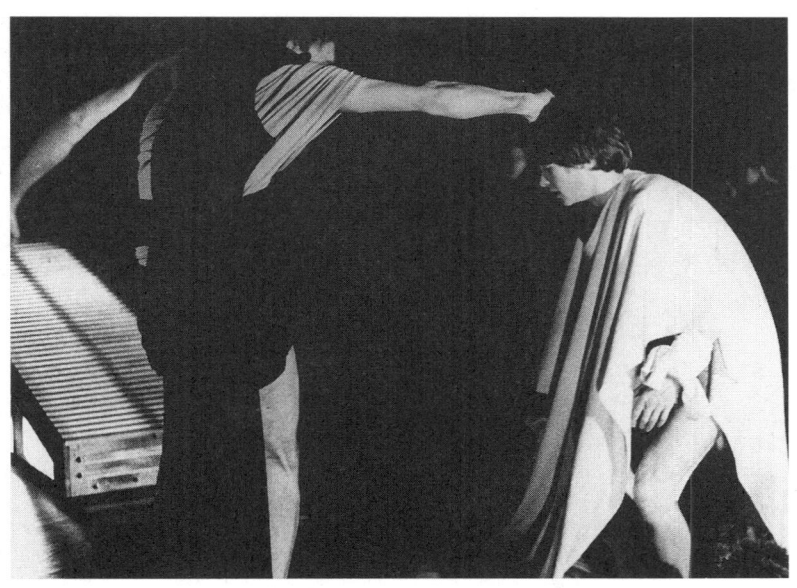

48. How does one become... a real man? 'Kaspar shall be your name'. *(Lars Göran Kjellstedt and Torgeir Wethal)*

3. Ferai, 1969.

Created in Holstebro.

220 performances from June 1969 to July 1970.

Actors: Ulla Alasjärvi, Maria Gilberti, Juha Häkkänen, Sören Larsson, Else Marie Laukvik, Iben Nagel Rasmussen, Carita Rindell, Torgeir Wethal.

Text by Peter Seeberg.

Adaptation and direction: Eugenio Barba.

The actors speak their own different Scandinavian languages.

Number of spectators: 60.

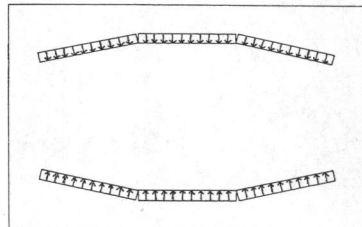 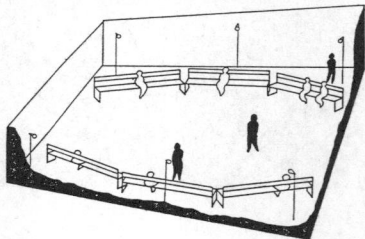

A Greek island or an island in the North Sea. There was once an autocratic king who kept order in the state and family through the fear of ruthless laws. He died. His place was taken by a just young man who loved peace and non-violence, who wanted to free the people from subjection to authority and to the gods, and who wanted to abolish prisons and treat criminals as sick patients to be rehabilitated. As in all fables, the young king wins both power and the daughter of the dead king as his bride. The performance begins where Kaspariana finished: with a struggle for the possession of a knife. The young prince who takes over exhibits another kind of violence: he surrenders the weapon and fights with his bare hands, a smile upon his lips, not violent like a ferocious dog but with a feline gentleness, harmonious, acrobatic, dancing, and revealing implacability only at the precise moment of the strike. He demonstrates the necessary use of violence to install a reign of non-violence, of force to ensure a reign of reason.

The struggle for power is no different from what took place before. But the fact that it now happens in the name of absolute principles of which no one has any concrete experience, allows for a certain nostalgia for the ordered tyranny of the deceased autocratic king. And the bride, the king's daughter, caught in the jaws of a double injustice, takes the law into her own hands and commits suicide. In vain, because that was what the young king needed. After mourning her briefly, he tramples on her mortal remains and his people follow him in bewilderment and awe.

49. *King Admetos:* 'We are all equal in this hour of democracy'. *(Torgeir Wethal and Juha Häkkänen)*

4. Min Fars Hus (My Father's House), 1972.

Created in Holstebro, between April 1971 and April 1972, while Odin Teatret discussed whether or not to become an agricultural commune.

322 performances from April 1972 to January 1974.

Actors: Jens Christensen, Malou Ilmoni (who left the group after the first few weeks of performances), Tage Larsen, Else Marie Laukvik, Iben Nagel Rasmussen, Ulrik Skeel, Torgeir Wethal.

Adaptation and direction: Eugenio Barba.

The actors speak a reinvented Russian. There is no plot. In spite of the original intentions at the start of the rehersals, the performance does not evoke the life and works of Dostoyevski, but is dedicated to him. In the context of the second half of the twentieth century, it is one of the most influential European performances: it is an experience, for the spectators, of which it is almost impossible to speak in 'objective' terms.

Number of spectators: 60.

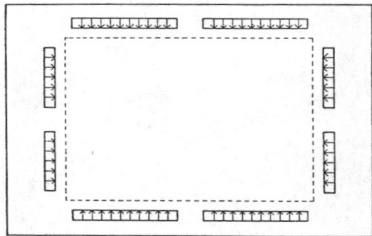 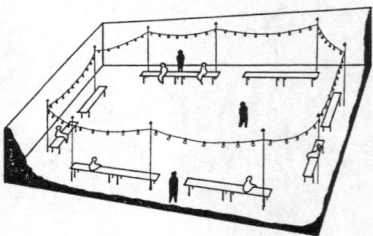

A small courtyard, in festive mood, festooned with coloured lights. Aristoctatic rooms, peasant hovels and muddy clearings in Dostoyevski's Russia. 'Paraclete! Paraclete!' With this call, the fire butterfly which hovers in the shadows, flutters down. A hand snuffs it out. The music swells through the pitch darkness, as though rising out of a well.

    'What is a great thought?'

    'Changing stones into bread, that is a great thought.'

    'Is it really the greatest?'

    'It is great, but not the greatest. When you no longer suffer the pangs of hunger, you say: now that my belly is full, what shall I do next?'

50. *The author:* 'What is a great thought?'. *The woman who knows how to dance:* 'Changing stones into bread, that is a great thought'. *The author:* 'Is it really the greatest?'. *The woman who knows how to dance:* 'It is great, but not the greatest. When you no longer suffer the pangs of hunger, you say: now that my belly is full, what shall I do next?' *(Else Marie Laukvik and Torgeir Wethal)*

5. Dansenes Bog (The Book of Dances), 1974.

Created in a courtyard in Carpignano, in southern Italy, during the summer of 1974 when the Odin has completed its first ten years of life and radically changes direction.

355 performances from July 1974 to January 1980, sometimes indoors but more often in the open air, in theatres and in squares; in the centres of big cities and in their suburbs; in psychiatric hospitals and prisons; at home (in Holstebro) and - its antipode - in Venezuelan Amazonia, in a shabono belonging to the Yanomani tribe of Karohi, with whom the French anthropologist, Jacques Lizot, was living when he helped the Odin to penetrate into the 'heart of darkness'. It was with this performance that the Odin carried out all its first theatre barters.

Actors: Roberta Carreri, Tom Fjordefalk, Tage Larsen, Else Marie Laukvik, Iben Nagel Rasmussen and Torgeir Wethal. (During the first few months Elsa Kvamme and Odd Strøm were also in the performance.)

Eugenio Barba's mise-en-scène consisted of a montage of numbers.

No limit to the number of spectators.

There is no story, but there are many characters: dwarfs, warriors, tall ladies on stilts, a dancing town crier who is taken prisoner. The performance is born out of the individual training of the actors, transformed through costumes, masks, music, banners and songs, and fixed in precise scores of actions, reactions and relationships. Rudimentary music: drums and a xylophone made out of bottles filled with differing amounts of water. For the final scene, Eugenio Barba and Torgeir Wethal worked on the acrobatic exercises in the training to reach a crescendo of solitary aggressivity. A dance of leaps and falls which apparently leaves the actor exhausted. The music becomes more impelling and the actor begins again. This grotesque acrobatic number is transformed into the final act of a bullfight, a killing, a cockfight. With ferocious spectacularity the actor flies through the air once more, falls, loses his mask, hides his face, flies into the air yet again and crashes to the ground on his back after a final somersault. One of the paradoxes of the actor is that his 'violence' is also his 'vulnerability'. Dance as virtuosity and virtue; vitality, colour, vehemence; soliloquy: 'I'm afraid/ The earth is grey/ And the sky's sadness gapes open/ Like the mouth of a skull.'

51. *Dance as virtuosity and virtue; vitality, colour, vehemence.* 'I'm afraid/ The earth is grey/ And the sky's sadness gapes open/ Like the mouth of a skull. *(Iben Nagel Rasmussen)*

6. Come! And the Day will be Ours, 1976.

Created between the summer of 1974 and the spring of 1976 in different phases and places: in a former tobacco repository in Carpignano (Italy); in Odin Teatret's 'white room' in Holstebro; in the village schoolroom of Ollolai in the Sardinian mountains.

180 performances from May 1976 to June 1980.

Actors: Roberta Carreri, Else Marie Laukvik, Iben Nagel Rasmussen, Tom Fjordefalk, Tage Larsen, Torgeir Wethal.

Dramaturgy and direction: Eugenio Barba.

In English, with fragments in the languages of the native Americans.

Number of spectators: 120

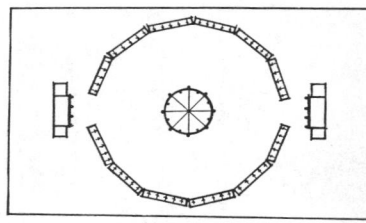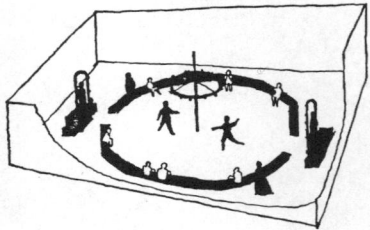

A small white circus ring with red velvet seats. Frontier territories. The Odin's first performance on a historical theme. A confrontation between peoples and cultures. It is as though each actor embodies a group, a tribe, a crowd of emigrants. Each action is the quintessence of an episode in history, the blueprint of a battle, an ambush, a social upheaval, a violent acculturation, a massacre whose occurrence is documented. The theme is the seduction and the slaughter which result from the clash between civilisations, as when the pioneers encountered the American Indians, the Frontier was pushed westwards, the prairies were conquered and, following the 'futile' victory of Little Big Horn, the reservations became the sole salvation for the 'savages'. Rape and rapture: surrender to force, surrender to a vision. The pride of becoming a prostitute in the brothels of Sonora.

52. Frontier territories. A clash between peoples and cultures. Rape and rapture: how one surrenders to force, surrenders to a vision. (Iben Nagel Rasmussen and Else Marie Laukvik)

7. Anabasis, 1977.

Created in Holstebro on the basis of experiences from the parades of the previous years, from the summer of 1974 onwards.

180 performances from April 1977 to September 1984.

Actors: Torben Bjelke, Roberta Carreri, Toni Cots, Tom Fjordefalk, Francis Pardeilhan, Tage Larsen, Else Marie Laukvik, Iben Nagel Rasmussen, Silvia Ricciardelli, Ulrik Skeel, Julia Varley, Torgeir Wethal. (Some of the actors only participated in one of the various versions.)

An itinerant performance, based on an elementary dramaturgy which exploits the basic opposition between the actors with their technical skills and the spectators that they encounter on their way.

No limit to the number of spectators and passers-by.

It unravels in streets and squares. A group of strangers making their way amongst strangers. From time to time the actors chat amicably with one of the spectators, but then this newly struck up relationship is suddenly interrupted by a call from their companions. Sometimes they make a halt, the spectators gather round them in a circle and the actors perform a grotesque number or an acrobatic dance. As soon as they have finished, they ignore the applause and continue their march in a tight group. With drums rolling, trumpets blasting and banners waving, they urge the crowd on or split it in two with their wedge-shaped formation. At times the giant figures on stilts collapse to the ground, while other figures suddenly appear on balconies or roofs, high on church spires, let themselves down into the square or street on a rope, start marching in the opposite direction, disperse, disorientate the people following them. A compact group which remains united until it reaches its goal. The reaching of the goal implies dissolution (therefore the title, which comes from the classical Greek Xenophon and his autobiographical and military odyssey, was not just a pretext). In the end, all the actors huddle together and are covered by a black sheet transforming them into a dark and shapeless monument, guarded by tall and lanky figures of death.

53. The passage of strangers amongst strangers. A compact group which remains united until it reaches its goal. The reaching of the goal implies dissolution. (Torgeir Wethal heading the march, in the foreground.)

8. The Million, 1978.

Created in Holstebro, Lima and Ayacucho (Peru), on the basis of scenic material prepared by the actors during travels, on their own or in small groups, in different parts of the world.

223 performances, indoors and in the open air, from September 1978 to October 1984.

Actors: Torben Bjelke, Roberta Carreri, Toni Cots, Tom Fjordefalk, Tage Larsen, Else Marie Laukvik, Francis Pardeilhan, Iben Nagel Rasmussen, Silvia Ricciardelli, Gustavo Riondet, Ulrik Skeel, Julia Varley, Torgeir Wethal. (Some of the actors only participated in one of the various versions.)

Direction: Eugenio Barba. The dramaturgy consisted of a montage of various musical and dance numbers representing the stages of a journey.

No limit to the number of spectators.

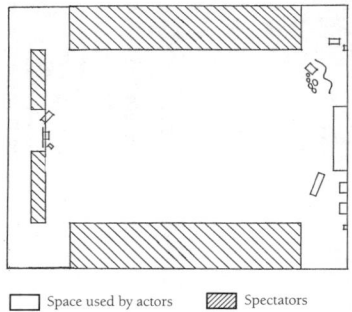

☐ Space used by actors   ▨ Spectators

A journey among the carnivals of different cultures, from India to Bali, from Japan to Brazil, from Africa to European ballroom dancing. A 'musical' à la Odin: a mocking album of exoticism whose figures of flesh and blood prance about in front of a strange traveller, clad like a missionary, with the spectacles of a short-sighted intellectual and the back pack of a tourist. The spectacularity and the candid joy of the opening scenes slowly reveal their opposites: dismay at the brutality which accompanies the explosions of life, the misfortunes which encompass the carnivals on the outskirts of empires, the exploitation and humiliation of women, the children with no future. This exotic album becomes one of meditation reduced to its essentials: love, abandonment, old age, death. For the civilised traveller who is intimidated and vulnerable, the journey becomes escape, distance, involuntary cynicism. A procession of the Magi sings a lullaby to the skeleton of a child: 'In a doorway in Bethlehem/ The Virgin and Saint Joseph ...'.

54. *A journey through the carnivals of different cultures. A musical album full of mocking exoticism.* 'As you travel beyond the seas/ across lands/ children will be singing./ Be happy and sleep, my child./ Death is watching you!'. (*In the foreground, Tage Larsen and Iben Nagel Rasmussen. Behind, from left to right, Toni Cots, Roberta Carreri and Tom Fjordefalk.*)

9. Brecht's Ashes (first version: 1980; second version: 1982).

Created in Holstebro, at the same time as The Million.

166 performances from March 1980 to October 1984.

Actors: Torben Bjelke (only in the first version), Roberta Carreri, Toni Cots, Tage Larsen, Francis Pardeilhan, Iben Nagel Rasmussen, Silvia Ricciardelli, Ulrik Skeel, Julia Varley, Torgeir Wethal.

Text and direction by Eugenio Barba, using a montage of Brecht's poetry and songs as well as other documents from the period. After Brecht's heirs withdrew their permission to use the texts, Barba composed a new montage which, instead of using Brecht's verses, often referred back to those of other authors who had inspired Brecht. The text is in German and is translated by the actor who plays Mack the Knife into the language of the country in which the performance is shown.

Number of spectators: 150.

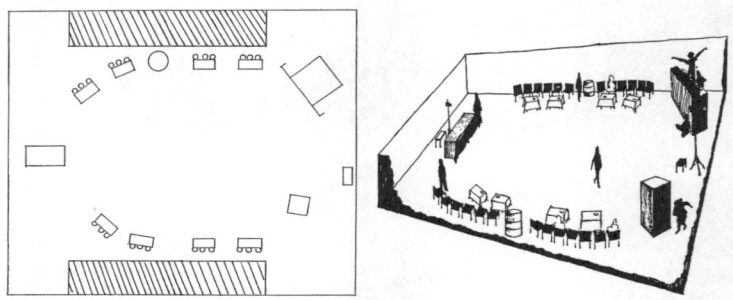

A crossing through nazism, World War II, the Thirty Years' War, the Un-American Activities Committee, until salvation arrives with Ulbricht's communist Berlin. In Brecht's *Ashes*, independent lines of actions are presented simultaneously, concentrating a double system of references into a single scene. These two characteristics of Eugenio Barba's dramaturgy are put to the service of an impressive historical tapestry which intertwines: 1. the biography of Bertolt Brecht; 2. historical events during his lifetime; 3. the transposition that these events underwent in Brecht's works. The writer's relatively secure years of exile are set against the deaths of distant friends; the Second World War melts into the Thirty Years' War as experienced by Mother Courage (when Kattrin, the mute, is captured, raped and put to death); the abjuration of Galileo is also Brecht's deposition before the Un-American Activities Committee. Powerful theatrical images are condensed into easily recognisable conceptual knots, as in satirical drawings and political cartoons. In the end, in Stalinist East Berlin with its grey and depressing atmosphere, the young and ingenuous Kattrin, who dances for joy over liberty and socialism, is suffocated by having the communist newspaper *Pravda* thrust down her throat ('Pravda' meaning 'Truth' in Russian).

55. *The fanatical and terrifying wave of History.* 'The night has twelve hours, but in the end daybreak comes'. *Brecht continued to tap away at his typewriter, crying out in a discordant voice:* 'Don't let yourselves be seduced!'. (*Roberta Carreri and Francis Pardeilhan*)

10. Marriage with God, 1984.

Created in Holstebro on the basis of material elaborated by the two actors.

210 performances from February 1984 to 1990.

Actors: César Brie and Iben Nagel Rasmussen.

Dramaturgy and direction by Eugenio Barba, based on fragments from Nijinski's diary and texts by St. Teresa of Avila, Jorge Luis Borges, St. John of the Cross, Vincent Gaeta, Miguel Hernández, Juan Ramón Jiménez and, above all, Jalal Ud-Din Rumi. The actors speak in the language of the place where the performance takes place.

Number of spectators: 150.

A small house in the snow and an elderly couple: Vaslav Nijinski and Romola de Pulszky. 'I'm thirsty. I have been mad for 33 years. I have lived with a madman for 33 years. I'm thirsty.' There is no difference between them: the two people on stage are one and the same person. They merge together, superimpose themselves, are two faces of a single reality. Ecstasy and madness are shown from the outside and from the inside: the stuttering of the visionary when *we* see him, and his greatness when he dances in the world which *he* sees. A performance about which it is difficult to speak according to 'objective' conventions, as with *Min Fars Hus*.

56. Ecstasy and madness are shown from the outside and from the inside: the stuttering of the visionary when we see him, and his greatness when he dances in the world which he sees.(CésarBrie)

11. The Story of Oedipus, 1984.

Created in Holstebro.

110 performances from February 1984 to 1990.

Actor: Toni Cots.

Text and direction: Eugenio Barba. The actor speaks in the language of the place where the performance takes place.

Number of spectators: 150.

On the road, a disillusioned storyteller is fleeing from Creon's city. A single actor portrays all the characters. Jocasta comes to life without being present: materially she is no more than a long, raven-black wig and a length of brocade animated by the actor who, at the same time, represents the young Oedipus. Under the brocade, however, the spectator 'sees' the passionate body of Jocasta, still young enough to love, responding to the caresses of the young warrior. In the emotion of the embrace, the queen says to her young king: 'You are just a boy! You could be my son!'. And the spectator experiences, in its simplest form, the refined cruelty of the superior powers and their joyful ravages as they fulfill to the letter that which human beings whisper in their happiest moments.

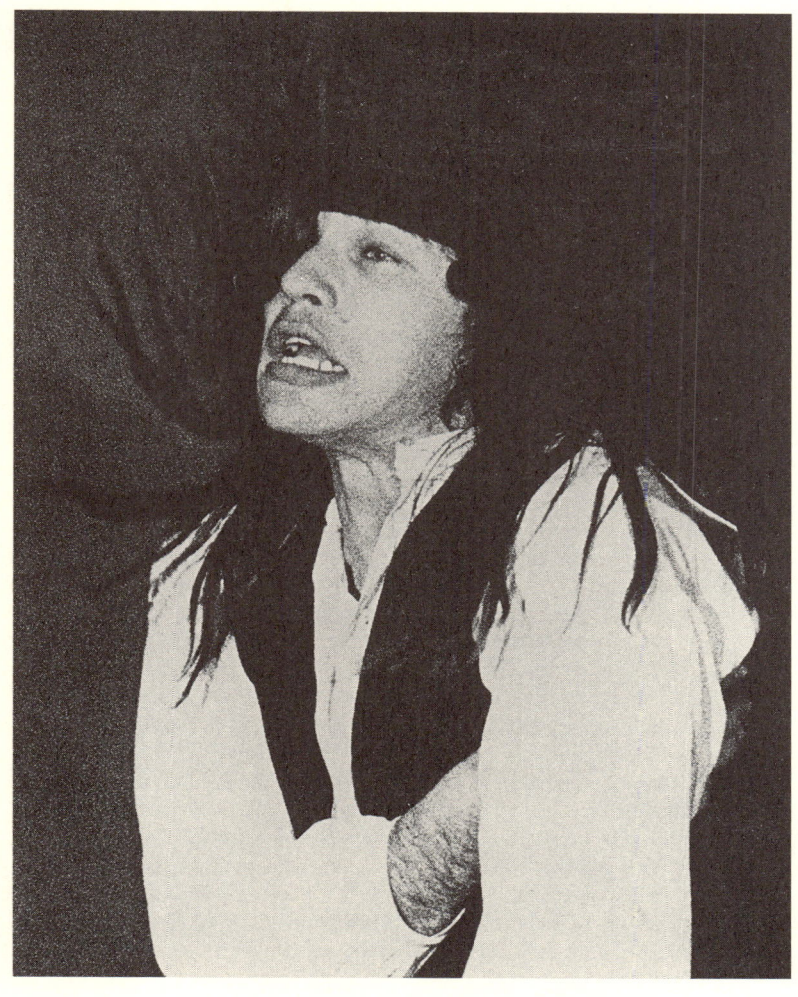

57. In the emotion of the embrace, the queen says to her young king: 'You are just a boy! You could be my son!'. And the spectator experiences, in its simplest form, the refined cruelty of the superior powers and their joyful ravages as they fulfill to the letter that which human beings whisper in their happiest moments. (Toni Cots)

12. The Gospel according to Oxyrhyncus, 1985.

Created in Holstebro, first in the 'white room' and later in the 'red room'.

214 performances from March 1985 to June 1987.

Actors: Roberta Carreri, Else Marie Laukvik, Tage Larsen, Francis Pardeilhan, Julia Varley, Torgeir Wethal.

Text and direction: Eugenio Barba. The actors speak a reinvented Coptic, Koine Greek and Yiddish.

Number of spectators: 190.

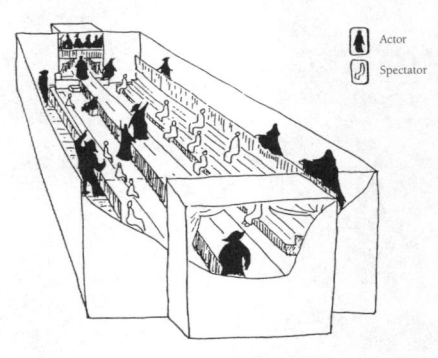

Actor

Spectator

A narrow catwalk between two flanks of spectators: 'Maran Ata! The Lord is coming! A child is born in Bethlehem. He will destroy Jerusalem. Kyrie Eleison. He has not come to bring peace'. The characters who speak and act before us on the narrow walkway which divides the spectators in two, live in an unspecified time and place, perhaps in the distant past, perhaps in the future. They use a language we cannot understand (Yiddish, Ancient Greek, Coptic). But there is a moment when the words reach us clearly, in our own language. An impressive turbaned figure of uncertain sex, looks us earnestly in the eyes and reads us the beginning of this exotic yet familiar Gospel: 'In the beginning was the Idea. And the Idea was with God. And the Idea was God. God is a devourer of men; that is why man is sacrificed to Him'.

In the end, all the Messiahs appear in a tableau, blood dripping from their mouths. All faith is transformed into ferocity, all thirst for the future becomes domination. Even the Jewish tailor's final dance - whose steps correspond to as many names for God - is executed amongst weapons and bones scattered about a battlefield. This pious man continues to pray and weep while he awaits the Messiah, not satisfied that he has already seen so many other cruel Messiahs in action. He is the most sincere, the most moving, the most honest character in the performance. His heart is brimming over with hope, but his head does not understand and his eyes do not want to see. Does his stubborn faith suggest, perhaps, that there is no end to the victories of fanaticism and that history teaches us nothing? Does he represent the innocent earth into which idolatry and violence can push their robust roots? Is he the incarnation of the saying according to which only good faith is worse than bad faith?

58. 'In the beginning was the Idea. And the Idea was with God. And the Idea was God. God is a devourer of men; that is why man is sacrificed to Him.' *All faith is transformed into ferocity, all thirst for the future becomes domination. (Tage Larsen)*

315

13. Judith, 1987.

Created in Holstebro on the basis of material elaborated by the actress.

235 performances from August 1987. Still being performed at the present time (September 1999).

Actress: Roberta Carreri.

Text: Eugenio Barba and Roberta Carreri. The actress speaks in the language of the country where the performance takes place.

Number of spectators: 150.

A white deck chair, a large fan, a bonsai, combs of mother-of-pearl, a decapitated head carved out of wood, long hat pins to pierce its eyes and tongue and for adorning the hair, a red dressing gown, a white silk night-dress. Through the justification of the biblical story of Judith, the performance explores the theme of violence and vulnerability, plunging into an ocean of luminous and murderous eroticism. That which in other productions comes to the surface only in flashes, is here disentangled and dilated, meticulously analysed and merged into the precision of a symphony. The story is told in full at the beginning. In the end, an amusing epilogue makes us suspect that the character speaking the monologues is not the protagonist, Judith, but her servant recalling her. (This is the servant we see in many famous paintings, often the most moving and fascinating character, carrying the head of Holofernes in a basket and following, almost as though in a dance, the footsteps of her mistress, somewhat stiff after her heroic exploit.) During the remainder of the performance, the underlying story is no longer present, its fronds ruffled and at the mercy of passing winds. We watch waves of feelings and passions intermingle, erasing the confines of moral maps, and above all we see a dazzling and almost purifying joy in horror.

59. 'I will prepare you a bed of silk/ I will cover you with my hair/ I will lie down beside you/ But a white horse awaits you/ It will tear you from my arms/ You will vanish behind a mountain peak.' *Waves of feelings and passions intermingle, erasing the confines of moral maps, and above all we see a dazzling and almost purifying joy in horror. (Roberta Carreri)*

14. Talabot, 1988.

Created in Chicxulub (Yucatan, Mexico) and then in Holstebro in the 'blue room', the smallest of Odin Teatret's working spaces. The performance retains the restricted dimensions of the small room in Yucatan where rehearsals started. All the scenes derive from mise-en-scène proposals by the actors and the theatre's collaborators.

279 performances from August 1988 to October 1991.

Actors: César Brie (later replaced by Falk Heinrich), Jan Ferslev, Richard Fowler, Naira Gonzalez (later replaced by Isabel Ubeda), Iben Nagel Rasmussen, Julia Varley, Torgeir Wethal.

Direction and text by Eugenio Barba (partly based on autobiographical material specially written by Kirsten Hastrup). Barba finalises the dramaturgy of the historical and biographical episodes chosen by the actors and the theatre's collaborators. Some of the text is spoken by the actors in their own language and some in the language spoken in the country where the performance takes place.

Number of spectators: 104.

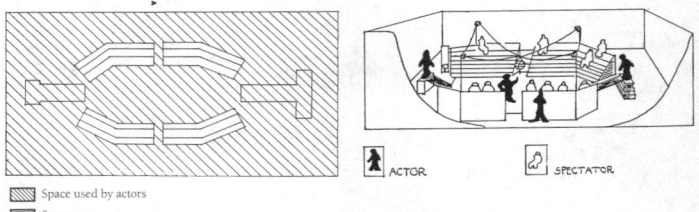

Space used by actors
Spectators

Amongst the 'hidden people' of the dead, Che Guevara is a Captain with feathers in his hat and resembling Cyrano de Bergerac. Light bones tinkle with a silver laughter. A baby is suckled with sand. A mound of refuse. And the true story, with a happy ending, of a living forty year-old Danish anthropologist with many children. After the performance, on the way out, a postcard is handed to each of the spectators in a sealed envelope. It shows an image from the performance: the Trickster, a strange elf with wings and a feline face, dancing around the mound of refuse from the performance which is piled up around a tree whose branches are tangled up in burnt barbed wire. On the other side of the postcard there is a quotation by Walter Benjamin on the Angel of History:

'His face is turned towards the past. There where *we* see a chain of events, *he* sees one single catastrophe which piles up wreckage upon wreckage throwing it at his feet. He would prefer to remain, awaken the dead and put back together what has been laid waste. But from paradise a storm blows, so violent that his wings become entangled and the Angel can no longer fold them together. The storm pushes him irresistibly towards the future on which he turns his back, while in front of him the mountain of wreckage rises towards the sky. This storm is what we call progress.'

60. *The true biography of a Danish anthropologist. A performance about distancing oneself from a familiar reality. An anthropologist, like an emigrant, abandons her own culture to live in another. In this way she discovers that part of herself which lives in exile.* 'Often I am happy, and yet I want to cry/ because nobody shares my happiness./ Often I am sad, and yet I have to laugh/ so that nobody notices my tears.' *(Julia Varley)*

15. Memoria, l990.

Created in Holstebro on the basis of material elaborated by the actress and the musician.

107 performances from March 1990 to March 1994.

Actress: Else Marie Laukvik. Musician: Frans Winther.

Text : Else Marie Laukvik in collaboration with Eugenio Barba and Frans Winther. Music: Frans Winther, and Yiddish songs. The actress speaks in the language used where the performance takes place.

Number of spectators: 30.

In a sitting room, before a steaming teapot, sit a storyteller and a strolling musician. Around them, on three small sofas and one row of chairs a small group of spectators is assembled. The violinist observes us with a quiet smile which sometimes verges on sarcasm. The woman, the storyteller, the priestess of the memory of horror (because they are here to remember the horror), looks at us as though she could see other faces through ours and wished to find in them the relief that comes with mercy. She speaks as though she were telling fairy tales. Two tales. Two true stories. They concern children, witnesses' accounts from the Nazi extermination camps, but which end happily. Hebrew and Yiddish songs. At times the storyteller appears to be haunted, obscured by her stories: she jumps with fright, her images become confused, she pauses, radiating a childlike panic. The violinist watches over her as though he were assisting a medium, a priestess whose supreme energy is constantly on the brink of aphasia or insanity. And then, when the two stories are ended, we see her fall into a state of mute serenity. She is brooding over something which shakes her and lulls her at the same time. The stories which she cannot forget come back to dispel her peace, to torment her, to urge her on, and she starts once more to narrate, following tracks which cancel each other out. The winds of the mind and the impossibility to forget toss her about like an autumn leaf. She slips from one sentence to the next, from one episode to another, mixes up people, forgets the words and finds them again, connects lives and events that do not belong together. Something essential is getting lost: not memory, but the strength and the words capable of transmitting it without succumbing. The performance ends as we look at the photographs of two writers' faces: a smiling Primo Levi and a melancholic Jean Améry, both Jews who had survived Auschwitz and committed suicide years later. 'Only two of us are left and we deal in bones.'

61. *In a sitting room, before a steaming teapot, sit a storyteller and a strolling musician. The Storyteller, the priestess of the memory of horror, looks at us as though she could see other faces through ours, and wished to find in them the relief that comes with mercy. 'Only two of us are left and we deal in bones.' (Frans Winther and Else Marie Laukvik)*

16. The Castle of Holstebro, (first version: 1990; second version 1999).

Created in Holstebro and on tour, based on material elaborated by the actress.

208 performances from November 1990 until now. Still being performed at the present time (September 1999).

Actress: Julia Varley.

Text: Julia Varley and Eugenio Barba. The actress speaks the language of the country where the performance takes place.

Number of spectators: 120.

In a red room we see a woman dressed in white and a cynical old jester with a skull for a head called Mister Peanut. Two characters in one person: 'If they see beard and moustache, they call it man. If they see long hair and breasts, they call it woman. But look! The soul inside is neither man nor woman.' This, more than any other of Odin Teatret's productions, refuses to cross the no-man's-land between the actor and the spectator. Here the autobiographical space is that of vulnerability. It is as though, while watching the fantasies of a woman shut in a room of her own, we descend step by step into the depths where youth dances with death, ingenuousness is the other face of foresight, and even love with all the irony of its many destinies can teach the truth. In the end, sitting on the floor, the actress holds in her arms the old and shrunken Mister Peanut as though he were her baby, an infant-grandfather to be suckled. Or Death, newly born.

62. 'If they see beard and moustache, they call it man. If they see long hair and breasts, they call it woman. But look! The soul inside is neither man nor woman.' *Youth dances with death, and ingenuousness is the other face of foresight. (Julia Varley)*

17. Itsi-Bitsi, 1991.

Created in Holstebro and on tour, on the basis of material elaborated by the actress.

205 performances from January 1991. Still being performed today (September 1999).

Actress: Iben Nagel Rasmussen. Musicians/actors: Jan Ferslev and Kai Bredholt.

Text: Iben Nagel Rasmussen. Text montage: Eugenio Barba. Musical adaptation by Jan Ferslev with the collaboration of Kai Bredholt. Performed in the language spoken where the performance takes place.

Number of spectators: 150.

Sun and snow. Empty space. Fragments of the actress's life at the beginning of the sixties: the different meanings of *journey*: 'We wanted to throw open the doors and yet they became doors with bars. When the doors closed, some of us found ourselves on the wrong side.' The actress tells of the years preceding her arrival at the Odin, years of hitchhiking round the world, of music and poetry, of political radicalism and drugs. It is her story, that of Erik Skaløe (the first beat poet to sing in Danish, who committed suicide in India in '68) and of their generation.

Eugenio Barba worked on Iben Nagel Rasmussen's autobiography as if it were a second hand memory and it was up to him to relive the story of the actress on a transcendental level. He contrasted events in her life with a 'double', inventing characters, situations, relationships which do not comment on the images but skip from one to another, leading them beyond the confines of autobiographical memory. Some fragments of the actress's previous performances are interwoven in *Itsi-Bitsi*, not as quotations and examples, but as revealing metaphors: the mute Kattrin from *Brecht's Ashes*, the wandering shaman from *Come! And the Day will be Ours*, the Trickster from *Talabot*.

63. *The different meanings of journey:* 'We wanted to throw open the doors and yet they became doors with bars. When the doors closed, some of us found ourselves on the wrong side'. *(Iben Nagel Rasmussen)*

18. Kaosmos, 1993.

Created in Holstebro.

216 performances from April 1993 to December 1996.

Actors: Kai Bredholt, Roberta Carreri, Jan Ferslev, Tina Nielsen, Iben Nagel Rasmussen, Isabel Ubeda, Julia Varley, Torgeir Wethal, Frans Winther.

Dramaturgy and direction: Eugenio Barba. The actors speak in their own mother tongue.

Number of spectators: 190.

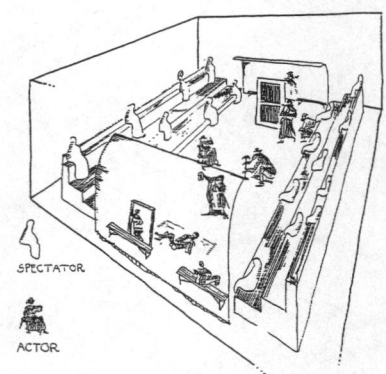

A village in the heart of Europe. Sickles harvest the corn and feet trample it. We are witnessing a world which ends happily, amidst some weeping and some melancholy, but above all with an insane self-confidence. It is a fascinating and sensuous village whose inhabitants are clothed in garments of the richest colours and textures, with ornamental hairstyles which are only to be seen in illustrations of ancient folklore or in books of fables. But this book of fables is plagued by war and modernity. *Kaosmos*'s subtitle is *'The Ritual of the Door'*, a door which remains closed to those who wait a lifetime to enter it. We therefore expect a performance about divisions, about insurmountable walls. But there are no divisions, distinctions, points of orientation. There is no inside and outside, no 'us' and 'them', no 'these' and 'those'. There is the door which is mobile, and the actors move it around from place to place, laying it flat on the ground like a box or a coffin, dragging it on their shoulders like a cross or standing it upright on its frame, dividing nothing from nothing. It is the negation of a door: with no house and no adjoining wall, it opens onto and separates from, in the abstract - or, if you prefer - fictitiously. Beside it, a peasant woman, looking like a village schoolteacher with spectacles on her nose, is vainly waiting to enter, as though the waiting, the entrances and exits, the comings and goings around that negation of a door, had a meaning. But they don't. Shutting in, shutting out are derisory expressions when you can bang the door and turn the handle as much as you like, but there is no inside and there is no outside. Order and Disorder, chaos and cosmos, they are all one: Kaosmos.

64. A book of fables, plagued by war and modernity. We are witnessing a world which ends happily, amidst some weeping and some melancholy, but above all with an insane self-confidence. 'It's going to rain/ come into the ark/ follow me/ it's going to rain.' (From left to right: Roberta Carreri, Isabel Ubeda, Tina Nielsen, Torgeir Wethal, Jan Ferslev and Kai Bredholt)

19. Inside the Skeleton of the Whale (1997).

Created in Holstebro between the end of 1996 and the beginning of 1997.

25 performances from February 1997, Still being performed at the present time (September 1999).

Actors: Kai Bredholt, Roberta Carreri, Jan Ferslev, Tage Larsen, Iben Nagel Rasmussen, Julia Varley, Torgeir Wethal, Frans Winther.

Dramaturgy and direction: Eugenio Barba.

The actors speak in the language used where the performance takes place.

A 'secret' performance for 50 spectators only.

'An evil and adulterous generation seeks after a sign! But no sign will be given except the sign of Jonas' (Matthew 12,39). This production derives from another one - *Kaosmos*- and is reborn becoming convivial yet secret. In a candle-lit room, between two rows of tables decked with white cloths, fifty spectators sit eating bread and olives and drinking wine while an 'empty ritual' takes place.

The skeleton is what is left when the theatre has lost everything that was intended to be seen and narrated, retaining only its inner support: the subterranean threads that guide the actors; the relationship between actors and spectators; the search for contact and for a fertile emptiness from which a stream of meaning can come gushing forth, differing for each spectator. Neither the costumes nor the colours nor the accessories from *Kaosmos* remain. Only the detailed pattern of each action is left, without the objects that were moved and manipulated by those actions.

The actors wear their everyday clothes. They move with an intensity and an inner necessity of their own, their motivations hidden to the spectators. The texts come partly form *Kaosmos* and partly from *The Gospel according to Oxyrhyncus* where they were spoken in archaic and incomprehensible languages. Here they are translated: they are heretical and blasphemous, transforming in a nihilistic way the words of the Holy Book. Condemnation is disguised as hope, and vice versa. The shadows seem so deep that light emanates from them. A sombre steadfast light, like a kernel of joy. And in this shared solitude, the drama - the meaning emerging from the web of actions - takes on a form and a consistency somewhere in the empty space which unites and distinguishes actors and spectators.

65. *A performance which derives from another performance. The words of the Holy Book become sarcastic, nihilistic, blasphemous. (From left to right: Roberta Carreri, Iben Nagel Rasmussen. Torgeir Wethal, Frans Winther and Jan Ferslev)*

20. Ode to Progress - A Ballet (1997).

Created in Holstebro, during the first few months of 1997.

41 performances from may 1997. Still being performed at the present time (September 1999). Can be performed both indoors and outdoors.

Actors: Kai Bredholt, Roberta Carreri, Jan Ferslev, Tage Larsen, Iben Nagel Rasmussen, Julia Varley, Torgeir Wethal, Frans Winther.

Dramaturgy and direction: Eugenio Barba.

The actors speak in the language used where the performance takes place.

Number of spectators: between 250 and 500 according to whether the performance takes place indoors or outdoors.

An invitation: 'Odin Teatret takes pleasure in presenting some representatives of the *hidden people*, who will sing praises of human conquests'. The 'conquests' are items taken from the Guinness Book of Records. The performance navigates on a sea of irony, accompanied by songs and hymns that have characterised the events of the 20th century. But from the depths of this irony unexpected phantoms appear. The stories recorded in the book - curious, banal or comic as they are - become grotesque, touching or tragic scenes full of pathos. The mother who has given birth to 50 children; the man who has had hiccups all his life; the woman who lived for ninety-nine years in a psychiatric hospital; the tireless labourer who toiled for more than a century; the tamer of large numbers of wild animals, all indicate a side of human behaviour which leaves us bewildered. The scores and masks belong to the Odin actors, but they undergo yet another transformation. The performance is a morality play as conceived by a libertine. A performance safari: the *hidden people* of goblins, fantasy animals, fairies and gnomes dances and celebrates the passage of the doubly wise animal *Homo sapiens-sapiens* into a new millennium - and is exterminated

66. The scores and masks which belong to the repertoire of Odin Teatret undergo yet another transformation. A morality play. A performance safari. (Julia Varley and Iben Nagel Rasmussen)

21. Mythos, 1998.

Created in Holstebro.

55 performances from May 1998. Still being performed at the present time (September 1999).

Actors: Kai Bredholt, Roberta Carreri. Jan Ferslev, Tage Larsen, Iben Nagel Rasmussen, Julia Varley, Torgeir Wethal, Frans Winther.

Text: Henrik Nordbrandt and Odin Teatret.

Dramaturgy and direction: Eugenio Barba.

The actors speak in their own mother tongue, with fragments in the language used where the performance takes place.

Number of spectators: 120.

A sea without water. A garden of stones. A graveyard. A pathway through time. Ground where severed hands grow like anemones. The battlefield when the fighting is over: 'I remember my mother / and the swallows skimming low / over the field where April rain / consoled the parched ones stretched in pain / through the truce of night that followed the battle./ I remember the parting groans / and the prayers of dying enemies, mingled there, / foes at dawn, but friends at dusk, / indifferent to glory and country, / deceived by the truth of a bullet. / Now we lie here in the mud. / Over us the swallows skim low / and all is hushed'.

A funeral wake is burying the revolution at the end of the century, enshrining it in the arid sea of myths, on the shore where Oedipus confronts Odysseus; where Medea meets Cassandra; where Orpheus faces Daedalus, lamenting his son who has fallen while in flight; and where Sisiphus labours eternally making and remaking the landscape.

The lines by the Danish poet Henrik Nordbrant, are transformed into the monologues and dialogues of the protagonists of the ancient myths and their modern younger brother: the myth of the Revolution. The latter continues its march even after death: it is epitomised in a South American rebel, a soldier of the 'Prestes Column'.

For Eugenio Barba, Oedipus and his companions are 'actors of ferocity'. He writes: 'We can imagine them, tired of killing and being killed, of pillaging and destroying, of raping and being raped. These are the protagonists of the myths of ancient Greece who, throughout the ages, have repeated their ferocious acts'.

Thomas Bredsdorff, literary advisor for the production, reflects *a posteriori* on its meaning: 'Odin Teatret stubbornly continues along its road. They never called themselves political when that was the fashion, but do so with pride today. What is it they want to change? If it is the world of theatre, they may as well forget it. Is it the world - which is as unaffected as it was thirty years ago? Hardly. What then?'

67. *A sea without water. Ground where severed hands grow like anemones.* 'Over us the swallows skim low, and all is hushed.' *(Tage Larsen, Roberta Carreri and Iben Nagel Rasmussen)*

EUROPEAN CONTEMPORARY CLASSICS/
THEATRE is a major series of ground-
breaking, authoritative works by scholars
and practitioners from throughout Europe. It
makes available, in English, new thinking on
the practice of theatre, its processes and
contexts. It aims to document innovative
methods, theories and approaches to
making and understanding theatre.

Other books already in the process of trans-
lation and production include:

Ingemar Lindh
Stepping Stones

Krysztof Plesniarowicz
*The Dead Memory Machine: Tadeusz
Kantor's Theatre of Death*

Franco Ruffini
Theatre and Boxing

Nicola Savarese
*Theatre and Performance Between East and
West*

Books already published by Black Mountain
Press:

Eugenio Barba
*Land of Ashes and Diamonds: My
Apprenticeship in Poland, followed by 26
Letters from Jerzy Grotowski to Eugenio
Barba*

 Black Mountain Press is a division of the Centre for Performance Research Ltd.

 *An Independent Theatre Organisation*
Located in Wales
Working Internationally

The Centre for Performance Research produces innovative performance work, promotes tours, collaborates and exchanges with theatre companies of international significance, arranges conferences, stages workshops, masterclasses and lecture demonstrations, publishes and distributes theatre books, mounts exhibitions and runs a multicultural resource centre for the performing arts.

Artistic Director: Richard Gough
Producer: Judie Christie
Publications Assistant: Rachel Rogers

CENTRE FOR PERFORMANCE RESEARCH
8 SCIENCE PARK, ABERYSTWYTH
SY23 3AH, WALES, UK
TEL: +44 (0) 1970 622 133
Fax: +44 (0) 1970 622 132
email: cprwww@aber.ac.uk
http://www.aber.ac.uk/-cprwww

THEATRE : SOLITUDE, CRAFT, REVOLT

Theatre, Solitude, Craft, Revolt is a highly illuminating and provocative professional autobiography by one of Europe's leading theatre directors. It is a collection of essays dating from 1964 to 1995 by Eugenio Barba, director, theorist and founder of Odin Teatret. As a chronicle of over thirty years' sustained work with a permanent ensemble, it reveals the meaning of his influential theatre practice, his life's work and guiding principles.

The book is a transformation of Barba's previous publication *Beyond the Floating Islands* (1985), focusing on theatre practice and the meaning, the 'why' of doing theatre. As such it forms the ideal companion to his other book *The Paper Canoe* (1995) which expands his theories on the work of the actor and also Theatre Anthropology.

The peculiar relationships between discipline and revolt (craft and its denial, training and its betrayal) are revealed as creative strategies throughout these texts. But most of all a singular capacity for mutation, which paradoxically affirms a will to remain oneself, protecting one's identity, emerges as a key to Barba's professional biography and explains in some way Odin Teatret's longevity. An illustrated appendix compiled by Fernando Taviani comprehensively catalogues the productions of thirty five-years' work.

*

EUGENIO BARBA

Eugenio Barba was born in southern Italy in 1936 and emigrated to Norway in 1954. From 1961-64 he studied theatre in Poland, spending three years with Jerzy Grotowski and writing the first book about him. In 1963, after a journey to India, he published an essay on *kathakali*, a theatre form which was not, at the time, extensively known in the West. He founded Odin Teatret in Oslo in 1964 and moved with it to Denmark in 1966, directing more than twenty performances to date which have toured regularly in Europe, North America and Latin America. In 1979 he founded ISTA, the International School of Theatre Anthropology, and has been awarded honorary doctorates from the Universities of: Århus, Denmark; Ayacucho, Peru; Bologna, Italy, and Montreal, Canada.

Of the books he has published, the following have been translated into English: *Beyond the Floating Islands* (PAJ Publications 1986), *The Paper Canoe* (Routledge 1995) and, in collaboration with Nicola Savarese, *A Dictionary of Theatre Anthropology: The Secret Art of the Performer* (CPR/ Routledge 1991), *Land of Ashes and Diamonds: My Apprenticeship in Poland, followed by 26 Letters from Jerzy Grotowski to Eugenio Barba* (Black Mountain Press 1999).